W9-CZH-987

Using IBM's ISPF
Dialog Manager

THE VAN NOSTRAND REINHOLD DATA PROCESSING SERIES

Series Editor: *Ned Chapin, Ph.D.*

IMS Programming Techniques: A Guide to Using DL/1
Dan Kapp and Joseph L. Leben

Reducing COBOL Complexity Through Structured Programming
Carma L. McClure

Composite/Structured Design
Glenford J. Myers

Reliable Software Through Composite Design
Glenford J. Myers

Flowcharts
Ned Chapin

A Programmer's Guide to COBOL
William J. Harrison

A Guide to Structured COBOL with Efficiency Techniques
and Special Algorithms
Pacifico A. Lim

CICS/VS Command Level with ANS COBOL Examples,
First Edition
Pacifico A. Lim

Managing Software Development and Maintenance
Carma L. McClure

Computer-Assisted Data Base Design
George U. Hubbard

Computer Performance Evaluation: Tools and Techniques
for Effective Analysis
Michael F. Morris and Paul F. Roth

Evaluating Data Base Management Systems
Judy King

Network Systems
Roshan Lal Sharma, Paulo T. deSousa, and Ashok D. Inglé

Logical Data Base Design
Robert M. Curtice and Paul E. Jones, Jr.

Decision Tables in Software Engineering
Richard B. Hurley

USING IBM'S ISPF DIALOG MANAGER
Under MVS, VM, and VSE

Howard Fosdick

VAN NOSTRAND REINHOLD DATA PROCESSING SERIES

VNR VAN NOSTRAND REINHOLD COMPANY
————————————————————— New York

Copyright © 1987 by **Van Nostrand Reinhold Company Inc.**
Library of Congress Catalog Card Number: 86-15900
ISBN: 0-442-22626-8

All rights reserved. No part of this work covered by the copyrights
herein may be reproduced or used in any form or by any means—
graphic, electronic, or mechanical, including photocopying, recording,
taping, or information storage and retrieval systems—without
permission of the publisher.

Manufactured in the United States of America.

Published by Van Nostrand Reinhold Company Inc.
115 Fifth Avenue
New York, New York 10003

Van Nostrand Reinhold Company Limited
Molly Millars Lane
Wokingham, Berkshire RG11 2PY, England

Van Nostrand Reinhold
480 La Trobe Street
Melbourne, Victoria 3000, Australia

Macmillan of Canada
Division of Canada Publishing Corporation
164 Commander Boulevard
Agincourt, Ontario MIS 3C7, Canada

15 14 13 12 11 10 9 8 7 6 5 4 3 2 1

Library of Congress Cataloging-in-Publication Data
Fosdick, Howard.
    Using IBM's ISPF dialog manager.
    (Van Nostrand Reinhold data processing series)
    Includes index.
    1. Interactive computer systems.   2. ISPF Dialog
Manager (Computer program).   3. IBM computers—Programming
I. Title.   II. Series.
QA76.9.I58F67   1987   005.2'25   86-15900
ISBN 0-442-22626-8

To P. F. P.

Contents

Series Editor's Foreword

ISPF grows in popularity with users of IBM computers for the convenience it offers, for the power it offers, and for the quick get-to-the-heart-of-it practicality it offers with interactive applications. Tapping these qualities well requires using Dialog Manager.

A simple example starts us off. Howard Fosdick builds up the example with facets that bring different aspects of Dialog Manager into focus. For each facet he shows us a way of using Dialog Manager to get the work done. In the process, we are shown screen formats, panel definitions, and option menus. For clarity and breadth, alternative dialogs in both COBOL and CLIST are presented.

Fosdick emphasizes common situations to be handled. After getting a good start, he brings in some file tailoring and table functions. Library access functions are the focus in the last part of the book. Useful facilities like providing "help" are covered, and the main differences between the large computer and the IBM PC versions of the ISPF Dialog Manager are described.

While ISPF is an IBM product, it has served as a de facto inspiration both for other IBM software aids and for non-IBM products and aids. Hence, learning the use of the ISPF Dialog Manager is an investment in our professional futures.

NED CHAPIN

Preface

The ISPF Dialog Manager is an IBM program product designed to aid application developers in creating interactive applications. The Dialog Manager helps programmers develop interactive systems of greater functionality in a fraction of the time previously required.

IBM vends the Dialog Manager as a strategic product. It is one of the vendor's few products available across the entire spectrum of its mainframes. The Dialog Manager operates with the MVS, VM, DOS/VSE, and SSX/VSE operating systems. It runs on the XT/370 and AT/370 microcomputers under the VM/PC operating system. And IBM has recently introduced a personal computer product modeled on the mainframe Dialog Manager, the EZ-VU Development Facility.

IBM's commitment to the Dialog Manager product is fast rendering it a de facto standard in the MVS and VM worlds. If you are a programmer or analyst, learning the ISPF Dialog Manager greatly increases your marketability. If you are a data processing or MIS manager, making informed decisions requires familiarity with this product. Indeed, for anyone working in these software environments, understanding the role and nature of the Dialog Manager is essential.

This book introduces the Dialog Manager. Using illustrations, it progressively describes a complete example application developed with the Dialog Manager. This well-documented coding example demonstrates a core subset of Dialog Manager facilities. It teaches you what you need to know first and prepares you for dealing with the vendor's reference manuals later.

This example dialog is provided in its entirety in two languages: COBOL, and the CLIST command language of MVS. This approach allows you to work with either language while comparing applications developed with compiled programs versus command procedures. The minor differences pertinent to using the Dialog Manager under the various operating systems are explained also.

I would appreciate any suggestions that will improve this book. Please write to me courtesy of the publisher.

Sometimes I feel as if I fight for no banner but my own. Then I realize that just as I often go out of my way to help someone, many others have done just that in their contributions to this book. It is my pleasure to acknowledge them here:

I called Gary DeWard Brown, unannounced and unexpected, at his home.

He gave me sound advice on finding a publisher for this book and a very helpful technical review.

I approached Gus Trujillo and Cindy Stegemeier of the GUIDE ISPF Project, also without warning, for their critique of the manuscript. Both were friendly and helpful.

I thank Michael P. Bouros, author of an excellent VSAM book, for his expert criticisms and friendly encouragement.

I express my appreciation to Ross Overbeek for his advice concerning this book and my other writings.

I thank Gerald Galbo, Mary Dorian, and all others at Van Nostrand Reinhold who worked on this book. I also wish to acknowledge the publisher's anonymous reviewers who contributed some excellent suggestions for improvement.

I thank Lee Fosdick for proofreading the manuscript.

Most of all, I owe great gratitude to two outstanding computer scientists, Dennis Beckley and Priscilla Polk, who read the manuscript for this book and my previous works. They have consistently provided me with technical reviews of the highest quality. I give them both my heartfelt thanks.

HOWARD FOSDICK

Abbreviations

ADF	Application Development Facility	ISPF	Interactive System Productivity Facility
APL	A Programming Language	JCL	Job Control Language
CICS	Customer Information Control System	MVS	Multiple Virtual Storage
CLIST	Command List	MVS/XA	Multiple Virtual Storage/Extended Architecture
CMS	Conversational Monitor System		
COBOL	Common Business Oriented Language	PC	Personal Computer
CP	Control Program	OS	Operating System
		OS/VS2	Operating System/Virtual Storage 2
CRP	Current Row Pointer		
CSP	Cross-System Product	PA keys	Program Attention keys
DB2	Database 2	PC-DOS	Personal Computer-Disk Operating System
DM	Dialog Manager		
DOS/VSE	Disk Operating System/Virtual Storage Extended		
		PDF	Program Development Facility
FORTRAN	Formula Translator	PF keys	Program Function keys
FORTRAN/VS	Formula Translator/Virtual Storage	PL/I	Programming Language/One
GDDM	Graphical Display Data Manager	RPGII	Report Program Generator II
ICCF	Interactive Computing Control Facility	SDF	Screen Design Facility
		SDU	Screen Development Utility
IMS	Information Management System		

SPF	System Productivity Facility (formerly Structured Programming Facility)	VM	Virtual Machine
		VMCF	Virtual Machine Communication Facility
SQL	Structured Query Language	VM/PC	Virtual Machine/ Personal Computer
SQL/DS	Structured Query Language/Data System	VM/SP	Virtual Machine/ System Product
SSX	Small Systems Executive	VSE	Virtual Storage Extended
SSX/VSE	Small Systems Executive/ Virtual Storage Extended	VSE/AF	Virtual Storage Extended/ Advanced Function
TSO	Time-Sharing Option		

Introduction

WHAT IS THE DIALOG MANAGER?

The ISPF Dialog Manager is an IBM program product designed to support the development of online, interactive applications. It is a software tool that enables applications developers to create interactive applications in a fraction of the time that would otherwise be required. The Dialog Manager makes it easy to develop full-screen applications having the sophisticated features associated with carefully designed online systems.

The Dialog Manager offers a number of important features to application developers. Its *display services* facilitate full-screen presentation of information from applications to the terminal, along with automatic editing of user input.* The Dialog Manager's *table services* permit entry and maintenance of data in two-dimensional tables and the saving of these data permanently on disk. *Message services* provide for context-sensitive display of informational and error messages and support an entire system of "help" and tutorial screens. The Dialog Manager contains a complete spectrum of *variable services* as well. These include the ability to associate variables with particular terminal users, the option to save such information across users' terminal sessions, and the provision of system information to application developers through what are referred to as *system variables*. Finally, the Dialog Manager can process files in order to perform dynamic variable substitution. These *file tailoring services* are useful in designing applications that set up and run background (or "batch") jobs at the request of terminal users.

The Dialog Manager is formally referred to as the Interactive System Productivity Facility (ISPF). It forms the basis for a separate program product, the Interactive System Productivity Facility/Program Devel-

---

Display services and other terms with which you may be unfamiliar are listed in the Glossary.

1

opment Facility (ISPF/PDF). You will be familiar with the Program Development Facility (PDF) as consisting of those menus and screens encountered after entering the command **ISPF** to the teleprocessing monitor. ISPF/PDF is composed of screens and supporting systems programs that help programmers run operating system utilities, edit and browse files, and execute various system language translators in foreground or background.

The Dialog Manager extends to the individual application developer features similar to those found in ISPF/PDF. Programmers can create interactive applications with a user interface similar to that of ISPF/PDF. These applications can use such ISPF functions as log file support, **EDIT** and **BROWSE** capability for files, and the split-screen option.*

For what kinds of applications might the Dialog Manager be useful? Examples cover the spectrum of online systems. Production systems involving the submission of batch jobs by non–data processing personnel are common. In these applications, the Dialog Manager services are used for file tailoring to permit users to change control information for each batch job submittal while still enforcing the kinds of data validation best implemented in online systems. Applications of this kind that the author has seen include a Time Card Reporting System, an Order Management System, and a Dialog Manager front-end to an offline data dictionary.

Other uses of the Dialog Manager benefit from its full-screen, interactive nature to support online query systems. Examples include a financial modeling system and a system for online generation of business graphs.

Many software vendors employ the Dialog Manager during the development of system products for sale to their clients. DATA-XPERT, vended by XA Systems Corporation, uses many of the Dialog Manager's facilities in providing licensees a general purpose file manipulation tool. Users can edit partitioned, ISAM, and VSAM data files from within a dialog that resembles ISPF/PDF (1). Information Planner, from Knowledgeware, Inc., similarly utilizes the Dialog Manager to support an information engineering approach to the information systems planning process (2). These products are only two examples of the many applications based on the Dialog Manager that are available in the marketplace (3).

The development of a wide variety of interactive applications requires software support of the kind provided by the ISPF Dialog Manager. Both MIS installations and software vendors increasingly use this product to aid in rapid development of new systems.

SUPPORTED OPERATING SYSTEMS

The ISPF Dialog Manager runs under a variety of operating systems. It runs in all three of IBM's major mainframe operating environments.

---

*Use of the **EDIT** and **BROWSE** features requires installation of ISPF/PDF as well as ISPF.

On large mainframes, the MVS operating system is included, and on smaller to midrange mainframes, the VSE operating system is included. Both operating systems are often referred to by a variety of acronyms. MVS is sometimes called OS, OS/VS2, MVS/TSO, MVS/SP, or MVS/XA; VSE is loosely referred to as DOS/VSE, VSE/ICCF, VSE/AF, or just DOS.

The Dialog Manager runs under the SSX/VSE operating system, a variant of the VSE environment for entry-level mainframes. This operating system is usually called SSX.

The Dialog Manager may also be installed under VM, an operating system whose use spans the mainframe spectrum. VM is sometimes referred to as VM/SP, VM/CMS, or VM/370. The Dialog Manager also runs under the microcomputer variant of the VM operating system, Virtual Machine/Personal Computer (VM/PC). VM/PC is supported on such microcomputers as the XT/370 and AT/370.

In this book, the operating systems supported by the ISPF Dialog Manager are generically referred to as MVS, VM, and VSE. VM includes reference to VM/PC, and VSE includes DOS/VSE and SSX/VSE.

Working with the Dialog Manager is essentially the same in all these environments. The coding differences that exist are quite minor. Any significant system-dependent differences will be discussed.

Within the various operating environments, the Dialog Manager supports a variety of languages for application development. Under the MVS and VM operating systems, these languages include COBOL, PL/I (Optimizer and Checkout), FORTRAN IV G1, and Assembler. The newest releases of the product add VS FORTRAN, Pascal, and APL2 to this list. The Dialog Manager also supports the CLIST interpretive command language under MVS and its counterpart under VM, the EXEC2 language. The latest version of the VM Dialog Manager additionally offers an interface to the REXX interpretive language.

In the VSE environment, the Dialog Manager supports the COBOL, PL/I, VS FORTRAN, RPGII, and Assembler languages. The Dialog Manager does not support a command language under VSE.

A Dialog Manager product is available for personal computers running the PC-DOS operating system; the product is called the EZ-VU Development Facility. Although it is modeled on the mainframe-based version of the Dialog Manager, EZ-VU has been heavily adapted to the PC-DOS environment. Since it requires substantial coding differences from the ISPF Dialog Manager, it is described in appendix E.

WHY LEARN THE DIALOG MANAGER?

In a world of proliferating languages and software tools, it is quite legitimate to ask why you should want to learn or use any particular product. There are a number of excellent reasons, however, for considering the Dialog Manager a product well worth learning. Some of these reasons have been alluded to already. For example, the ISPF

Dialog Manager presents a coherent application interface across the three major mainframe operating systems: MVS, VM, and VSE. Thus, those who learn to use the Dialog Manager will develop skills applicable to all three of the major mainframe operating systems. Moreover, these skills have even broader application because of the growing use of VM/ PC on microcomputers and the existence of a similar product for personal computers. Surely few other software products of any kind enjoy such a broad base.

The spread of the Dialog Manager across these different operating environments presents other advantages as well, including a higher degree of program portability and a consistent application interface for end users across systems. Perhaps most important is the fact that the ISPF Dialog Manager represents a strategic product. IBM has rarely positioned other software products for such wide availability across machines and operating systems.

The importance of the Dialog Manager can also be seen in its increasing use at MIS installations. The ISPF Dialog Manager is emerging as one of those few products that attains widespread use at mainframe data processing installations. It is fast becoming a de facto standard at MVS and VM sites. And its use as a development tool by software vendors has already been mentioned. Software houses consider the Dialog Manager a key tool in their development of systems products.

In the final analysis, an argument for the value of learning the Dialog Manager should be based on the merits of the product. There is little question that ISPF offers broad functionality and that it shortens development time, as any system designer knows, the ultimate justification for the use of a software tool.

OUR APPROACH

This book presents the use of the Dialog Manager in a straightforward manner. It is pragmatic in that it emphasizes the most frequently used features of the product.

Our approach presents a usable subset of the Dialog Manager facilities first and then progressively expands this subset to provide a fuller understanding of the product's capabilities. The book emphasizes a simple way to use the Dialog Manager rather than focusing on complicated alternatives. Since the objective is practical, the book eschews discussion of tricky or obscure programming practices.

Following introductory material on Dialog Manager concepts, we examine a working application system developed with the Dialog Manager as an example. This example system is progressively expanded throughout the book in order to supply a coding example for additional Dialog Manager features. Use of a single programming system example throughout the book lends consistency and coherence to the discussions, while culminating in a realistic example of a Dialog Manager-based application.

Complete coding of the example system is provided in two languages: COBOL and the CLIST command language of MVS. The examples written in these two languages are functionally identical. The sample application is completely duplicated in these two languages for two reasons. First, you need only have knowledge of either the COBOL or MVS CLIST language to use this book. Second, you can compare the use of the Dialog Manager with a compiled programming language with its use with an interpreted command language. The COBOL and CLIST versions of the example were thoroughly tested on an MVS computer. Figures containing example code are located at the end of the chapters to which they apply.

In both language examples, full documentation is contained in the programs themselves, and all are completely explained in the text. The textual description assumes use of the MVS operating system to facilitate clear explanation of the sample application. As with the COBOL and CLIST languages, MVS was selected as meeting the requirements of the majority of users. Where use of the Dialog Manager varies for VM and VSE users, however, I explain the differences in using the Dialog Manager under these operating systems.

The appendixes to this book supplement the text with supporting information. They include a list of vendor's reference manuals and a detailed description of library definitions required by the Dialog Manager. The library definitions were excluded from the main text because of their technical nature and the fact that most users will program at installations where this preliminary work has already been done for them.

Although *Using IBM's ISPF Dialog Manager* is not intended to replace the vendor's reference manuals, the value of this book's complete index should be obvious. You can make most effective use of this book by using the vendor's manuals as supporting reference materials. You are urged to perform your own programming experiments while reading.

REFERENCES

1. Murphy, Leslie L., "XA Systems Use of ISPF," paper presented at GUIDE 60 session number MP-7294, November 1984, San Francisco. XA Systems Corporation is located in Santa Clara, California.
2. Knowledgeware Inc., *Using Information Planner* and *Installing Information Planner*. Both manuals are vended by Knowledgeware Inc., Ann Arbor, Michigan. Revised February 1984.
3. There are over 70 IBM program products that interface with ISPF, as well as at least 60 products from other vendors. See the *GUIDE ISPF Project Newsletter* for current listings of these products.

1
Dialog Manager Concepts

WHAT IS A DIALOG?

The Dialog Manager aids application designers in developing interactive applications called *dialogs*. A dialog is a system of programs and predefined display screens put together so as to present the terminal user with a meaningful sequence of screens in order to accomplish work. A typical dialog is a Time Card Reporting System. The terminal user enters this dialog by typing a single command into the system. Once engaged in this dialog, the user encounters a series of screens designed to enable him or her to accomplish work relevant to time reporting. After exiting this self-contained application system, the user may go on to do other work on the terminal.

A dialog can be conceived of as a series of programs and screens. It is much like what is often referred to as an interactive *script* except that scripts are line-oriented interactions between the terminal user and an application system. A dialog written with the Dialog Manager is a *full-screen* application. Information is presented to (and accepted from) the terminal user in units of a full screen at a time. Dialogs take advantage of the capabilities of the 3270 family of terminals (and other full-screen devices such as the 3178 and 3180 terminals and the 3290 series).

Dialogs can look much like the ISPF dialog one encounters after entering ISPF/PDF by typing in the command **ISPF** to a teleprocessing monitor like TSO or CMS. By entering **ISPF,** the user is presented with a complete application system designed to aid in program development. The user can choose selections from a main menu that allow him or her to run operating system utilities, browse and edit files, and run various system language processors in either foreground or background. The dialog is supported by such features as context-sensitive messages, a full "help" or tutorial system, split-screen capability, and a log file.

The particular application entered by typing **ISPF** is called ISPF/

PDF, or PDF.* The Dialog Manager makes it possible to develop dialogs that look much like PDF. The same features evident in the PDF dialog are available to individual application developers through use of the Dialog Manager.

DIAGRAMMING DIALOGS

Because a dialog consists of user-developed programs and screen displays, it can be diagramed. First, though, some refinement of terms is required. The user-programmed portions of dialogs are termed *functions*. Functions may be written in any language supported by the Dialog Manager.

Screen display panels consist of *data entry panels* and *menus*. Data entry panels are full-screen displays that the user views and through which he or she may optionally enter data. Some data entry panels are simple *output display panels*, which only display information. Menus are screen displays that present a collection of alternative actions; you are expected to select one action. Menus are also referred to as *selection panels*.

Two dialogs are diagramed in diagrams 1-1 and 1-2. In diagram 1-1, Dialog A begins with display of a menu. Since this is the first menu

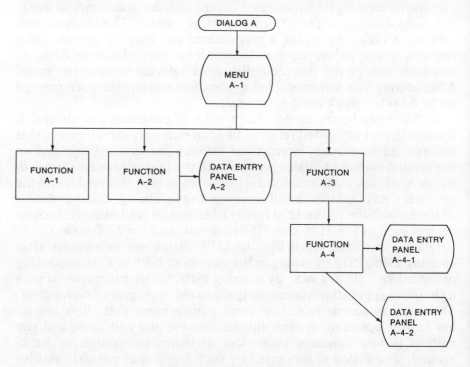

Diagram 1-1. Dialog A.

---

*Entry to ISPF/PDF may be site-dependent. See your system administrator in this case.

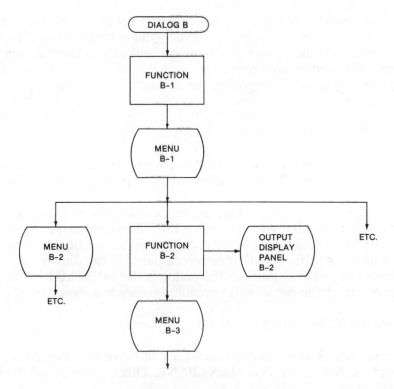

Diagram 1-2. Dialog B.

you see upon entering this dialog, it is called the *application master menu*. From this menu, Menu A-1, you can select one of several functions. The first option executes Function A-1, and the second choice runs Function A-2. Function A-2 displays Data Entry Panel A-2 and prompts you for data input through this screen. Function A-3 is also accessible from the dialog's master menu. Function A-3 selects Function A-4, which interacts with you through two data entry panels under its control.

Dialog B shows that a dialog can also begin with a function (diagram 1-2). Function B-1 performs some unspecified processing (perhaps initialization processing, for example) and then presents Menu B-1 on the screen. From Menu B-1, you might select a subsystem menu, Menu B-2, or you might select Function B-2, which displays information via panel B-2 and then passes control to Menu B-3.

In both diagrams, dialogs are conceived of as a hierarchically arranged scheme of menus, data entry panels, and programmed functions. The developer of the dialog can arrange the logic of the application in myriad ways using these basic elements. A dialog diagram is valuable when initially designing the dialog application and in documenting the system after it is developed. The hierarchical structure embodied in the diagram serves to define the dialog's logical design in the same manner that a flowchart describes the logical processing of a program.

A diagram of a dialog presents the *user view* of the system; that is, along with pictures of the screen panels, you can easily visualize what interaction with the system at a terminal looks like. The diagram also conveys the *application overview*, or the relationships between the functions and panels comprising the dialog.

ROLE OF THE DIALOG MANAGER

User-developed dialogs run under the control of the Dialog Manager. Therefore the Dialog Manager can provide applications with many services.

As diagrams 1-1 and 1-2 suggest, you can initiate any locally developed dialog through invocation of the ISPF Dialog Manager. One piece of information that must be included in this invocation command is the name of the first function or screen panel in the dialog.

The command that initiates the dialog is the **ISPSTART** command. An example of the use of this command to begin a dialog is:

ISPSTART PANEL(MENUPANL)

This command starts a dialog under the control of the Dialog Manager whose first display panel is **MENUPANL**. Other examples of the **ISP-START** command are:

ISPSTART PGM(PROGFUN)

and

ISPSTART CMD(CLISTFUN)

In the first instance, the Dialog Manager is initiated, and it executes program function **PROGFUN**. This program function might be written in COBOL, PL/I, FORTRAN or Pascal, depending on the choice of the application developer and the availability of these languages on the system. In the second case, a dialog is started under the Dialog Manager, and dialog processing begins with command language function **CLISTFUN**.

A user-developed dialog is thus initiated under the control of the Dialog Manager by entering the **ISPSTART** command. Parameters indicate whether dialog processing begins with display of a menu panel or execution of a command language or program function. More specific examples of starting dialogs are provided in the next chapter. For now, it is important to understand that the processing for any user-developed dialog must occur under the control of the Dialog Manager.

Although any dialog starts with the **ISPSTART** command, you do not necessarily have to enter this command yourself. **ISPSTART** can be entered in several ways besides direct entry. One approach is for the command to be executed automatically upon logon. Under the MVS operating system, this means that the TSO LOGON procedure accomplishes the appropriate **ISPSTART** command. In the VM environment, the CMS **PROFILE EXEC** performs this same function.

Another method is to include the **ISPSTART** command in a command procedure. Thus an MVS CLIST or VM EXEC2 or REXX command procedure issues the proper command to start a dialog, and you only have to execute this command procedure.

Another alternative is to make the user-developed dialog selectable from the ISPF/PDF master menu or a submenu. An installation thus presents a locally implemented dialog application as an option on the familiar ISPF/PDF menus after you enter the command **ISPF** to your teleprocessing monitor (either TSO under MVS or CMS under VM).

You can initiate a dialog:

1. by direct entry of the **ISPSTART** command,
2. via logon (MVS/TSO LOGON procedure or VM/CMS **PROFILE EXEC**),
3. through a command procedure (MVS CLIST or VM EXEC), or
4. by bundling user-developed dialog(s) as choices on the ISPF/PDF menus and reaching these applications through the familiar **ISPF** command.

In practice, the third method is probably most common.

The fourth approach is especially significant in that it demonstrates that the ISPF Dialog Manager is conceptually an extension of the operating system. ISPF and user-developed dialogs can be combined into an installation-configured *shell* surrounding the operating system. Derived from the UNIX environment, the concept of a shell refers to software that intercedes between the terminal user and the operating system, presenting a new software personality.

The user-developed portion of an ISPF-based shell is nearly code compatible across operating systems when written in portable languages; the Dialog Manager is *cross-systems compatible*. Program products that are cross-systems compatible feature a high degree of code compatibility and a similar user interface across the variety of operating systems for which they are available.

REQUESTING DIALOG MANAGER SERVICES

Since dialogs run under the Dialog Manager, it is appropriate that they request services from the Dialog Manager through service calls. Such Dialog Manager features as panel display services, table services, message services, and file tailoring services are invoked in this fashion. Functions coded as compiled programs or command procedures make service calls to ISPF to request Dialog Manager services. From a compiled programming language, the service invocation is achieved by calling a special service interface routine, **ISPLINK**. For example, from a COBOL program, calls take this general form:

CALL 'ISPLINK' USING service-name parameter1 parameter2 . . .

From command procedure functions, these service invocations are performed through the **ISPEXEC** command and take the form:

ISPEXEC service-name parameter1 parameter2 . . .

Much of this book illustrates requests for and use of ISPF Dialog Manager–provided services, so it is not important to feel comfortable with service invocation formats yet. The point is that such service requests are the basic mechanism through which user-developed functions make use of the Dialog Manager's facilities.

DIALOG MANAGER SERVICES

Dialog Manager facilities can be divided into two categories. One group consists of those features of the product that must be explicitly invoked by user-developed functions. For example, the Dialog Manager's display services permit display of a data entry screen; this service must be specifically invoked by a user-programmed function. The other class of features are those that exist inherently as part of the ISPF Dialog Manager environment. These features exist as fundamental characteristics of any dialog because that dialog must run under the control of the Dialog Manager. For example, the hierarchical control structure is an inherent characteristic of Dialog Manager applications. Other examples include the *online tutorial system* and the built-in *split-screen* capability. The *online tutorial system* appears to behave in a manner similar to the "help" screens you encounter when interacting with ISPF/PDF. Thus, you view a context-sensitive "help" panel from anywhere in a dialog merely by depressing the **HELP** program function key. (This key is normally program function key 1.) You return to your panel of origin by pressing the **END** program function key. This "help" screen facility is built into any user-developed dialog (assuming that the designers created the necessary tutorial panel definitions).

Split screen capability allows you to divide your screen horizontally into two logical portions and interact with copies of the dialog application in both logical screens. This feature is provided by the Dialog Manager in a manner totally transparent to user dialogs. You need take no special action to enable the user to use split-screen capability from within a dialog you develop.

Whereas tutorial and split-screen features are an inherent part of the Dialog Manager environment, user dialogs must explicitly invoke the system's *display services*. The service invocations allow you to develop a function that displays an output display panel, a data entry panel, or a menu. Users can enter data by the data entry panels, and the panel definition provides for automatic input editing of data by the Dialog Manager. Informational and error messages and tables maintained by the Dialog Manager's *message services* can also be displayed.

Table services permit functions to invoke the appropriate service commands to create and maintain data as two-dimensional arrays. These tables exist in main memory during a dialog and can be permanently saved on disk. Service invocations allow access to table rows either *sequentially* or *directly* via one or more keys. When more than one data element is specified as key, ISPF treats these data items like a concatenated key. In other words, where direct access is defined for a table with more than one key, all keys are used simultaneously (there is no provision for "alternate" or "secondary" key access). Tables may be used by more than a single dialog and table services ensure data integrity when used properly.

File tailoring services are invoked by dialog functions to prompt the Dialog Manager to tailor (process) specifically designated sequential files dynamically. File tailoring substitutes values for dialog variables occurring in the input *skeleton* file, producing a sequential output file. The input skeleton itself is never altered. Functions often use this class of services to create background jobs for submission to the operating system.

Variable services provide for the grouping of dialog variables into groups, or *pools*. The Dialog Manager recognizes three basic pools of variables: the *function*, *shared*, and *application profile* pools. The function pool is the group of dialog variables associated with a specific function; the shared pool consists of the dialog variables held in common among all functions in a single dialog; and the application profile pool consists of variables saved for each terminal user across terminal sessions. Values in the application profile pool represent individual terminal users.

Thus variable services provides a group of service commands that permit functions to manipulate variables in terms of the three pools. Services exist to copy and update variables between functions and pools and between the various pools themselves. How these variable services operate are illustrated and explained in depth through the program examples.

The Dialog Manager also provides *system variables*. These contain system and environmental information that may be useful to user-developed functions.

Finally, there are several miscellaneous services that functions may invoke through the Dialog Manager. These include the ability to place the user into the ISPF editor through the **EDIT** facility and the corresponding ability to allow him or her to **BROWSE** (view) files.* Dialogs may also utilize the ISPF log file in order to create a file of dialog messages that may be retained or printed when the dialog interaction terminates. Last, the **CONTROL** service permits functions to regulate various defaults of the Dialog Manager's operation. This enables dialog functions to set certain parameters concerning screen display and error handling.

DIALOG COMPONENTS

User-developed dialogs consist of several key components. Panels and functions have been mentioned. It is now appropriate to expand this

---

*Use of the **EDIT** and **BROWSE** services requires installation of ISPF/PDF.

list and enumerate the parts that comprise dialogs. Typical dialogs include all or some of the following elements:

Functions. Functions contain the processing logic in the dialog. Functions may be written as command procedures or in compiled programming languages.

Panels. Full-screen display panels communicate information. The panels may be menu panels, data entry panels, or output display panels. The Dialog Manager also supports tutorial or "help" screens. Messages may optionally be displayed on panels.

Messages. Messages may be displayed to provide explanatory, warning, or error information. Functions can designate messages for display on particular panels or on the next panel displayed. Messages can also be displayed automatically in response to invalid user input data or as the result of the user depressing the **HELP** program function key.

Tables. Dialog developers may define tables of information to be maintained under the auspices of the Dialog Manager. A table is simply a two-dimensional array of information. Tables can be temporary (they exist only during the dialog) or permanent (they are retained across sessions). Permanent tables may be used by only one dialog or by multiple dialogs. The Dialog Manager provides a lock mechanism to ensure the integrity of tables concurrently referenced by more than one dialog function or user.*

File Tailoring Skeletons. A *skeleton* is a sequential file processed by the Dialog Manager's file tailoring services to produce a sequential output file. This processing may involve dynamic variable substitution, which is automatically performed by the Dialog Manager. Often this service is used to configure dynamically Job Control Language statements that are submitted to the operating system as a batch job.

Individual Profile Datasets. Profile datasets contain variables saved per terminal user across terminal sessions. They customize dialogs for each user.

COMPONENT LIBRARIES

The dialog elements discussed already are created by the dialog developer as needed and placed into the appropriate *component libraries*. The library requirements are as follows:

Functions. Program functions must be compiled and linked with the **ISPLINK** interface service routine and placed into a load module library known to the Dialog Manager. Functions coded as command procedures must similarly reside in command procedure libraries.

---

*The manual *ISPF Dialog Management Services* contains details concerning proper use of ISPF's table integrity features.

Panels. A *panel definition* is coded for each panel used in the dialog. These panel definitions reside in a panel library known to the Dialog Manager. A special (and very simple) notation is used to define panels (this language is explored later in this book). Panel definitions are entered directly into the panel library; no compile or preprocessing of panel definitions prior to their use by the Dialog Manager is required. The same panel definition can be used by more than one function regardless of whether the functions are coded as command procedures or in compiled programming languages.

Messages. Messages are written in a simple, structured format (described later in this book). Messages written in this format are called *message definitions*. All message definitions are placed in a message library known to the Dialog Manager.

Tables. Tables may be *temporary* (they exist only in main memory during a dialog) or *permanent* (they are written to disk and saved across sessions). Permanent tables are stored on disk in a table library known to the Dialog Manager.

File Tailoring Skeletons. Like panel definitions, *skeleton definitions* for file tailoring services are entered by the dialog developer directly into a skeleton library known to the Dialog Manager. Skeleton definitions do not require any compile or preprocessing step prior to their use in a dialog.

Diagram 1-3 provides a schematic view of the various libraries the Dialog Manager uses to keep track of dialog components. As the diagram shows, a user dialog runs under control of the Dialog Manager, which itself runs under control of the operating system. The Dialog Manager references the libraries. Several additional groups of files are shown in this figure. The *file tailoring output files* contain the results of the file tailoring process on skeleton definitions; the *log file* supports the Dialog Manager's log facility; and the *profile datasets* save variables for each user across terminal sessions.

The encoding of functions, panel definitions, messages, and skeleton definitions required in dialog development is illustrated in the examples in subsequent chapters. These are distinct dialog elements; developing a dialog means creating these components as needed.

All dialog components reside in libraries that are defined to the Dialog Manager. You will likely be in a programming environment where component libraries have already been defined for your use. In such a situation, ask your supervisor or project team members about the names of these libraries. Installations or project teams typically write a command procedure to specify the various component libraries to the Dialog Manager for running and testing dialogs.

If you are on your own, you will find details of library allocation for using the Dialog Manager in appendix A. This information is separated from the text of this book because of its technical nature and because such information is operating-system and site-dependent. Most readers will not need to read this appendix. For those who do, we suggest examining appendix A after reading the next chapter.

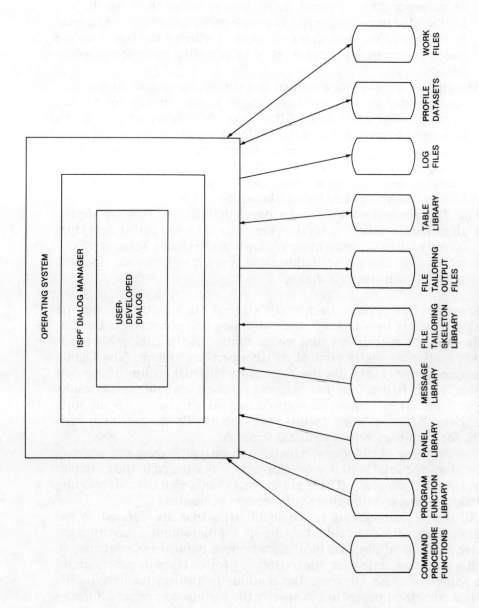

Diagram 1-3. Dialog manager libraries.

VM AND VSE DIFFERENCES

The body of this book addresses use of the Dialog Manager under the operating system of the majority of readers, MVS. Separate sections at the end of each chapter note any differences in the VM and VSE environments.

There is only one minor respect in which use of the Dialog Manager under VM differs from what has been stated already. This is that functions written in a compiled programming language do not have to be linked prior to their use under the Dialog Manager, as in MVS. Instead program functions may either be

1. compiled only (in **TEXT** or object module format), or
2. compiled and linked edited (in load module format).

There are several unique aspects of using the Dialog Manager under VSE compared to MVS. First, VSE users may program functions in one of several compiled languages (including COBOL, PL/I, and VS FORTRAN). VSE users do not have the option to encode functions in a command language.

Second, the manner in which a dialog is initiated under ICCF is slightly different. A dialog is started from an ICCF terminal by use of an ICCF procedure. Assuming that this procedure is called **ISPSTART**, initiating a dialog whose first action is display of a menu panel named **MENUPANL** is achieved by:

    ISPSTART 'PANEL(MENUPANL)'

A dialog that begins with program processing can be initiated with

    ISPSTART 'PGM(PROGFUN) LANG(COBOL)'

or

    ISPSTART 'PGM(PROGFUN) LANG(PLI)'

The VSE environment requires use of the **LANG** keyword to convey to the Dialog Manager which programming language the program function is written in.

CHAPTER REVIEW

The remainder of this book provides a step-by-step explanation of an example dialog designed to illustrate use of the Dialog Manager. A brief summary of the concepts presented is appropriate because you must understand these concepts to understand the rest of this book.

The Interactive System Productivity Facility is an IBM program product also known under the names ISPF, the ISPF Dialog Manager, and the Dialog Manager. In this book, we usually refer to it by the last two names.

Diagram 1-4 shows that the ISPF Dialog Manager is conceptually an extension to the host operating system. Programmers develop on-line, interactive applications called *dialogs* using ISPF. A dialog permits full-screen, conversational interaction between a terminal user and the computer. As diagram 1-4 indicates, programmer-developed dialogs run under the control of the Dialog Manager.

The Dialog Manager provides a wide variety of services to its dialog applications. These services are generally classified as display services, table services, message services, variable services, file tailoring services, and miscellaneous services.

All Dialog Manager services are invoked from programmer-developed dialogs via the **CALL** facility of compiled programming languages or the **ISPEXEC** command in command procedure languages. These interfaces are depicted in diagrams 1-5 and 1-6, respectively. Dialogs may be written in a variety of programming languages, and several languages may be used within a single dialog.

ISPF permits maximum flexibility in the design of dialogs. As described already in the chapter and shown in diagrams 1-1 and 1-2, dialogs may be organized or structured in any manner desired. Selection panels (or menus), program or command functions, data entry panels, and data display panels may be arranged within a dialog as appropriate.

Dialogs may also be thought of in terms of their major components.

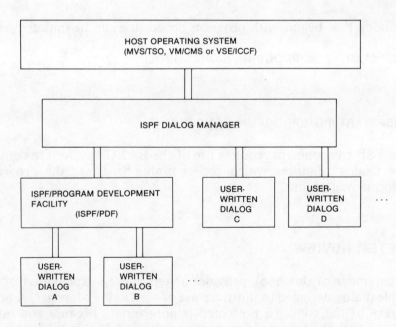

Diagram 1-4. Dialogs run under control of the ISPF Dialog Manager.

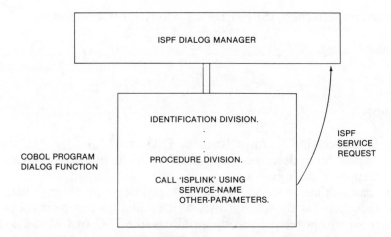

Diagram 1-5. *Program dialog functions* run under and request services of the ISPF Dialog Manager.

Typical dialogs include: program or command procedure *functions*; data entry, display, or menu *panels*; error and warning *messages*; *tables* for data storage; and file tailoring *skeletons*. These dialog components are stored in the component libraries described already in the chapter and illustrated in diagram 1-3.

IBM vends a separately purchased program product based upon the ISPF Dialog Manager, the ISPF/Program Development Facility, (ISPF/PDF, or just PDF). ISPF/PDF is a dialog designed to aid in the development of ISPF-based dialogs (as well as to perform other tasks). As a dialog, ISPF/PDF runs under the control of the ISPF Dialog Manager and makes use of ISPF Dialog Manager services.

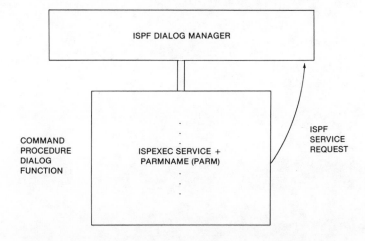

Diagram 1-6. *Command procedure dialog functions* run under and request services of the ISPF Dialog Manager.

Programmers enter ISPF/PDF by entering the commands

ISPF

or

PDF

to the teleprocessing monitor (such as TSO or CMS).*

This book later describes how ISPF/PDF helps programmers develop their own dialogs.

You can initiate user-developed dialogs in one of several different ways. Diagram 1-4 shows that user-written dialogs can be invoked directly from within teleprocessing monitors like TSO or CMS. The text has already described several approaches. Diagram 1-4 also indicates that user-developed dialogs can be listed as selectable options from the ISPF/PDF menus. In this case, you enter ISPF/PDF and then select the locally written dialog from the ISPF/PDF application master menu or a submenu.

You should now have a conceptual understanding of the role and purposes of the ISPF Dialog Manager and how user-written dialogs can make use of its many services. Do not be concerned if the material seems abstract at this point. The remainder of this book provides concrete examples of how to use the many Dialog Manager facilities mentioned in this chapter.

---

*Invocation of ISPF/PDF is sometimes site-dependent. See your system administrator in this case.

2
A Simple Dialog

This chapter presents a complete example of a dialog. The example shows how to initiate the dialog under control of the Dialog Manager, create a menu panel definition, and run a function selected from the application master menu panel. This example also shows you how to exit from the dialog.

As with all the other example dialogs in this book, the code has been tested under the MVS operating system. Differences for VM and VSE environments are covered at the end of the chapter.

If you do not have associates who can aid you in specifying the necessary dialog component libraries, you will wish to read appendix A on how to define libraries to the Dialog Manager. Because the example code in appendix A is modeled on the dialog of this chapter, you should review this chapter prior to reading the appendix.

THE DIALOG

The example dialog is shown in diagram 2-1. When the user enters a command, dialog processing is initiated. The menu panel called **WMENU2** is displayed on the screen (figure 2-1). The application is entitled West Department Accounts Receivable. Its purpose is to support an online accounts receivables reporting system for a department in a large company.

In subsequent chapters, this example dialog will be expanded to show a complete accounts receivable reporting system for a department within a company implemented using the Dialog Manager. The West Department Accounts Receivable system allows users to view the master file of accounts receivable records and to produce reports based on that master file for their own or other cost centers within the company.

For now, the sample dialog is highly simplified in order to concentrate on the basics of dialog creation. Thus, only two options appear on this application master menu: (1) the user selects a function that will

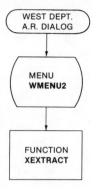

Diagram 2-1. Dialog diagram example.

extract data from another system within the company to create the master file for this application or (2) the user exits the dialog. At the arrow next to the **SELECT OPTION** message, the user enters the choice. This choice must be either **1** or **X,** or an error message results. If the user enters **1** from this menu, the selected function is executed, and the user again views this master menu. If the user enters **X** or **x** (lower case), the dialog and the Dialog Manager are exited, and the screen displays the prompt of the operating system's teleprocessing monitor (**READY** for MVS/TSO, and **R;** for VM/CMS).

IMPLEMENTATION

The command the user enters to initiate this dialog is the name of a CLIST (MVS command list procedure). In this particular system, the command procedure is called **XDM2.** Thus the user enters

XDM2

to initiate the dialog, assuming that the operating system knows the location of the library in which this CLIST resides. The function of this CLIST is to indicate the proper dialog component libraries to the Dialog Manager and to issue the appropriate **ISPSTART** command. Figure 2-2 lists the code of this CLIST in full. As it contains certain installation-dependent code, the only command from this CLIST that concerns us at this time is

ISPSTART PANEL(WMENU2)

This is the last command executed in the CLIST, **XDM2.** It starts the Dialog Manager and indicates that the master menu panel **WMENU2** should be displayed. How this panel appears was illustrated in figure 2-1.

The panel definition for menu **WMENU2** is listed in figure 2-3. The panel definition is written using a simple notation and is directly entered into the panel definition library.

The panel definition consists of three parts. The sections are indicated by the following words, each of which must begin in column 1 of the panel definition:

)BODY
)INIT
)PROC

The end of the panel definition is indicated by **)END**. Each section of the panel definition has a specific purpose, and the sections of the panel definition must appear in the order shown. Although almost all panel definitions contain these three sections, only the **)BODY** section and the **)END** keyword are required by the Dialog Manager. Most panel definitions also contain other sections that are described later in this book.

The purpose of the **)BODY** section is to define the format of the panel as it will display on the screen. This section describes the *literal information* that appears on the screen and any *variable fields*. Literal information refers to character strings that appear on the screen exactly as written in the panel definition. Variable fields are those whose display will be determined by their contents at the time of screen display. Variables can be used for output of information or they can be *user-modifiable,* meaning that data may be entered into these fields.

Preceding each literal and variable displayed on the screen, the panel definition contains an *attribute character* or *attribute byte*. The attribute character indicates the manner in which the information will be displayed on the screen. Fields can be displayed as high or low intensity and as protected fields or user-modifiable fields. Protected and user-modifiable fields are referred to as *text* and *input* fields, respectively.

These default attribute characters are provided by the Dialog Manager:

% (percentage sign)   = text (or protected) field, high intensity
+ (plus sign)   = text (or protected) field, low intensity
— (underscore)   = input (user-modifiable) field, high intensity

Thus, in figure 2-3, the first line to appear on the screen is a title line for the system containing dashes and the phrase **WEST DEPARTMENT ACCOUNTS RECEIVABLE**. This literal appears highlighted on the first line of the terminal display. Two blank lines follow the first line. On line 4 appears the **SELECT OPTION** = = = > phrase, also a protected, high-intensity field. Immediately after the arrow is an input field. Whatever the user enters into this field displays in high intensity as the user types it. The remainder of the screen contains two literals, designating selectable options. In both cases, the option number itself is highlighted, and the explanation of the option appears as a low-intensity protected field. Notice that the screen display of figure 2-1 does not indicate highlighted versus low-intensity display fields because it is a screen picture reproduced through use of a printer. Conventional printers cannot distinguish between high- and low-intensity display fields.

The panel definition section specified by the keyword)INIT describes *initialization processing*, or that which the Dialog Manager is to do prior to display of this panel. This initialization section normally describes how to initialize variables prior to screen display. In the case of the **WMENU2** panel definition, the values of two variables are set. **.HELP** is called a *control variable;* that is, it is a predefined variable that pertains to the display of the panel. The **.HELP** control variable indicates the name of the "help" panel definition to display if the user presses the **HELP** program function key.* In this case, this variable is set to **WH001**, so **WH001** must be the member name of a panel definition for a "help" or tutorial panel. If the user presses the **HELP** program function key, the Dialog Manager displays the panel definition library member named **WH001**. (This assumes such a panel has been defined by the dialog developers.) After reading this "help" panel, the user presses the **END** program function key to return to viewing panel **WMENU2**. The Dialog Manager's tutorial services are described in greater detail later.

ZPRIM is one of a number of *system variables*. System variables communicate information between the dialog and the Dialog Manager. For example, a value of **YES** in **ZPRIM** indicates that menu panel **WMENU2** is the primary option menu in this application. In other words, **WMENU2** is the *application master menu*. System variables, and the manner in which they are used in dialogs, are discussed later. For now, it is important only to recognize that system variables begin with the letter **Z**, just as control variables begin with a period (.). Dialog developers should avoid naming their own dialog variables with names beginning with the letter **Z**.

The *processing section* of the panel is indicated by the keyword)PROC. This section of the panel definition describes processing that the Dialog Manager will perform after the panel has been displayed. This section typically specifies data validation and translation the Dialog Manager performs on user input fields. In the case of menu **WMENU2**, the user enters a command option into the system variable **ZCMD**. This input must then be translated into an appropriate selection action by the Dialog Manager, as indicated in the processing section of the display panel definition for **WMENU2**. The *built-in function* **TRANS** is used for this purpose. Its simple format is:

> **TRANS (variable valueA, valueB valueC, valueD . . .)**

The variable occurring after the left parenthesis is analyzed to determine its contents. If it contains **valueA**, it is translated into **valueB**, and if it contains **valueC**, it is translated into **valueD**. The multiple pairs of values after the variable within the translate statement indicate pairs of current values and their respective translated values.

---

*Depressing a program function key (PF key) issues the ISPF command assigned to that key. This book assumes default ISPF key assignments, with PF1 assigned to the **HELP** command, PF3 to the **END** command, PF4 to the **RETURN** command, and so forth. However, these default key assignments may vary by dialog or installation.

In the panel definition, the system variable **ZCMD** is set through the user's data input on line 4 of the screen. The processing section uses the **TRANS** built-in function to analyze the value of **ZCMD**. If the value of **ZCMD** is **1**, it is translated into the character string **CMD(XEXTRACT)**; if its value is **X**, it is translated into the string **EXIT**. A space is translated into a space, and the "none of the above" condition, indicated by an asterisk (*), results in display of an ISPF-provided error message for an invalid menu selection.

The general format of the processing portion of a menu panel definition is:

```
&ZSEL = TRANS ( &ZCMD
                value, 'string'
                value, 'string'
                         .
                         .
                         .
                '  ',  '  '
                *,  '?'  )
```

In the menu panel definition, the command input system variable **ZCMD** is always translated to the appropriate value and then assigned to the system variable **ZSEL**. The Dialog Manager knows to implement the menu selection depending on the value of **ZSEL**. In the case of panel **WMENU2**, selection of option 1 means **ZSEL** is set to the character string value **CMD(XEXTRACT)**. Similar to its appearance on the **ISPSTART** command, **CMD(XEXTRACT)** indicates the command procedure function called **XEXTRACT** should be executed. If the **XEXTRACT** function were written in a compiled programming language, it would be executed through the encoding of this string: **PGM(XEXTRACT)**.

After execution of the function, the menu panel **WMENU2** is redisplayed. Selection of the option **X** results in **ZSEL** containing the string **EXIT**, the keyword the Dialog Manager recognizes as specifying an exit terminating the dialog.

The processing section of this panel definition indicates that entering a space, or entering nothing, from menu **WMENU2** simply redisplays the panel. Entry of an invalid option is caught by the translation value of * (asterisk), which results in setting **ZSEL** to ? (question mark). The Dialog Manager displays the default error message of **INVALID OPTION** in the rightmost corner of the screen display. This is illustrated in figure 2-4. Because **2** was incorrectly entered as an option, the Dialog Manager responded **INVALID OPTION**.

EXECUTING THE FUNCTION

Consider what happens when option 1 is selected from the menu panel.

First, the processing section of the menu panel definition translates the input to **CMD(XEXTRACT)**. This is assigned to system variable **ZSEL**, and since this is a menu panel, the Dialog Manager knows to pass control to function **XEXTRACT**. The keyword **CMD** tells the Dialog Manager this is a command procedure function rather than a program function. Program functions are indicated by **PGM**.

The CLIST that executes is contained in figure 2-5. You need not inspect the code of this command procedure in detail. Its function is merely to set up and run a program. That program performs the work of reading input data from external files and translating these data into the master file format for the West Department Accounts Receivable system.

Neither this CLIST nor the program it executes invokes the Dialog Manager's services. The CLIST does not contain any **ISPEXEC** statements. Recall that command procedures invoke Dialog Manager services through use of the **ISPEXEC** command.

Since the command procedure does not invoke the Dialog Manager to display a data entry or output display panels, the next screen the terminal user sees is a redisplay of the **WMENU2** menu panel.* Thus, when a function completes execution, control returns to the next higher level panel or function in the hierarchy expressed through the dialog diagram. Selecting option 1 from the application master menu therefore results in execution of the **XEXTRACT** function and redisplay of the master menu.

VM AND VSE DIFFERENCES

In the VM environment, the Dialog function **XEXTRACT** could be written as an EXEC2 command procedure. The CLIST **XDM2,** which starts the dialog, could similarly be written in the EXEC2 language. Details on what this procedure should contain are given in the appropriate section of appendix A.

Notice that under VM, the Dialog Manager does *not* support the EXEC command language. **&TRACE** must occur in the first line in the command procedure to specify use of the EXEC2 language.

The latest version of the Dialog Manager, Version 2, supports use of the REXX language in addition to EXEC2. Details on ISPF Version 2 are provided in chapter 12.

The VSE environment does not support use of a command language. All dialog functions must be written in compiled programming languages.

---

*Actually, this particular CLIST specifies the option **CONTROL MSG**. This CLIST option means that informational messages from CLIST commands and statements will display on the terminal. The user selects option 1 from the menu, and the CLIST's informational messages list on the screen. After the user presses the **ENTER** key, menu **WMENU2** will be redisplayed. All CLISTs in this book specify **CONTROL MSG** because these programs were written for demonstration purposes. To execute the command procedure with immediate redisplay of the menu **WMENU2** and no intervening CLIST messages (as stated in the text), the CLIST control options should include **CONTROL NOMSG.** CLISTs in production environments normally specify command procedure options to eliminate CLIST-generated messages. All display messages should be sent via the Dialog Manager's services.

Rather than invoking an ISPF dialog through a CLIST, VSE users start an ISPF application from a terminal running under ICCF through specification of an ICCF procedure. This ICCF procedure invokes ISPF, as discussed in chapter 1. Similar to the use of the **ISPSTART** command shown in that chapter, VSE menu selections require use of the keywords **PGM** and **LANG** in the character strings assigned to system variable **ZSEL**.

Figure 2-1. **WMENU2** screen as displayed.

```
-------------- WEST DEPARTMENT ACCOUNTS RECEIVABLE --------------------------


SELECT OPTION ===>


   1    EXTRACT DATA FROM MASTER FILES

   X    EXIT
```

Figure 2-2. XDM2 CLIST.

```
00010000   PROC 0
00020000   CONTROL MSG NOFLUSH
00030000   /*****************************************************************/
00040000   /* NAME: XDM2                              BY: H. FOSDICK      */
00050000   /*                                                            */
00060000   /* PURPOSE: THIS CLIST SETS UP THE ENVIRONMENT NECESSARY      */
00070000   /* TO ENTERING THE 'WEST DEPARTMENT ACCOUNTS RECEIVABLE'      */
00080000   /* SYSTEM.  IT ALLOCATES ALL LIBRARIES REQUIRED BY THE USER   */
00090000   /* WHEN ENTERING A DIALOG MANAGER APPLICATION, THEN ISSUES    */
00100000   /* THE 'ISPSTART' COMMAND TO SELECT THE APPLICATION MASTER    */
00110000   /* MENU.                                                      */
00120000   /*                                                            */
00130000   /*****************************************************************/
00140000
00150000   /*                                                            */
00160000   /*   FREE ANY PREVIOUS ISPF/DIALOG MANAGER ALLOCATIONS:       */
00170000   /*                                                            */
00180000
00190000   FREE FILE(ISPPLIB ISPMLIB ISPSLIB ISPTLIB ISPPROF ISPTABL ISPLLIB)
00200000
00210000
00220000   /*                                                            */
00230000   /*   ALLOCATE THE PANEL LIBRARIES:                            */
00240000   /*                                                            */
00250000
00260002   ALLOCATE FILE(ISPPLIB) DA(PROGRAMS.TEST    'SYS1.PANELS')  SHR REUSE
00270000
00280000
00290000   /*                                                            */
00300000   /*   ALLOCATE THE MESSAGE LIBRARIES:                          */
00310000   /*                                                            */
00320000
00330002   ALLOCATE FILE(ISPMLIB) DA(PROGRAMS.TEST    'SYS1.MSGS')  SHR REUSE
00340000
00350000
00360000   /*                                                            */
00370000   /*   ALLOCATE THE SKELETON JCL LIBRARIES:                     */
00380000   /*                                                            */
00390000
00400002   ALLOCATE FILE(ISPSLIB) DA(PROGRAMS.TEST    'SYS1.SKELS')   SHR REUSE
00410000
00420000
00430000   /*                                                            */
00440000   /*   ALLOCATE THE TABLE INPUT LIBRARIES:                      */
00450000   /*                                                            */
00460000
00470002   ALLOCATE FILE(ISPTLIB) DA(PROGRAMS.TEST    'SYS1.TABLES')  SHR REUSE
00480000
00490000
00500000   /*                                                            */
00510000   /*   ALLOCATE THE USER PROFILE LIBRARY:                       */
00520000   /*                                                            */
00530000
00540000   ALLOCATE FILE(ISPPROF) DA('&SYSUID..ISPF.PROFILE') OLD REUSE
00550000
00560000
00570000   /*                                                            */
00580000   /*   ALLOCATE THE TABLE OUTPUT LIBRARY:                       */
00590000   /*                                                            */
00600000
00610001   ALLOCATE FILE(ISPTABL) DA(PROGRAMS.TEST)  SHR REUSE
00620000
00630000
00640000   /*                                                            */
00650000   /*   ALLOCATE THE PROGRAM FUNCTION LOAD LIBRARY:              */
00660000   /*                                                            */
00670000
00680000   ALLOCATE FILE(ISPLLIB) DA(C.LOAD)  SHR REUSE
00690000
00700000
00710000   /*                                                            */
00720000   /*   ISSUE THE 'ISPSTART' COMMAND TO DISPLAY THE MASTER       */
00730000   /*   APPLICATION MENU TO THE USER:                            */
00740000   /*                                                            */
00750000
00760000   ISPSTART PANEL(WMENU2)
```

Figure 2-3. WMENU2 panel definition.

```
)BODY
%-------------- WEST DEPARTMENT ACCOUNTS RECEIVABLE ----------------------------
%
%
%SELECT OPTION ===>_ZCMD+
%
%
%  1  +EXTRACT DATA FROM MASTER FILES
%
%  X  +EXIT
%
%
)INIT
   .HELP     = WH001
   &ZPRIM    = YES
)PROC
   &ZSEL = TRANS( &ZCMD
                  1,'CMD(XEXTRACT)'
                  X,'EXIT'
                ' ',' '
                  *,'?' )

)END
```

Figure 2-4.   WMENU2 screen as displayed with error message.

```
------------ WEST DEPARTMENT ACCOUNTS RECEIVABLE ------------ INVALID OPTION

SELECT OPTION ===> 2


  1    EXTRACT DATA FROM MASTER FILES

  X    EXIT
```

Figure 2-5. XEXTRACT CLIST function.

```
00010000    PROC 0
00020000    CONTROL MSG NOFLUSH
00030000    /****************************************************************/
00040000    /* NAME: XEXTRACT                        BY: H. FOSDICK        */
00050000    /*                                                            */
00060000    /* PURPOSE: THIS CLIST SETS UP AND RUNS A PROGRAM UNDER       */
00070000    /* CONTROL OF THE DIALOG MANAGER.  AFTER COMPLETION, THE      */
00080000    /* USER RETURNS TO THE APPLICATION MASTER MENU.               */
00090000    /*                                                            */
00100000    /****************************************************************/
00110000
00120000    DELETE ACCT.OUT
00130000    FREE FILE(SYSIN)
00140000
00150000    /*                                                            */
00160000    /*   ALLOCATE ALL REQUIRED FILES, EXECUTE THE DATA            */
00170000    /*   EXTRACTION PROGRAM, AND RETURN TO THE APPLICATION MENU:  */
00180000    /*                                                            */
00190000
00200000    ATTRIB    ATTR1 BLKSIZE(6000) LRECL(200) RECFM(F B)
00210000    ALLOCATE FILE(OUTFILE) DA(ACCT.OUT) NEW SPACE(1) CYL USING(ATTR1)
00220000    ALLOCATE FILE(INFILE)   DA(SESSION.TEXT(GRAPHIN)) SHR
00230000    ALLOCATE FILE(SYSIN)    DA(PROGRAMS.PLI(VPLANNER)) SHR
00240000    CALL W.LOAD(TRANPROG)
00250000
00260000
00270000    /*                                                            */
00280000    /*   FREE ALLOCATED FILES AND EXIT WITH RETURN CODE OF 0:     */
00290000    /*                                                            */
00300000
00310000    FREE FILE(INFILE SYSIN OUTFILE)
00320000    FREE ATTRLIST(ATTR1)
00330000
00340000    EXIT CODE(0)
```

③

Expanding the Example Dialog

This chapter, and the several that follow, build on the example dialog of chapter 2. Together they revise that simple dialog into a much broader example that addresses the most frequently used features of the Dialog Manager. The result is a complete and realistic example dialog application that aids in describing use of the Dialog Manager and explaining its strengths as a programming tool.

The example application implemented through the use of the Dialog Manager is called the West Department Accounts Receivable system. It is an accounts receivable reporting system for a particular department of a large company, the West Department.

Through this Dialog Manager–based application system, users can view online the invoice records in the departmental accounts receivable master file. They can produce a simple report of this file and can update their own job accounting parameters used in the submission of the report program. They can also run a Distribution Report program, which prints a multipart report of accounts receivable for the particular cost and sub-cost centers of the company. The different parts of this report are distributed to the appropriate employees in each cost and sub-cost center within the company. A special subsystem within the West Department Accounts Receivable system allows users to update cost and sub-cost centers (and the report control date) so that the parts of the Distribution Report are sent to the appropriate people within the company.

Do not worry if the underlying rationale of the West Department Accounts Receivable application is not entirely clear to you. The nature of this sample dialog becomes apparent as it is described in subsequent chapters.

REVISING THE MASTER MENU

In developing a more ambitious version of the West Department Accounts Receivable reporting system, the first thing to be done is to revise the application master menu. Figure 3-1 shows that the previous menu definition of figure 2-3 has been used as a basis for development of a more comprehensive master menu. Figure 3-1 is the master menu for the COBOL implementation of the sample dialog.

The primary difference in this new form of the dialog master menu is the addition of several more options. Option 1 is the same as previously; its role in this application is to create the master file used by other functions in the application. Selection of option 1, **EXTRACT DATA FROM MASTER FILES**, refreshes the master file used as input by the other functions in this system, from its source files maintained by another application system. Option 2 allows users to view the extracted data file (the master file for this dialog application) as that file has been created through the execution of the function selected by option 1. Option 2 illustrates the Dialog Manager services for the viewing and editing of files under dialog control.

Option 3 permits users to enter and update employee accounting information. These data are used as source information for options 4 and 5. Thus, option 3 demonstrates how to save and update information associated with a particular terminal user through the Dialog Manager, and it also illustrates how this information can be picked up and used by other dialog functions.

Options 4 and 5 allow users to produce either of two accounts receivable reports. One is referred to as the *Simple Report;* the other is called the *Distribution Report.* In terms of the example system, these options illustrate various aspects of the Dialog Manager's file tailoring services. Option 5 additionally demonstrates some of the features of the Dialog Manager's table services.

Finally, option 6 displays a menu for a subsystem through which users can enter and update accounting control card data. This information is utilized by the Distribution Report program of menu option 5 so that different parts of that report can be distributed to the appropriate employees in the proper cost and sub-cost centers of the company. The several functions executed through the submenu of option 6 show extensive use of the Dialog Manager's table services. The format of this submenu and its functions are described later in the book.

As in the earlier form of the master application menu, entering **X** from the master menu permits exit from the dialog.

Appendixes C and D contain the dialog diagram for this example system. It is not necessary to inspect this diagram at this time; it is merely included in the appendixes for future reference.

Figure 3-1 therefore contains a menu panel description for a complete system to provide an accounts receivable function for the West Department in a corporation. This example provides the basis for a coding illustration and discussion of the most important features of the Dialog Manager throughout the remainder of this book.

In figure 3-1, the manner in which additional selectable topics are added to the menu is apparent. The)**BODY** section of the panel definition adds several literals to describe additional menu options. When adding lines to the body of the panel definition, remember not to add more lines than can display on the terminal.

The initialization section, following the)INIT keyword, is also expanded. It shows the use of two more system variables, **ZHTOP** and **ZHINDEX**. **ZHTOP** tells the Dialog Manager which is the topmost panel definition in the hierarchy of tutorial or "help" panels. This is usually the table of contents for the tutorial system. **ZHINDEX** similarly denotes the name of the panel definition library member that provides the index panel (or the first index panel, if there are more than one) for the hierarchy of tutorial panels.

Because the manner in which the tutorial system works under the Dialog Manager merits discussion in its own right, chapter 8 fully describes it. For now, it is important to realize that the Dialog Manager supports a complete system of "help" screens, which includes index panels and a table of contents. These screens are related in a hierachical fashion, allowing users to navigate them as necessary to retrieve relevant tutorial information. The tutorial system is completely implemented as a feature of the Dialog Manager.

The processing section of the screen panel definition includes additional options corresponding to those in the body section of the menu. Option 2, for example, will execute a function called **CBROWSE** under Dialog Manager control. This option is written in a compiled programming language, as designated by the keyword **PGM**. Other options similarly execute other COBOL programs (for technical reasons explained later, options 4 and 5 execute CLISTs, which then use Dialog Manager services to execute COBOL functions). Option 6 displays the menu for the Accounting Control Administration Subsystem. The **PANEL** keyword informs the Dialog Manager that **WSAMENC** is a panel definition in the panel library. Like Figure 3-1's **WMENUC** panel definition, **WSAMENC** is a menu or selection panel.

There is one other aspect of interest in this menu panel definition. The *truncation* built-in function is used to truncate the system variable **ZCMD**, input by the user, at the first period. This truncation function is performed by the Dialog Manager prior to the **TRANS** function because it is nested within parentheses. The truncation function allows termination of the user input after a certain number of characters. For example, the statement

```
&SAMPLE = TRUNC (&VARA,2)
```

truncates the variable **&VARA** after the first two characters and then assigns these two characters to variable **&SAMPLE**. In the case of figure 3-1, **ZCMD** is truncated at the first period so as to implement a feature of the Dialog Manager called the *jump function*. The jump function permits users to navigate directly through the hierarchical structure of the dialog. In this system, for example, users could enter **6.2** from this primary menu. This would cause them to enter option 2 of the subsystem menu **WSAMENC** directly, bypassing display of that menu.

The nesting of the **TRUNC** function within the option selection statement has a simple purpose. Most menus in production systems use this feature of the Dialog Manager. The primary menu definition of figure 3-1 provides a good model for defining menu panels.

CLIST SYSTEM MASTER MENU

The menu panel definition of figure 3-1 is used in the COBOL implementation of the example dialog system. The CLIST sample system must use a different, though highly similar, version of this same menu definition. The reason is that the Dialog Manager's selection of functions from a menu requires an indication of the language encoding of the selected function. In the processing section of figure 3-1, the **PGM** keyword indicates that options 2 and 3 are written in a compiled programming language. The CLIST version of the sample dialog requires the **PGM** keyword to be altered to **CMD** because CLISTs implement these functions. Figure 3-2 shows how the menu definition has been altered to designate that the CLIST command language (or the command language EXEC2 under VM) has been used to develop the selectable functions.

It is important to note that in the parallel COBOL and command language implementations of the example dialog, both versions use the same panel definitions for data entry panels, output display panels, and tutorial or "help" panels. The only panel definitions that are different are those for the menu panels, a difference forced by the Dialog Manager's selection service requirement that menu panels indicate whether functions are written as command procedures or compiled programs. The Dialog Manager does not require information to distinguish which language is used beyond whether it is a command or a compiled language. (The VSE environment is an exception to this rule in that it requires an indication concerning which compiled language is used for each program function.)

The result of this requirement regarding menu panel definitions is that the COBOL and CLIST implementations of the example dialog use all the same panel definitions except those defining menus. These implementation-dependent menu panels include those shown in figures 3-1 and 3-2, as well as those defined as the menu panels for the Accounting Control Administration Subsystem (selectable as option 6 from the master menu). These subsystem menu panels will be examined later.

Figure 3-1. WMENUC panel definition.

```
)BODY
%-------------- WEST DEPARTMENT ACCOUNTS RECEIVABLE ----------------------------
%
%
%SELECT OPTION ===>_ZCMD+
%
%
%  1  +EXTRACT DATA FROM MASTER FILES
%
%  2  +VIEW EXTRACTED DATA FILE
%
%  3  +ADD / UPDATE YOUR EMPLOYEE ACCOUNTING PARAMETERS
%
%  4  +RUN BATCH RECEIVABLES SIMPLE REPORT
%
%  5  +RUN BATCH RECEIVABLES DISTRIBUTION REPORT
%
%  6  +ACCOUNTING CONTROL ADMINISTRATION SUBSYSTEM
%
%  X  +EXIT
%
%
)INIT
    .HELP    = WH001
    &ZHTOP   = WH001
    &ZHINDEX = WH000
    &ZPRIM   = YES
)PROC
    &ZSEL = TRANS( TRUNC (&ZCMD,'.')
                   1,'CMD(XEXTRACT)'
                   2,'PGM(CBROWSE)'
                   3,'PGM(CPROFILE)'
                   4,'CMD(SUBREPTS)'
                   5,'CMD(SUBREPTC)'
                   6,'PANEL(WSAMENC)'
                   X,'EXIT'
                 ' ',' '
                   *,'?' )

)END
```

Figure 3-2. WMENU panel definition.

```
)BODY
%-------------- WEST DEPARTMENT ACCOUNTS RECEIVABLE --------------------
%
%
%SELECT OPTION ===>_ZCMD+
%
%
%  1   +EXTRACT DATA FROM MASTER FILES
%
%  2   +VIEW EXTRACTED DATA FILE
%
%  3   +ADD / UPDATE YOUR EMPLOYEE ACCOUNTING PARAMETERS
%
%  4   +RUN BATCH RECEIVABLES SIMPLE REPORT
%
%  5   +RUN BATCH RECEIVABLES DISTRIBUTION REPORT
%
%  6   +ACCOUNTING CONTROL ADMINISTRATION SUBSYSTEM
%
%  X   +EXIT
%
%
)INIT
   .HELP    = WH001
   &ZHTOP   = WH001
   &ZHINDEX = WH000
   &ZPRIM   = YES
)PROC
   &ZSEL = TRANS( TRUNC (&ZCMD,'.')
                 1,'CMD(XEXTRACT)'
                 2,'CMD(XBROWSE)'
                 3,'CMD(XPROFILE)'
                 4,'CMD(XREPTS)'
                 5,'CMD(XREPTC)'
                 6,'PANEL(WSAMENU)'
                 X,'EXIT'
               ' ',' '
                 *,'?' )

)END
```

4

Developing Dialog Functions

BROWSE AND EDIT SERVICES

Selecting option 2 from the master menu of figure 3-1 or 3-2 executes a function that permits the terminal user to view the master file created by option 1. Recall that this is the master file of accounts receivable invoice records for West Department. The function invokes the Dialog Manager **BROWSE** service. For readers familiar with ISPF/PDF, browsing a file is one of the options provided in that dialog's master menu. Invocation of the **BROWSE** service from a user-developed dialog employs the same **BROWSE** service as ISPF/PDF except that it places the terminal user directly into viewing the file; it bypasses display of the **BROWSE** entry panel.*

Figure 4-1 shows what users see after selecting option 2 from the master menu. They view the accounts receivable master file and use the appropriate program function keys to scroll upward and downward while viewing that file. The ISPF/PDF tutorial system for the **BROWSE** service is also available at this time. If the user presses the **HELP** program function key, he or she views the **BROWSE** "help" panels of ISPF/PDF. After reading these tutorial panels, the user presses the **END** program function key to return to browsing the accounts receivable master file. When the user finishes examining the master file, he or she presses the **END** program function key to return to the master menu of figure 3-1 or 3-2.

COBOL IMPLEMENTATION

The COBOL implementation of this function is called by the master menu of figure 3-1. The load module for this program resides in the

---

*Use of the **BROWSE** and **EDIT** services requires installation of the ISPF/PDF program product.

program function library available to the Dialog Manager, and the member is named **CBROWSE**. The COBOL source code is provided in figure 4-2.

In the example program, the function allows the user to view the accounts receivable master file by calling the **ISPLINK** service interface routine of the Dialog Manager. This occurs in the first sentence of the PROCEDURE DIVISION of the program. This statement is encoded as:

CALL 'ISPLINK' USING BROWSE FILENAME.

In this call, the variable **BROWSE** defines the service requested of the Dialog Manager.* Service requests are declared as variables eight characters long in the program's WORKING-STORAGE SECTION. The variable **FILENAME** must define sufficient storage space to hold a standard data set name as defined by the operating system under which the program is run. Under MVS, data set names can be up to 44 characters long.

The COBOL program ends by setting its return code to 0. Since Dialog Manager service invocations result in return codes accessible to user-developed dialog functions, it is appropriate that the dialog functions issue return codes as well. These function return codes are useful in communicating success or failure to higher-level functions in the dialog hierarchy.

This program function could have as easily allowed the user to *edit* the accounts receivable file as browse it. The user could edit the accounts receivable file with all the features of ISPF/PDF edit made available. In a manner similar to that of the **BROWSE** service, the user would be placed directly into editing the file, bypassing display of the initial ISPF/PDF edit panel. After editing, the user presses the **END** program function key to save the file and exit the editor. Then the user returns to the master menu of figure 3-1.

The coding of an **EDIT** service call within a function is analogous to that of the **BROWSE** invocation. To provide the capability to edit the subject file, the program would merely have issued this service call instead of that shown for **BROWSE**:

CALL 'ISPLINK' USING EDIT FILENAME.

where the variable **EDIT** is an eight-character field containing the character string **EDIT** as the service name.

The utility and power inherent in giving users the capability to browse and edit files through encoding a single statement within a function should be self-evident. This capability is a special feature of Dialog Manager–based applications. Both the **EDIT** and **BROWSE** services provide the full features of the ISPF/PDF system. It is not possible to offer similar capability from transactions developed under teleprocessing monitors such as IMS/DC or CICS.

---

*The COBOL examples in this book use static linkage. Dynamic linkage avoids re-linking as new releases of ISPF become available.

SERVICE INVOCATIONS FROM OTHER PROGRAMMING LANGUAGES

Although this book concentrates on COBOL as the compiled programming language for developing the example dialog, it is worth mentioning the call formats used in other languages. These formats are all analogous to their COBOL counterparts. For example, PL/I programs access Dialog Manager services in this format:

```
CALL ISPLINK (service-name, parameter1, parameter2 . . . );
```

PL/I programs require appropriate declarations for the external routine entry point and return code:

```
DECLARE ISPLINK ENTRY EXTERNAL
         OPTIONS (ASM, INTER, RETCODE) ;

DECLARE PLIRETV BUILTIN;
```

PL/I programs access Dialog Manager return codes through the **PLIRETV** built-in function. This is analogous to accessing ISPF return codes through the COBOL special register **RETURN-CODE**.

FORTRAN programs use this general format for service calls:

```
LASTRC = ISPLNK (service-name, parameter1, parameter2 . . . )
```

LASTRC is an integer variable where the return code from the Dialog Manager call is accessible. Notice that FORTRAN refers to the interface module as **ISPLNK**, a six-character name, because FORTRAN allows only six characters in a called module's name.

CLIST IMPLEMENTATION

Figure 4-3 shows the CLIST implementation of option 2 of the master menu of figure 3-2. The CLIST source code is contained in a command procedure library, and the member is named **XBROWSE**. Remember that this code duplicates the function of the COBOL program of figure 4-2.

As with all the other CLISTs in this example dialog, the **CONTROL MSG** statement specifies that informational messages from the command procedure commands and statements will appear on the terminal. This option is used because this system was designed for demonstration purposes. In a production system, **CONTROL NOMSG** is more appropriate because it specifies that no CLIST messages appear on the screen. The terminal display services of the Dialog Manager should be used for display of all messages and panels.

The first Dialog Manager service invocation in the CLIST is:

```
ISPEXEC CONTROL ERRORS CANCEL
```

This is an example invocation of the ISPF environment **CONTROL** service. The **ERRORS** keyword specifies what action the Dialog Manager should take in event of error. An *error* is defined as a return code of 12 or higher from any Dialog Manager service. **CANCEL** specifies that this dialog terminate when an ISPF service invocation results in an error. The Dialog Manager will automatically write an error message to the ISPF log file, and a panel will display to describe the error situation.

The other option for the **ERRORS** keyword is **RETURN**. Use of this parameter means that control returns to the dialog on error. The write to the log file and the display of the error panel do not occur, and the dialog function can inspect the system variable called **ZERRMSG** to retrieve the ID of the system error message. Thus, the **CONTROL** service is useful for error trapping should you desire to override the default of **CANCEL**. The **CONTROL** service also permits control over various options relating to screen display modes.

Once the control environment has been initialized, **XBROWSE** lets the user browse the accounts receivable master file through this statement:

ISPEXEC BROWSE DATASET (ACCT.OUT)

The **DATASET** keyword is followed by a valid MVS data set name in parentheses. Of course, since this data set name is not enclosed in single quotation marks (or apostrophes), the TSO user prefix is automatically affixed to the data set name. Similar to the COBOL program, this function could also specify that the service effect browsing of a partitioned dataset member, as in:

ISPEXEC BROWSE DATASET ('LOGONID.PDS.NAME(MEMBER)')

Under MVS, both the **BROWSE** and **EDIT** services also have keywords to specify the volume serial and password of the subject data set.

Like its COBOL counterpart, the CLIST **XBROWSE** exits issuing a return code of 0.

VM DIFFERENCES

The **BROWSE** and **EDIT** services are two of the few system-dependent commands of the Dialog Manager. This is because both refer to file names, and data set naming conventions are determined by the host operating system.

In the VM environment, the COBOL call format for these services is:

CALL 'ISPLINK' USING BROWSE FILEID MEMBER.
or EDIT

The **FILEID** parameter specifies an area in WORKING-STORAGE containing the filename, filetype, and optionally the filemode of the CMS file to browse (or edit). This CMS file specification must be enclosed in parentheses. Its maximum length, including the parentheses, is 22 characters.

The **MEMBER** parameter indicates the member to browse (or edit) within a MACLIB or TXTLIB. If it is not specified for a MACLIB or TXTLIB, the member selection list is displayed for these libraries. If the **FILEID** does not refer to a MACLIB or TXTLIB, the **MEMBER** parameter is ignored.

There are also some considerations to mention concerning EXEC2 command procedure functions under VM. First, the EXEC2 language must be used rather than the EXEC language. EXEC2 is specified through use of the **&TRACE** control statement as the first line within the procedure. Second, the **&PRESUME** statement commonly appears near the beginning of CMS procedures to permit omission of **&SUB-COMMAND** and **ISPEXEC** in the requests for ISPF services:

```
&PRESUME &SUBCOMMAND ISPEXEC
```

To cancel the subcommand environment, issue **&PRESUME** without any operands. Another difference in using EXEC2 is that EXEC2 variables that occur as parameters within parentheses must be followed by a blank prior to the closing parenthesis. Assuming the **&PRESUME** statement has not been specified, a sample VM service invocation appears like this:

```
&SUBCOMMAND ISPEXEC DISPLAY PANEL(&PANL )
```

where **&PANL** specifies the panel named in the **DISPLAY** service.

VSE DIFFERENCES

Under VSE, the data set names referred to in the **BROWSE** and **EDIT** calls must conform to the operating system's file naming conventions. VSE users can apply these services to members of libraries and sequential data sets. Because an explanation of the VSE data set naming conventions requires more space than is available here, you may refer to the discussions of the **BROWSE** and **EDIT** services provided in the chapter "Description of Services" in the vendor's reference manual *ISPF Dialog Management Services*.

Language coding requirements also differ slightly under VSE. For example, the internal documentation of the COBOL function in figure 4-2 shows that in VSE, the program must have a LINKAGE SECTION definition to capture the ISPF return code. The first field in the LINKAGE SECTION should provide storage for the return code. Naming this field **RETURN-CODE** allows for greater code compatibility with programs developed for the MVS and VM environments.

VSE PL/I programs require these statements:

DECLARE ISPLINK EXTERNAL ENTRY OPTIONS(ASM INTER);
DECLARE PLIRETV BUILTIN;

The Dialog Manager return code is accessible through the built-in function **PLIRETV**.

FORTRAN service calls appear the same as described for MVS and VM.

No programs run under VSE may use phase overlay structures. Detailed considerations concerning compiler and link editor options are explained in the manual *ISPF Dialog Management Services*.

Figure 4-1. Browsing the accounts receivable master file.

```
 BROWSE - POLK01.ACCT.OUT --------------------------- LINE 000000 COL 001 080
 COMMAND ===>                                             SCROLL ===> HALF
 ********************************* TOP OF DATA *********************************
 HEADER RECORDS   03                            ORDER: PRE-SORT
 CUSTNO   ITEMNO   QTY  COST  DS INVDATE  RECDATE  INVNO   CRSNO  RTE  TRUCKID
 ----------------------------------------------------------------------------
 JLM1423 E7714-17 02 0443.45 0 12/23/84 12/23/84 N888-236 992932 004 CANEXP1202
 AKD3092 W7711-03 01 2092.44 0 12/12/84 12/23/84 K434-929 383839 003 AMNEXP1029
 JLM1423 Q9829-09 12 0023.12 1 12/19/84 12/23/84 L982-911 992932 004 CANEXP1202
 LLL8828 E9282-00 01 0292.12 0 12/17/84 12/19/84 L911-903 929182 001 REDBLL0011
 TTY1939 E7714-17 01 0443.45 0 12/09/84 12/19/84 K939-999 934333 001 REDBLL0011
 DDC8483 E9984-00 11 0393.22 0 12/09/84 12/19/84 K882-992 920230 001 REDBLL0011
 JLM1423 E7714-17 01 0443.45 0 12/11/84 12/14/84 K393-011 393921 004 CANEXP2201
 JLM1423 W9992-09 25 0024.78 2 12/03/84 12/07/84 K911-002 484839 004 CANEXP0111
 KLD3943 T3984-39 X4 0054.99 4 12/11/84 12/22/84 K129-932 237483 007 FBNTRK0332
 VMB4984 P6759-29 01 0053.38 0 12/17/84 12/19/84 K937-119 374751 003 AMNEXP8291
 TTY1939 T3984-39 X2 0054.99 4 12/12/84 12/19/84 K274-903 919383 001 REDBLL0011
 JVC5847 T1293-02 X7 0102.45 5 12/12/84 12/17/84 K495-293 048684 007 FBNTRK3029
 KLD3943 I0293-10 01 0029.93 0 12/03/84 12/10/84 K938-093 789384 007 FBNTRK9382
 KLD3943 02392-02 01 0012.36 0 12/09/84 12/10/84 K993-022 972824 007 FBNTRK9382
 III9349 Y3209-09 01 0129.34 0 12/09/84 12/13/84 K348-343 383475 005 ATRAIL2392
 UEI3434 Q3943-34 01 0015.34 0 12/12/84 12/13/84 K349-232 285242 004 CANEXP1206
 JLM1423 E7714-17 01 0443.45 0 12/14/84 12/13/84 K239-231 349573 004 CANEXP1213
 SDL3492 02392-99 01 2322.44 0 12/14/84 12/16/84 K292-232 383473 006 ALLRAC3932
```

Figure 4-2 CBROWSE COBOL function.

```
IDENTIFICATION DIVISION.                                           00010000
PROGRAM-ID. CBROWSE.                                               00020000
*******************************************************************00030000
*   NAME: CBROWSE                              BY: H. FOSDICK *00040000
*                                                             *00050000
*   PURPOSE: THIS ROUTINE ALLOWS A USER TO VIEW A DATASET     *00060000
*   VIA THE ISPF 'BROWSE' FACILITY UNDER THE DIALOG MANAGER.  *00070000
*                                                             *00080000
*   NOTE: IT ASSUMES THE DATASET TO BROWSE EXISTS.            *00090000
*                                                             *00100000
*******************************************************************00110000
ENVIRONMENT DIVISION.                                              00120000
DATA DIVISION.                                                     00130000
                                                                   00140000
                                                                   00150000
WORKING-STORAGE SECTION.                                           00160000
                                                                   00170000
01   BROWSE              PIC X(8)     VALUE 'BROWSE  '.             00180000
01   FILENAME            PIC X(45)    VALUE 'ACCT.OUT'.             00190001
                                                                   00200000
*******************************************************************00210000
*   UNDER VSE, INCLUDE A LINKAGE SECTION TO DEFINE THE RETURN *00220000
*   CODE ISSUED BY ISPF:                                      *00230000
*                                                             *00240000
*LINKAGE SECTION.                                             *00250002
*77  RETURN-CODE    PIC 9(8)     COMP-4.                      *00260002
*                                                             *00270000
*******************************************************************00280000
                                                                   00290000
                                                                   00300000
PROCEDURE DIVISION.                                                00310000
                                                                   00320000
                                                                   00330000
*                                                                  00340000
*   PUT THE USER INTO ISPF 'BROWSE' FACILITY FOR THE ACCOUNTING    00350000
*   MASTER FILE:                                                   00360000
*                                                                  00370000
                                                                   00380000
    CALL 'ISPLINK' USING  BROWSE  FILENAME.                        00390000
                                                                   00400000
                                                                   00410000
*                                                                  00420000
*   RETURN WITH RETURN CODE OF 0:                                  00430000
*                                                                  00440000
                                                                   00450000
    MOVE 0 TO RETURN-CODE.                                         00460000
    GOBACK.                                                        00470000
```

Figure 4-3. XBROWSE CLIST function.

```
00010000     PROC 0
00020000     CONTROL MSG NOFLUSH
00030000     /*****************************************************************/
00040000     /* NAME: XBROWSE                        BY: H. FOSDICK      */
00050000     /*                                                          */
00060000     /* PURPOSE: THIS CLIST ALLOWS THE USER TO VIEW A DATASET    */
00070000     /* VIA THE ISPF 'BROWSE' FACILITY UNDER THE DIALOG MANAGER. */
00080000     /*                                                          */
00090000     /* NOTE: IT ASSUMES THE DATASET TO BROWSE EXISTS.           */
00100000     /*                                                          */
00110000     /*****************************************************************/
00120000
00130000     /*                                                          */
00140000     /*  SET UP THE ENVIRONMENT FOR THE CLIST:                   */
00150000     /*                                                          */
00160000
00170000     ISPEXEC  CONTROL  ERRORS  CANCEL
00180000
00190000
00200000     /*                                                          */
00210000     /*  PUT THE USER INTO ISPF 'BROWSE' FACILITY FOR THE        */
00220000     /*  ACCOUNTING MASTER FILE:                                 */
00230000     /*                                                          */
00240000
00250000     ISPEXEC  BROWSE  DATASET (ACCT.OUT)
00260000
00270000
00280001     EXIT CODE(0)
```

5

Functions That Maintain
User Data

The third option selectable from the master menus of figures 3-1 and 3-2 allows users to enter and update their employee accounting parameters. These parameters consist of several fields of information used by the dialog functions of master menu options 4 and 5 as job accounting data for the online submission of batch report programs. This employee accounting information is saved on a **per user** basis. Different values are retained for each terminal user.

This function is best understood by looking at the data entry panel it displays (figure 5-1). In the figure, the first panel line contains the dialog title, and the fourth line contains a phrase that describes this function. Both literals are displayed as nonmodifiable and high intensity because the % (percentage sign) is used as their attribute character.

Several lines down, the system variable **ZUSER** is displayed as a highlighted text field. This line displays the terminal user's ID. Thus, if the logon ID is **ZHMF01**, that information will be inserted into the screen display at this location by the Dialog Manager.

The next several lines contain three input fields, designated by the __(underscore) attribute character. These fields are displayed in high intensity to allow for updating. If the fields do not exist or have values, they are displayed as nulls or blanks.

The initialization section of this panel definition merely sets the control variable **.HELP** to the name of the associated tutorial or "help" panel. When the tutorial system is described later, we will look at the "help" panels for this dialog and the manner in which they are interconnected.

The processing section describes actions the Dialog Manager takes after the user has entered data into the **&PROJECT, &CLOCKID**, and **&ASSIGN** fields. The verify statement, **VER,** automatically verifies that the user-entered fields meet certain criteria. If any field fails verification, the Dialog Manager automatically displays a short message in the upper right-hand corner of the display screen (overlaying some of the literal dashes, as seen in the example in figure 2-4). These error messages are context sensitive; that is, the message displayed is appropriate to the error in the incorrect field. For example, an incorrectly entered numeric field results in the message:

MUST BE NUMERIC

A field that must be entered but was not entered at all results in the message:

ENTER REQUIRED FIELD

If the user presses the **HELP** program function key in response to the error message, a longer and more explanatory form of the message automatically appears on the third line of the screen. The third screen line is the default position for display of the longer error messages.

In this panel definition, the verify statement for the **&PROJECT** field states that this field must be nonblank (entered by the user). The field **&CLOCKID** must also be nonblank, and as well, the keyword **NUM** specifies that it must contain a numeric value. The third field, **&ASSIGN**, must be nonblank and must match the picture clause **'A999,99AA'**. As in many other programming languages, single quotation marks indicate a string field that describes an edit pattern. This string indicates that the input must consist of an alphabetic character, followed by three digits, followed by the literal , (comma), followed by two more digits, and then two more alphabetic characters. *Alphabetic characters* are defined as the set of characters containing all upper- and lower-case letters of the alphabet and the symbols # (pound sign), $ (dollar sign), and @ ("at" sign). *Alphabetic characters* are thus letters of the alphabet plus what are referred to as the *national symbols*. *Numeric characters* are defined as the digits 0 through 9. The verify statement, then, is the mechanism through which the Dialog Manager performs automatic input validation for user-developed dialog functions.

There is one further question concerning this panel definition: how many characters can be entered for each of the three modifiable fields? This is determined by the number of character positions between the attribute characters in the display for each of the input fields. Thus, the user could enter a **&PROJECT** field of up to eight characters; the same is true for the **&CLOCKID** field. The positioning of the trailing + (plus sign) attribute character limits the number of characters the user can enter for each of these fields. In these two cases, the minimum number of characters that can be entered has been established by the **NONBLANK** keyword in the verify statement: the user must enter at least one nonblank character in each field matching the **VER** statement criteria. The **&ASSIGN** field must be nine characters long. This criterion results from the specification of the **NONBLANK** keyword and the **PICT** clause.

This data entry panel definition will be used by both the COBOL and the CLIST implementations of the dialog example. Recall that only the menu panel definitions must be different in each of these two systems.

Figure 5-2 shows how this panel definition will look when displayed. This screen allows the user to update his or her employee accounting parameters by overtyping their current values. The first time the user encounters this display, the data input fields appear blank. The user then enters his employee accounting data.

COBOL IMPLEMENTATION

The COBOL implementation of this function is contained in figure 5-3. The member name in the program function library for this program is **CPROFILE**. The user selects this function for execution as option 3 from the master menu of figure 3-1.

The WORKING-STORAGE SECTION of the program shows declaration of the storage space for variables used as parameters in calls requesting Dialog Manager services. Similar to the previous COBOL program named **CBROWSE**, these variables are declared as eight characters long unless there is a reason for the Dialog Manager to require variables of alternative length. In this program, the service call types, the name of the data entry panel, and the message identifiers are defined as eight bytes long.

In the COBOL program's PROCEDURE DIVISION, the first call to the Dialog Manager is a **VGET** service call:

```
CALL 'ISPLINK' USING VGET
                     VARLIST
                     PROFILE.
```

The purpose of this call is to retrieve the variables specified by **VARLIST** from a Dialog Manager–maintained group of variables called the *application profile pool*. The profile pool is a collection of variables maintained by the Dialog Manager (as directed by user-developed functions through several different services) on a per user basis across terminal sessions. Functions use the profile pool to store data for each terminal user across sessions.

If the variables do not yet exist when this COBOL sentence is executed, the Dialog Manager issues a return code of **8**. This value is accessible via the **RETURN-CODE** special register of the COBOL program. If the variables do exist in the profile pool, the service return code is **0**, and the three fields named by the variable **VARLIST** are updated.

For clarity of illustration, this program does not check the return code issued by this particular service call. Similar to other programs in the example dialog, return codes are checked only where they are critical to the logic of the functions. This is because this demonstration system's design has been adapted for the purpose of readability. Code for a production system would embody a greater degree of error checking than that contained in this sample system. In production environments you will probably want to check all Dialog Manager return codes, as well as perform the greatest degree of data validation possible in each panel definition. The reference manual *ISPF Dialog Management*

Services provides information on all return codes issued by the Dialog Manager.

The **VGET** service call refers to the program variable **VARLIST**. Examination of this variable shows that the program initialized it to this character string:

(PROJECT ASSIGN CLOCKID)

These three variable names are written in what the Dialog Manager refers to as *name-list* format. In the name-list format, multiple variable references are enclosed in parentheses; a single variable can be enclosed in parentheses or not. If a single variable is not enclosed in parentheses and if it is fewer than eight characters in length, it should be followed by a trailing blank. This book follows the widely used convention of always enclosing any name-list in parentheses. For consistency and simplicity, this approach is recommended.

The last parameter in the **VGET** service call, **PROFILE**, specifies that the application profile pool is referenced in the **VGET** service. The purpose of the profile pool has been explained. An alternative to the **PROFILE** parameter is to specify the *shared variable pool*, a group of variables accessible to all functions of the same dialog but not saved across sessions. This is indicated through the **SHARED** keyword. A third possible parameter is **ASIS**, which requests copying the value(s) from the shared pool and, if they do not exist there, from the profile pool.

The next COBOL sentence displays a data entry panel via the **DISPLAY** service. The variable **PANEL-NAME** tells the Dialog Manager which panel definition in the panel library to display. The variables displayed on the screen for fields **&PROJECT**, **&ASSIGN**, and **&CLOCKID** will be those retrieved by the **VGET** service so that the user can change them as desired. If no variables were retrieved (if the user has not yet established them through previous use of this menu option), these fields will display as blank or nulls on the display screen.

The message ID referenced on the **DISPLAY** statement refers to a message in the message definition library that displays on this panel. This is message **WDAR001A**, which tells the user to update the displayed information as desired. The *short form* of the message definition will display in the uppermost right-hand 24 characters of the display screen, as seen previously in figure 5-2. Should the user press the **HELP** program function key, he or she will then view the *long form* of the message on line 3 of the display. This message provides a more complete explanation of up to 78 characters in length. Later in this chapter, we will discuss how message definitions are created in the message library.

After displaying the data entry screen, the program checks the return code from the **DISPLAY** service. If it is **0**, the user entered the input data and pressed the **ENTER** key. If it is **8**, however, the user pressed the **END** or **RETURN** program function key. The program logic checks to see if this return code in the special register **RETURN-CODE** is **0**. If it is, the function executes a Dialog Manager **VPUT** command to update the variables of the name-list in the application profile pool. The **VPUT** service format is similar to that of **VGET**. The program then executes a **SETMSG** call to set up an appropriate completion message. The message definition in the message component library is named **WDAR001B**, similar to the message name ID contained in the previous **DISPLAY** statement.

If the user pressed the **END** or **RETURN** keys while viewing panel definition **WPAN1**, the program merely executes a **SETMSG** service to display the message **WDAR000A**. This message informs the user that no update of employee accounting information took place because the **END** key was pressed.

The **SETMSG** service always sets up the message that will be displayed on the *next panel* the user views, regardless of what that next panel is. Therefore, whichever of the **SETMSG** statements are executed in this program will result in the appearance of the designated message on the master menu panel of figure 3-1 because the program always returns to a display of that panel when it is through executing. Thus, after viewing the data entry panel of this function, panel definition **WPAN1**, the user will either update the employee accounting information and press the **ENTER** key or exit the transaction without update by pressing the **END** key. In either case, the user returns to the dialog master menu with a message appropriate to the action he or she chose in the upper right-hand corner of the menu display.

Use of the **SETMSG** service is different from specifying the message reference parameter on a **DISPLAY** request. **SETMSG** identifies a message that will appear on the next panel displayed, regardless of which panel that is. **SETMSG** does not specify which panel will be shown next. On the other hand, the **DISPLAY** service tells the Dialog Manager which panel to display. This service may optionally designate a message in the message library to superimpose on the panel display.

CLIST IMPLEMENTATION

Figure 5-4 shows the CLIST version of this same dialog function. The CLIST is selected by option 3 from the master menu of figure 3-2. In this CLIST, **ISPEXEC** is first invoked to set control parameters for the environment. This statement is common to all the CLISTs in this dialog. Then the **VGET** command retrieves the fields **&PROJECT**, **&ASSIGN**, and **&CLOCKID** from the application profile pool. This command illustrates the manner in which name-lists are encoded in CLISTs.

As in the COBOL example, the Dialog Manager issues a return code of either **0** or **8** from the **VGET** service. **0** means that the variables specified in the name-list were copied from the profile pool; **8** indicates that they do not exist. The subsequent panel displays the proper values for these variables, or, in their absence, blanks or nulls.

The panel display request of the **DISPLAY** statement shows how keywords are used to reference the various parameters in CLIST invocations of ISPF services. The **PANEL** keyword tells which panel the

Dialog Manager should display, and the **MSG** keyword designates the message to appear on the panel.

After display of the panel, the CLIST checks the return code issued by this service through the **&LASTCC** variable. As in the COBOL program, this test enables the CLIST to discover whether the user input data with intent to update his or her employee accounting parameters, or whether he or she pressed the **END** or **RETURN** keys to exit the function. In the former case, the CLIST updates the application profile through the **VPUT** service and then sets up a message to appear on the next screen through a **SETMSG** invocation. In the latter instance, the CLIST merely invokes the **SETMSG** service to indicate that processing has terminated.

As in the example of the COBOL program, the CLIST exits with a return code of **0**.

MESSAGE DEFINITIONS

The examples demonstrated the manner in which messages are designated through the **SETMSG** service and the optional message parameter of the **DISPLAY** service. It is now appropriate to explore the message services of the Dialog Manager in greater detail.

As in the case of panel definitions, message definitions are encoded in a particular format and reside in their own component library. All the messages for this dialog, used by both the COBOL and the CLIST implementations of the example dialog, reside in the message library member named **WDAR00**. These messages are reproduced in figure 5-5. As the figure shows, each message in this member starts with a unique eight-character *message ID* identifying the message to the Dialog Manager. Then follows a *short-form message* (or *short message*) of up to 24 characters, enclosed in single quotation marks. Next occurs the optional keyword that specifies whether the terminal alarm is to sound when the message is displayed. This parameter may be encoded as **.ALARM = YES** or **.ALARM = NO**. If the parameter is omitted, the default is **.ALARM = NO**. The second line of the message definition contains up to 78 characters of the *long-form message* (or *long message*). Like the short-form message, this too is enclosed in apostrophes. Message definitions may contain substitutable dialog variables if desired. For example, in message **WDAR005H**, the Dialog Manager will dynamically substitute values for the variables **&COSCTR** and **&SUBCTR** before display of the message.

Messages such as these are displayed during panel displays by the **DISPLAY** service, through the **SETMSG** service, or other panel display services. The short-form message appears in the upper right-hand corner of the screen. If the user then presses the **HELP** program function key, the long form of the message appears (by Dialog Manager convention) on line 3 of the display screen. If the user presses the **HELP** program function key again, he or she will see the tutorial panel referred to by the current setting of the **.HELP** control variable. This value can be set in the initialization section of the panel definition. It can also be set by an optional parameter in the message definition. If it appears, the **.HELP** value in the message definition value overrides that set in the panel definition when the message displays. The fullest form of message definitions is as follows:

> **MSGID 'SHORT MESSAGE' .HELP = PANELID .ALARM = NO**
> **'LONG FORM OF THE MESSAGE UP TO 78 CHARACTERS'**

One somewhat complicated aspect of the message definition format concerns what constitutes a valid message ID. A valid ID contains between four and eight characters (inclusive). The first group of from one to five characters must be alphabetic (**A–Z,** and the national symbols #, $, and @). These are followed by three required numeric digits, followed by one additional optional alphabetic character. The message library member name in which a message definition resides is determined by truncating the message ID after the second digit of the numeric portion of the message ID. The member name for the message definitions of figure 5-5 is thus **WDAR00.**

In this sample dialog, all message definitions have been placed in the single library member shown in figure 5-5. In larger systems, you can take advantage of the message ID naming conventions to split messages among several library members in some logical fashion. One approach is to relate each panel to all messages that can be displayed on that panel. For example, for a panel named **NCC000,** all messages displayable on this panel reside in the member named **NCC00** in the message library.

Naming conventions such as these are often extended to dialog panel and function names as well. For example, digits within panel member names can be used to express the relative positions or levels of the panels within the hierarchical dialog structure. Ask your project leader or system administrator about Dialog Manager message, panel, function and skeleton naming conventions in use at your installation. Also, the GUIDE International Corporation ISPF Project publishes extensive information on naming conventions and standards.

Figure 5-1. WPAN1 panel definition.

```
)BODY
%-------------- WEST DEPARTMENT ACCOUNTS RECEIVABLE ----------------------------
+
+
%ADD / UPDATE EMPLOYEE ACCOUNTING INFORMATION:
+
+
+    FOR  LOGON ID: %%ZUSER
+
+
+    PROJECT NUMBER %===>_PROJECT +
+    CLOCK ID       %===>_CLOCKID +
+    ASSIGNMENT     %===>_ASSIGN   +
+
+
+
+
+
+
)INIT
   .HELP  = WH004
)PROC
   VER (&PROJECT, NONBLANK)
   VER (&CLOCKID, NONBLANK, NUM)
   VER (&ASSIGN,  NONBLANK, PICT, 'A999,99AA')

)END
```

Figure 5-2. WPAN1 screen as displayed.

```
------------ WEST DEPARTMENT ACCOUNTS RECEIVABLE --- ADD/UPDATE EMPLOYEE DATA


ADD / UPDATE EMPLOYEE ACCOUNTING INFORMATION:


   FOR   LOGON  ID:   ZHMF01


   PROJECT NUMBER   ===>  1112222
   CLOCK ID         ===>  11504
   ASSIGNMENT       ===>  C137,14AA
```

Figure 5-3. CPROFILE COBOL function.

```
IDENTIFICATION DIVISION.                                              00010000
PROGRAM-ID. CPROFILE                                                  00020000
****************************************************************************00030000
*  NAME: CPROFILE                                  BY: H. FOSDICK *00040000
*                                                                  *00050000
*  PURPOSE: THIS ROUTINE DISPLAYS A DATA ENTRY PANEL TO THE        *00060000
*  USER, INTO WHICH HE ENTERS CERTAIN EMPLOYEE ACCOUNTING          *00070000
*  INFORMATION.  THIS DATA IS THEN PERMANENTLY SAVED UNDER         *00080000
*  THE USER'S ISPF PROFILE.                                        *00090000
*                                                                  *00100000
****************************************************************************00110000
ENVIRONMENT DIVISION.                                                 00120000
DATA DIVISION.                                                        00130000
                                                                      00140000
                                                                      00150000
WORKING-STORAGE SECTION.                                              00160000
                                                                      00170000
                                                                      00180000
*  SERVICE CALL TYPES:                                                00190000
                                                                      00200000
01  VGET                PIC X(8)     VALUE 'VGET    '.                00210000
01  VPUT                PIC X(8)     VALUE 'VPUT    '.                00220000
01  DISPLAY-PANEL       PIC X(8)     VALUE 'DISPLAY '.                00230000
01  SETMSG              PIC X(8)     VALUE 'SETMSG  '.                00240000
                                                                      00250000
                                                                      00260000
*  REFER TO THE PROFILE POOL IN 'VGET' AND 'VPUT' CALLS:              00270000
                                                                      00280000
01  PROFILE             PIC X(8)     VALUE 'PROFILE '.                00290000
                                                                      00300000
                                                                      00310000
*  THE DATA ENTRY PANEL TO DISPLAY TO THE USER:                       00320000
                                                                      00330000
01  PANEL-NAME          PIC X(8)     VALUE 'WPAN1   '.                00340000
                                                                      00350000
                                                                      00360000
*  VARIABLES TO MANIPULATE IN THE PROFILE POOL:                       00370000
                                                                      00380000
01  VARLIST             PIC X(24)                                     00390000
                        VALUE  '(PROJECT ASSIGN CLOCKID)'.            00400000
                                                                      00410000
*  MESSAGES:                                                          00420000
                                                                      00430000
01  EMPLOYEE-DATA-UPDATED-MSG PIC X(8)  VALUE 'WDAR001B'.             00440000
01  PROCESSING-TERMINATED-MSG PIC X(8)  VALUE 'WDAR000A'.             00450000
01  ADD-UPDATE-DATA-MSG       PIC X(8)  VALUE 'WDAR001A'.             00460000
                                                                      00470000
                                                                      00480000
                                                                      00490000
PROCEDURE DIVISION.                                                   00500000
                                                                      00510000
                                                                      00520000
*                                                                    00530000
*  GET EXISTING EMPLOYEE ACCOUNTING DATA FROM USER PROFILE:          00540000
*                                                                    00550000
                                                                      00560000
     CALL 'ISPLINK' USING  VGET                                       00570000
                           VARLIST                                    00580000
                           PROFILE.                                   00590000
                                                                      00600000
                                                                      00610000
*                                                                    00620000
*  DISPLAY EMPLOYEE ACCOUNTING DATA ON DATA ENTRY SCREEN.            00630000
*  IF IT DOESN'T EXIST, DISPLAY BLANKS INSTEAD:                      00640000
*                                                                    00650000
                                                                      00660000
                                                                      00670000
     CALL 'ISPLINK' USING  DISPLAY-PANEL                              00680000
                           PANEL-NAME                                 00690000
                           ADD-UPDATE-DATA-MSG.                       00700000
                                                                      00710000
     IF RETURN-CODE = 0                                               00720000
                                                                      00730000
                                                                      00740000
*                                                                    00750000
*  ADD OR UPDATE THE EMPLOYEE DATA IN THE USER'S PROFILE:            00760000
*                                                                    00770000
                                                                      00780000
          CALL 'ISPLINK' USING  VPUT                                  00790000
                                VARLIST                               00800000
                                PROFILE                               00810000
                                                                      00820000
                                                                      00830000
*  SET UP THE UPDATE MESSAGE FOR THE TERMINAL USER:                  00840002
*                                                                    00850000
                                                                      00860000
                                                                      00870000
          CALL 'ISPLINK' USING  SETMSG                                00880000
                                EMPLOYEE-DATA-UPDATED-MSG             00890000
```

```
*                                                              00900000
*                                                              00910000
*    ELSE, IF USER HIT THE 'END' KEY, SET UP A 'PROCESSING     00920000
**   TERMINATED' MESSAGE FOR THE APPLICATION_MASTER MENU:      00930000
*                                                              00940000
                                                               00950000
                                                               00960000
      ELSE                                                     00970000
                                                               00980000
          CALL 'ISPLINK'  USING  SETMSG                        00990000
                                 PROCESSING-TERMINATED-MSG.    01000000
                                                               01010000
                                                               01020000
                                                               01030000
      MOVE 0 TO RETURN-CODE.                                   01040000
      GOBACK.                                                  01050000
```

Figure 5-4. XPROFILE CLIST function.

```
00010000   PROC 0
00020000   CONTROL MSG NOFLUSH
00030000   /*****************************************************************/
00040000   /* NAME: XPROFILE                        BY: H. FOSDICK       */
00050000   /*                                                           */
00060000   /* PURPOSE: THIS CLIST DISPLAYS A DATA ENTRY PANEL TO THE    */
00070000   /* USER, INTO WHICH HE ENTERS CERTAIN EMPLOYEE ACCOUNTING    */
00080000   /* INFORMATION.  THIS DATA IS THEN PERMANENTLY SAVED UNDER   */
00090000   /* THE USER'S ISPF PROFILE.                                  */
00100000   /*                                                           */
00110000   /*****************************************************************/
00120000
00130000   /*                                                           */
00140000   /*   SET UP THE ENVIRONMENT FOR THE CLIST:                   */
00150000   /*                                                           */
00160000
00170000   ISPEXEC  CONTROL  ERRORS  CANCEL
00180000
00190000
00200000   /*                                                           */
00210000   /*   GET EXISTING EMPLOYEE ACCOUNTING DATA FROM USER PROFILE */
00220000   /*                                                           */
00230000
00240000   ISPEXEC  VGET  (PROJECT ASSIGN CLOCKID) PROFILE
00250000
00260000
00270000   /*                                                           */
00280000   /*   DISPLAY EMPLOYEE ACCOUNTING DATA ON DATA ENTRY SCREEN.  */
00290000   /*   IF IT DOESN'T EXIST, DISPLAY NULLS INSTEAD:             */
00300000   /*                                                           */
00310000
00320000   ISPEXEC  DISPLAY PANEL(WPAN1) MSG(WDAR001A)
00330000
00340000
00350000   /*                                                           */
00360000   /*   IF NORMAL RETURN CODE (USER DID NOT HIT 'END' KEY):     */
00370000   /*                                                           */
00380000
00390000   IF &LASTCC = 0 THEN DO
00400000
00410000      /*                                                           */
00420000      /*   ADD OR UPDATE THE EMPLOYEE DATA IN THE USER'S PROFILE:  */
00430000      /*                                                           */
00440000
00450000      ISPEXEC  VPUT  (PROJECT ASSIGN CLOCKID) PROFILE
00460000
00470000
00480000      /*                                                           */
00490000      /*   SET UP A COMPLETION MESSAGE FOR DISPLAY ON NEXT SCREEN, */
00500000      /*   THEN EXIT TO APPLICATION MASTER MENU:                   */
00510000      /*                                                           */
00520000
00530000      ISPEXEC  SETMSG  MSG(WDAR001B)
00540000
00550000      END
00560000
00570000
00580000   /*                                                           */
00590000   /*   ELSE, IF USER HIT THE 'END' KEY, SET UP A "PROCESSING   */
00600001   /*   TERMINATED" MSG TO SHOW ON THE APPLICATION MASTER MENU: */
00610000   /*                                                           */
00620000
00630000   ELSE +
00640000      ISPEXEC SETMSG MSG(WDAR000A)
00650000
00660000
00670000   EXIT CODE(0)
```

Figure 5-5. Error message definitions.

```
WDAR000A  'PROCESSING TERMINATED '                 .ALARM=NO
'NO ACTION TAKEN ON PREVIOUS PANEL BECAUSE YOU HIT THE "END" KEY'

WDAR001A  'ADD/UPDATE EMPLOYEE DATA'               .ALARM=NO
'ADD NEW EMPLOYEE ACCOUNTING DATA OR UPDATE EXISTING INFORMATION'

WDAR001B  'EMPLOYEE DATA UPDATED'                  .ALARM=NO
'EMPLOYEE ACCOUNTING DATA HAS BEEN ADDED OR UPDATED'

WDAR002A  'ENTER "T" OR "A" '                      .ALARM=YES
'ENTER EITHER "T" OR "A" FOR OUTPUT CLASS'

WDAR002B  'ENTER "1" OR "2" '                      .ALARM=YES
'ENTER "1" FOR STANDARD FORMS, "2" FOR NO BACKGROUND PATTERN'

WDAR002C  'ENTER "MM/DD/YY" '                      .ALARM=YES
'ENTER REPORT CONTROL DATA IN FORM "MM/DD/YY" '

WDAR002D  'ENTER "W", "E" OR "S" '                 .ALARM=YES
'ENTER REPORT REGION STATUS OF WEST, EAST OR SOUTH '

WDAR002E  'ENTER JOB CONTROL DATA'                 .ALARM=NO
'ENTER JOB ACCOUNTING AND REPORT CONTROL INFORMATION'

WDAR002F  'REPORT JOB SUBMITTED'                   .ALARM=NO
'THE BACKGROUND REPORT PROGRAM HAS BEEN SUBMITTED TO THE SYSTEM'

WDAR003A  'ENTER "1", "2" OR BLANK'                .ALARM=YES
'ENTER "1" FOR STANDARD FORMS, "2" FOR NO PATTERN, BLANK FOR DEFAULT'

WDAR004A  'NO CONTROL DATA EXISTS'                 .ALARM=YES
'NO ACCOUNTING CONTROL DATA EXISTS TO BE VIEWED'

WDAR004B  'ENTER ACCOUNTING DATA'                  .ALARM=NO
'ENTER THE REQUESTED COST AND SUB-COST CENTERS'

WDAR004C  'ENTRY NOT FOUND'                        .ALARM=YES
'NO ACCOUNTING CONTROL DATA EXISTS FOR COST CENTER &COSCTR - &SUBCTR '

WDAR004D  'ENTER FOUR DIGITS'                      .ALARM=YES
'ENTER A FOUR DIGIT CENTER CODE'

WDAR004E  'PRESS "END" KEY TO EXIT'                .ALARM=NO
'PRESS THE "END" KEY WHEN THROUGH VIEWING THIS SCREEN'

WDAR005A  'ENTER "A", "U", OR "D" '                .ALARM=YES
'ENTER "A" FOR ADD, "U" FOR UPDATE, OR "D" FOR DELETE TRANSACTION'

WDAR005B  'ENTER COST CENTER CODES'                .ALARM=NO
'ENTER THE CODES FOR THE COST AND SUB-COST CENTERS'

WDAR005C  'PRESS "ENTER" TO PROCESS'               .ALARM=NO
'PRESS THE "ENTER" KEY TO ADD, UPDATE OR DELETE THE INFORMATION SHOWN'

WDAR005D  'DATA HAS BEEN ADDED'                    .ALARM=NO
'COST CENTER ACCOUNTING INFORMATION HAS BEEN ADDED'

WDAR005E  'DATA HAS BEEN UPDATED'                  .ALARM=NO
'COST CENTER ACCOUNTING INFORMATION HAS BEEN UPDATED'

WDAR005F  'DATA HAS BEEN DELETED'                  .ALARM=NO
'COST CENTER ACCOUNTING INFORMATION HAS BEEN DELETED'

WDAR005G  'NO SUCH COST CENTER'                    .ALARM=YES
'THERE IS NO ENTRY TO UPDATE OR DELETE FOR THE COST CENTER ENTERED'

WDAR005H  'INVALID ADD ATTEMPT'                    .ALARM=YES
'COST CENTER INFORMATION FOR CENTER &COSCTR - &SUBCTR ALREADY EXISTS'

WDAR006A  'DATA FOUND, PRESS ENTER'                .ALARM=NO
'CONTROL DATA IS DISPLAYED, PRESS "ENTER" TO SEARCH AGAIN'

WDAR006B  'SCAN FAILED, PRESS ENTER'               .ALARM=YES
'NO MATCH WITH YOUR PARAMETERS WAS FOUND, PRESS "ENTER" TO SEARCH AGAIN'

WDAR006C  'ENTER SCANNING FIELDS'                  .ALARM=NO
'ENTER THE DATA YOU WISH MATCHED IN THE SCAN OF THE CONTROL DATA'
```

⑥

Functions That Perform File Tailoring

This chapter expands the discussion of the example dialog to cover a major facility provided by the Dialog Manager: file tailoring services. File tailoring services are invoked through dialog functions in order to process sequential files. This processing includes the ability to dynamically substitute values for variables that occur in the input file and to conditionally generate particular file skeleton lines into the output file. Other features include the ability to imbed additional file skeletons into the subject file and the capability to process tables maintained by the Dialog Manager against the skeleton file. The output of the file tailoring process can be sent to a temporary file, accessible to dialog functions, or to an output file previously defined to the Dialog Manager.

The file tailoring services of the Dialog Manager are frequently used in data processing installations to create systems that are sometimes referred to as *online batch* or *batch online*. In a batch online system, users enter data in an online environment, such as that provided by Dialog Manager–based dialogs. This facilitates online validation of data required by the system. Online input editing of user-input data is more advanced than that provided by traditional batch systems because error messages are sent to the terminal user in real time, permitting immediate correction of invalid input data.

After entering the data required by the application, the user submits the background job that uses these data to the system. This provides the traditional advantages of batch processing: large or expensive jobs can be scheduled to maximize use of system resources. The installation can ensure that a large job does not hit the system at an inappropriate time, resulting in high processing costs or ruining online response time for other users. For example, the batch job could be scheduled overnight. Thus, batch online systems attempt to combine the advantages of interactive and background systems. These systems afford the data editing advantages of online, interactive systems while retaining the inherent scheduling advantages of batch systems.

The Dialog Manager provides a high degree of interactive flexibility through its dialog structure, and it features the traditional online advantage of real-time input data editing. Much of this data editing is transparent to the dialog functions, as seen in the verification capabilities built into the screen definition language. The Dialog Manager's file tailoring services provide the mechanism through which dialogs can tailor the necessary Job Control Language (JCL) statements to configure batch jobs dynamically, as based on the user's input. The file tailoring capability allows the dialog to submit background jobs to the system. The generated job stream can be saved for scheduling by the machine operators at a later time.

The sample dialog provides a typical example of the way the Dialog Manager is used to create this kind of system and illustrates the value of this approach. The file tailoring examples are selectable as options 4 and 5 from the master menus represented in figures 3-1 and 3-2. (Recall that figure 3-1 is the COBOL implementation of the sample system master menu and that figure 3-2 is its CLIST implementation counterpart.)

In selecting option 4 from the master menu of figure 3-1, the user requests that the West Department Accounts Receivable system run a large report program. This program produces a listing of accounts receivable, based on a control date the user supplies. Since the report of option 4 is based on a single control date, it is referred to as the Simple Report.

In selecting option 5 from the master menu, the user similarly requests that the system run a large report program. This report also produces an accounts receivable listing based on control date information; however, this version of the report program is called the Distribution Report because it generates accounts receivable report listings for multiple users. The resultant listing is separated in the Operations Room, and portions of this Distribution Report are sent to different users throughout the organization. In order to accomplish report distribution accurately, this version of the report program accepts additional control parameter information through an additional file. The control data in this extra file are produced from data stored in a permanent table maintained through the Dialog Manager.

The dialog function selected by option 4 of the master menu requests that the user input certain data to the function. The data entry panel requesting this information appears as seen in figure 6-1, and the panel definition generating this screen display appears in figure 6-2. As shown in these figures, the user is requested to input two kinds of data: job control accounting information and a control date. The control date represents a key piece of control information to the report program.

After the dialog function receives this information, it requests that the Dialog Manager file tailoring services process a skeleton file containing the JCL to run the Simple Report program. Through the dynamic variable substitution capability of the Dialog Manager, the function has the ability to insert the job accounting information into the file skeleton. It thereby generates batch-mode JCL with the proper job accounting parameters. The dialog function also places the control date information entered into an in-stream input file that is part of the file skeleton. The function then submits the file skeleton it has just tailored, via the Dialog Manager, as a background job to the operating system. The user returns to the master menu of figure 3-1 with a message stating that the Simple Report job has been submitted for background processing.

If the user selects option 5 from the master menu, his or her interaction with the dialog appears quite similar. Although the user executes a different dialog function than he or she would through option 4, the data entry screen looks nearly identical to that seen above. This screen is defined as shown in figure 7-1, and it requests the same information as the panel of figure 6-2. What is the difference, then, between options 4 and 5 of the master menu? Option 5 submits the Distribution Report program to the system. This program refers to one more input file than does the Simple Report, a file that contains user distribution information and an appropriate control date for each user. This extra file is generated for this batch job by the dialog function through the file tailoring services of the Dialog Manager, and the data inserted are drawn from a table of control information created and maintained through the Dialog Manager's table services. The programs that create and maintain the table of control information comprise all the functions selectable from the submenu of the Accounting Control Administration Subsystem, option 6 of the master menu of figures 3-1 and 3-2. They are examined in later chapters covering the Dialog Manager's table services.

Thus, the dialog functions of menu options 4 and 5 aid in providing correct job accounting and control date information to ensure proper running of the selected report program. The user is shielded from the complexities and opportunities for error inherent in directly altering JCL by the online capabilities of the dialog and the data validation facilities of the Dialog Manager. At the same time, the resource-hungry report programs are submitted as batch jobs, freeing the user for other tasks at the terminal and ensuring that the system can run these background jobs when most appropriate.

COBOL IMPLEMENTATION OF MENU OPTION 4

When the user selects option 4 from the master menu of figure 3-1, the menu selects a CLIST named **SUBREPTS** for execution. This CLIST is reproduced in figure 6-3. The CLIST runs the COBOL program to implement this menu option, and after that program has run, it checks its return code. If the program successfully tailored the file skeleton to create a Simple Report batch job, the CLIST receives a return code of 0, and it submits the output file from the file tailoring to the operating system as a background job. If the COBOL program could not create the JCL for a background report job successfully, the program returns a non-0 return code, and the CLIST does not submit a batch job for processing.

The sole reason for this CLIST is that under the MVS operating system, it is easier to submit a job stream to the operating system via a CLIST than through a COBOL program. Thus the **SUBREPTS** CLIST runs the COBOL program function and, if appropriate, submits the batch report job.

In this brief CLIST, the first command invokes the ISPF **SELECT** service. The purpose of this service is to transfer control from one dialog function to another, *with the knowledge of the Dialog Manager*. In other words, the Dialog Manager knows that control has been transfered to a lower-level function in the dialog's function hierarchy. The Dialog Manager is aware that a program function called **CREPTS** is to be started, and it provides full ISPF support to this new function. The **SELECT** service is the basic mechanism in the Dialog Manager by which a discrete function in the functional hierarchy is invoked. If the COBOL program **CREPTS** had been started not through a Dialog Manager **SELECT** service invocation but through such standard CLIST commands to run programs as the **CALL**, **LOADGO**, or **RUN** commands, the Dialog Manager would not be aware that the CLIST had started a lower-level dialog function, and the services of the Dialog Manager would not be available to the program **CREPTS**. The execution of the COBOL program would be transparent to the Dialog Manager: the program would not be able to issue calls for Dialog Manager services.

During debugging, I made this mistake. The **SELECT** statement was not used to start the COBOL program. Instead the standard MVS **CALL** command was encoded. This meant that any of the COBOL program's CALLs to the Dialog Manager to alter the terminal user's screen display were invalidated. From the viewpoint of the terminal user, selection of option 4 resulted in redisplay of the master menu. All that happened was that the master menu blinked!

Of course, there are cases where you will want to initiate a subroutine or subprogram that is transparent to the Dialog Manager and where, in effect, the Dialog Manager considers that subprogram as merely a routine within the calling function. An example of this occurred in master menu option 1. Recall that this option executes a CLIST that **CALLs** or runs a program to extract data from files external to the example dialog. That program did not make use of any Dialog Manager services, so it was not necessary to invoke the Dialog Manager **SELECT** service in order to run it.

The COBOL program initiated by this CLIST is shown in figure 6-4. This program displays the screen of figure 6-2, through which it receives job accounting and control date information. Then the program tailors a file skeleton to generate an appropriate JCL stream to create the Simple Report. If this tailoring process succeeds, the COBOL program passes a return code of 0 to the calling CLIST. The **SUBREPTS** CLIST then submits the JCL tailored by the COBOL program to the operating system as a background job.

The PROCEDURE DIVISION of the COBOL program starts on line 112 in the listing. (Line numbers consist of the first four digits on the far right-hand side of the code in figure 6-4.) The first action of the COBOL program is to define the dialog variables it uses to the

Dialog Manager. Where a program function will directly manipulate, compare, test, or initialize dialog variables such as occur in a panel definition, these dialog variables must be defined by the program function via the **VDEFINE** service. Another way to state this is that **VDEFINE** calls establish addressability between the Dialog Manager and the variables internal to a program function. This link enables program functions to manipulate dialog variables from within the program code.

The paragraph **DEFINE-VARIABLES**, (program lines 220-258) accomplishes this. The format of the **VDEFINE** call is:

```
CALL 'ISPLINK' USING VDEFINE
               name-list
               variable
               format
               length.
```

where **name-list** states the symbolic name to be used by ISPF when referencing the specified variable(s), **variable** specifies the program variable whose storage space is used, **format** describes the data type of the program variable (for example, **CHAR** for character variables, **FIXED** for binary integer variables, and **BIT** for bit string variables), and **length** specifies the length of the program variable storage, in bytes. The **name-list** parameter tells ISPF the name of the dialog variable used in the panel definition of figure 6-2, and the other parameters name and define the associated variable in the COBOL program. In this manner, the COBOL program can manipulate dialog variables referenced in the panel definition directly.

After establishing this link between internal program variables and their corresponding dialog variables, the program executes a **VGET** call to retrieve three variables from the application profile pool. Recall that these employee accounting variables are placed into the application profile by the function selected from master menu option 3. This program assumes that the profile pool variables exist and are valid.

The program next initializes the dialog variables that appear on the screen of figure 6-2 when this screen is displayed. The variables appearing on the screen can be initialized in this manner only because of the **VDEFINE** calls executed previously. When the screen panel displays to the user, the **&CLASS** field will contain **A**, the **&FORMS** field is **1**, and the **&STATUS** field displays **W**.

The program calls the **DISPLAY** service to generate the panel of figure 6-1. If the user enters the job accounting and control date information and presses the **ENTER** key, the program receives a RETURN-CODE of **0**. It then executes an ISPF service call to open the skeleton file to tailor. This is the **FTOPEN** call of program lines 160 and 161. The **FTOPEN** command begins the file tailoring process and through the **TEMP** operand specifies that the results of file tailoring will be written to a temporary output file. This file is automatically allocated by the Dialog Manager, and it may later be accessed through the system variable **ZTEMPF**. If **TEMP** is not specified, the Dialog Manager writes the file tailoring output to the library previously allocated for this purpose (see appendix A).

The next service call in the program is the **FTINCL** service. This ISPF invocation specifies the file or *skeleton* that the Dialog Manager should tailor. In this instance, the skeleton member name is **WSKEL1**. Figure 6-5 reproduces the code of **WSKEL1**.

The program calls the **FTCLOSE** service to terminate the file tailoring process. If this call contains a file name, this file is the member of the tailoring output library that will contain the results of the file tailoring process. In the case of this program, the file tailoring output is written to a file named in system variable **ZTEMPF**, allocated by the Dialog Manager. Under no cicumstances are the contents of the input skeleton altered; file tailoring produces an output file only.

After the file tailoring process is completed, the program moves **0** to program variable **RETURN-STATUS**. This variable saves the return code issued by this program to indicate the success or failure of its file tailoring attempt to the calling CLIST. Remember that the calling CLIST uses this return code to decide whether it should submit the file tailoring output as a background job to the operating system. An intermediate variable like **RETURN-STATUS** is required to save the program's return code because intervening calls to the Dialog Manager reset the **RETURN-CODE** special register.

If the user did not enter information in response to the display of the panel of figure 6-2, then the return code from the **DISPLAY** service is non-0. In this case, the COBOL program sets **RETURN-STATUS** to **4** and uses the **SETMSG** service to set up a "processing terminated" message on the next screen.

Before the program exits, it performs a paragraph that executes a **VDELETE** service call for each variable previously defined through a **VDEFINE** call. **VDELETE** removes definitions of function variables.

The program's last action before termination is to set its return code. This involves moving the value in **RETURN-STATUS** to the **RETURN-CODE** special register. Then the program exits.

Program termination results in return of control to the CLIST shown in figure 6-3. This CLIST tests the COBOL program's return code via the variable **&LASTCC**. If it is **0**, the CLIST uses the MVS **SUBMIT** command to submit the file tailoring output as a background job to the operating system.

Look at these lines of the CLIST in detail:

```
ISPEXEC VGET ZTEMPF SHARED
SUBMIT '&ZTEMPF'
```

The first line retrieves the value of **ZTEMPF** from its location in the shared variable pool. By definition, **ZTEMPF** is the system variable containing the default data set name for file tailoring output, and this variable resides in the shared variable pool. This **VGET** invocation is therefore necessary before executing the **SUBMIT** of the file as a background job to the operating system. Without the **VGET** invocation, the **SUBMIT** command results in the error message:

THIS STATEMENT HAS AN UNDEFINED SYSTEM VARIABLE.

FILE TAILORING PROCESS

Let us take a closer look at the file skeleton tailored by this COBOL program. Figure 6-5 shows this skeleton. It exists as a member in the file skeleton input library and is named **WSKEL1**.

WSKEL1 looks similar to a standard file of MVS Job Control Language (JCL) statements; however, there are several differences. First, notice that some JCL statements contain dialog variables. For example, the first line contains the three profile pool variables retrieved by the COBOL program from the application profile. These dialog variables are preceded by the **&** (ampersand), and the Dialog Manager replaces them with their current respective values during the file tailoring process. The first variable occurring in the first line of the file is a system variable, **ZUSER**. The Dialog Manager dynamically substitutes the user's ID into this variable in exactly the same manner it does when processing the panel definition of figure 6-2. Periods (.) are placed after variable names where concatenation with the character string following the dialog variable is required. For example, if the value of **&NAME** is **FOSDICK**, then:

&NAME.,BN

results in:

FOSDICK,BN

after variable substitution.

Skeleton lines such as the first one in **WSKEL1**, which consist of intermixed text and variables, are called *data records*. File skeletons may also contain *control records*. Control records are identified by a right parenthesis in column 1. The lines beginning with the symbols **)CM**, **)SEL**, and **)ENDSEL** are control records.

)CM identifies *comment lines*. Similar to their role in many programming languages, comment lines are ignored by the Dialog Manager during file tailoring and exist only for the purpose of explanation.

The **)SEL** and **)ENDSEL** keywords bracket a group of one or more data records. Depending on the truth of the condition identified on the **)SEL** statement, the data records between the **)SEL** and its corresponding **)ENDSEL** are included in the file tailoring output file. In the first **)SEL** statement:

)SEL   &FORMS = 1

if the value of the variable **&FORMS** is **1**, the statement

//SYSPRINT DD SYSOUT=A,DCB=BLKSIZE=133

is included in the output file. If the **)SEL** condition is not true, then the JCL statement is not included in the output file.

The effect of the two)**SEL** control statements in this skeleton is to test the value the user entered for **&FORMS** in the input panel of figure 6-1. If **1** was entered, the generated report contains the above **SYSPRINT** statement. If **2** was entered, **&FORMS** will be **2**, and the **SYSPRINT** statement for the report specifies:

//SYSPRINT DD SYSOUT = A,FLASH = NONE,DCB = BLKSIZE = 133

The result is that the Simple Report will print on lined paper if the user enters **1** for **&FORMS**, or it will print on unlined paper (as designated by **FLASH = NONE**) if he or she entered **2** for **&FORMS**.

Figure 6-6 reproduces the generated file tailoring output for the input values entered by the panel display pictured in figure 6-7. The employee accounting information used in the file tailoring process is as pictured in figure 5-2. Make sure that you understand how the COBOL program tailored the skeleton file **WSKEL1** in order to produce this job stream.

CLIST IMPLEMENTATION
OF MENU OPTION 4

The CLIST version of the COBOL program is contained in figure 6-8. It is selected as option 4 from the master menu of the CLIST-based dialog, figure 3-2. Like other functions in this book, this CLIST uses the same panel and file skeleton definitions as its COBOL counterpart. These are contained in figures 6-2 and 6-5, respectively.

The CLIST implementation of this function is considerably shorter than the COBOL version, for several reasons. First, command procedures are interpreted and do not have to declare variables as do programs in compiled languages like COBOL. This difference is an attribute of interpreted versus compiled languages and has nothing to do with the Dialog Manager. Second, command procedures do not have to use the **VDEFINE** service to make their use of dialog variables explicit to the Dialog Manager. The **VDEFINE** and **VDELETE** commands are for the use of program functions only. This is a key difference in writing dialog manager functions between compiled languages and command procedures. Last, the CLIST is shorter than its COBOL counterpart because the COBOL program had to be **SELECT**ed by a CLIST for execution. This was because the COBOL program relies on its originating CLIST to submit its file tailoring output as a batch job to the operating system. In figure 6-8, of course, the CLIST submits the background job for execution itself.

The **XREPTS** CLIST first initializes its environment through use of the **CONTROL** service. It then retrieves the employee accounting data from the application profile. Recall that these data are created and maintained in the application profile pool by the function of option 3 of the master menu of figure 3-2.

Next, the CLIST initializes the variables that appear on the data entry panel. Unlike the COBOL program function, no **VDEFINE**s are required in order to do this. The CLIST displays the data entry panel and then tests **&LASTCC** to see if the input data were entered. If they were, these lines are executed:

```
ISPEXEC   FTOPEN   TEMP
ISPEXEC   FTINCL   WSKEL1
ISPEXEC   FTCLOSE
```

The first statement initializes the file tailoring process, indicating that the output of this procedure will be written to a temporary dataset automatically allocated by the Dialog Manager. The second line informs ISPF that the file skeleton is named **WSKEL1**. The last line terminates file tailoring.

The next two statements in the CLIST are these:

```
ISPEXEC   VGET   ZTEMPF   SHARED
SUBMIT '&ZTEMPF'
```

The first statement ensures that the second will refer to a valid file name. Then the CLIST submits the background job to the operating system.

Whether this CLIST submits a background job to the system, the **SETMSG** command provides an appropriate action message. The CLIST exits issuing a return code of **0**.

VM AND VSE DIFFERENCES

There are no significant differences in ISPF file tailoring services in the VM and VSE environments; however, there are system dependencies in considering what file skeletons might contain. The example in this chapter tailors a file containing generalized MVS JCL. Obviously a JCL skeleton in the VSE environment would contain DOS JCL. Under VM, JCL skeletons could include whatever is appropriate to the target batch facility.

Besides tailoring background job submissions, the Dialog Manager's file tailoring services can process other kinds of statements. For example, under MVS and VM, these services could be used to process text files for submission to DCF SCRIPT. As another example, files can be tailored to produce reports directly. The example in the next chapter demonstrates file tailoring against an ISPF-maintained table that produces an in-stream input data set for a batch job.

Under VSE, the **SELECT** service is similar to the **ISPSTART** command in that it requires reference to the language of the program selected. As discussed in chapter 1, the **LANG** keyword is used for this purpose.

Figure 6-1. WPAN2 screen as displayed.

```
------------ WEST DEPARTMENT ACCOUNTS RECEIVABLE ----- ENTER JOB CONTROL DATA


RUN BATCH ACCOUNTS RECEIVABLE SIMPLE REPORT:


   FOR  LOGON ID:  ZHMF01


   YOUR LAST  NAME    ===>
   DISTRIBUTION CODE ===>
   OUTPUT  CLASS     ===> A            (EITHER 'T' OR 'A')
   FORMS SELECTION   ===> 1            (EITHER '1' OR '2')

   REPORT CONTROL DATE   ===>          (IN FORM 'MM/DD/YY')
   REPORT CONTROL STATUS ===> W        (EITHER 'W', 'E' OR 'S')
```

Figure 6-2. WPAN2 panel definition.

```
)BODY
%-------------- WEST DEPARTMENT ACCOUNTS RECEIVABLE ----------------------------
+
+
%RUN BATCH ACCOUNTS RECEIVABLE SIMPLE REPORT:
+
+
+    FOR   LOGON ID: %&ZUSER
+
+
+    YOUR LAST   NAME  %===>_NAME     +
+    DISTRIBUTION CODE%===>_DIST+
+    OUTPUT   CLASS    %===>_CLASS+        (EITHER 'T' OR 'A')
+    FORMS SELECTION   %===>_FORMS+        (EITHER '1' OR '2')
+
+    REPORT CONTROL DATE  %===>_CDATE   +(IN FORM 'MM/DD/YY')
+    REPORT CONTROL STATUS%===>_STATUS+  (EITHER 'W', 'E' OR 'S')
+
+
)INIT
   .HELP  = WH005
)PROC
   &NAME = TRUNC (&NAME, 8)
   VER (&NAME, NONBLANK, ALPHA)
   VER (&DIST, NONBLANK, PICT, 'NNNN')
   VER (&CLASS,NONBLANK, LIST, T, A, MSG=WDAR002A)
   VER (&FORMS,NONBLANK, LIST, 1, 2, MSG=WDAR002B)
   VER (&CDATE,NONBLANK, PICT, '99/99/99', MSG=WDAR002C)
   &STATUS = TRUNC (&STATUS, 1)
   VER (&STATUS,NB, LIST, W, E, S, MSG=WDAR002D)
)END
```

Figure 6-3. SUBREPTS CLIST function.

```
00010000   PROC 0
00020000   CONTROL MSG NOFLUSH
00030000   /*******************************************************************/
00040000   /* NAME: SUBREPTS                          BY: H. FOSDICK        */
00050000   /*                                                              */
00060000   /* PURPOSE: THIS CLIST RUNS A COBOL PROGRAM TO PERFORM          */
00070000   /* FILE TAILORING ON A SKELETON TO SET UP A BATCH JOB.          */
00080000   /* THIS CLIST CHECKS THE RETURN CODE FROM THAT PROGRAM,         */
00090000   /* AND SUBMITS THE BATCH JOB IF THAT RETURN CODE WAS ZERO.      */
00100000   /*                                                              */
00110000   /*******************************************************************/
00120000
00130000
00140000   /*                                                              */
00150000   /*   RUN THE COBOL PROGRAM VIA THE ISPF 'SELECT' SERVICE:       */
00160000   /*                                                              */
00170000
00180000   ISPEXEC  SELECT  PGM(CREPTS)
00190000
00200000
00210000   /*                                                              */
00220000   /*   IF RETURN CODE FROM PROGRAM WAS 0, SUBMIT THE BATCH JOB:*/
00230000   /*                                                              */
00240000
00250000   IF &LASTCC = 0 THEN DO
00260000
00270000       ISPEXEC  VGET  ZTEMPF  SHARED
00280000       SUBMIT '&ZTEMPF'
00290000       END
00300000
00310000
00320000   EXIT CODE(0)
```

Figure 6-4. CREPTS COBOL function.

```
IDENTIFICATION DIVISION.                                            00010000
PROGRAM-ID. CREPTS.                                                 00020000
************************************************************************00030000
*  NAME: CREPTS                                   BY: H. FOSDICK *00040000
*                                                                  *00050000
*  PURPOSE: THIS ROUTINE ILLUSTRATES FILE TAILORING SERVICES.      *00060000
*  AFTER RECEIVING USER-ENTERED DATA THROUGH ITS DATA ENTRY        *00070000
*  PANEL, THE ROUTINE RUNS FILE TAILORING SERVICES AGAINST         *00080000
*  A SKELETON JCL FILE FOR RUNNING THE ACCOUNTS RECEIVABLE         *00090000
*  BATCH SIMPLE REPORT PROGRAM.                                    *00100000
*                                                                  *00110000
*  NOTE: THIS ROUTINE ASSUMES THE PROFILE VARIABLES ARE VALID.     *00120000
*                                                                  *00130000
************************************************************************00140000
ENVIRONMENT DIVISION.                                               00150000
DATA DIVISION.                                                      00160000
                                                                    00170000
                                                                    00180000
WORKING-STORAGE SECTION.                                            00190000
                                                                    00200000
                                                                    00210000
*  SERVICE CALL TYPES:                                              00220000
                                                                    00230000
01  VGET                  PIC X(8)     VALUE 'VGET    '.            00240000
01  DISPLAY-PANEL         PIC X(8)     VALUE 'DISPLAY '.            00250000
01  FTOPEN                PIC X(8)     VALUE 'FTOPEN  '.            00260000
01  FTINCL                PIC X(8)     VALUE 'FTINCL  '.            00270000
01  FTCLOSE               PIC X(8)     VALUE 'FTCLOSE '.            00280000
01  SETMSG                PIC X(8)     VALUE 'SETMSG  '.            00290000
01  VDEFINE               PIC X(8)     VALUE 'VDEFINE '.            00300000
01  VDELETE               PIC X(8)     VALUE 'VDELETE '.            00310000
                                                                    00320000
                                                                    00330000
*  REFER TO THE PROFILE POOL IN THE 'VGET' CALL:                    00340000
                                                                    00350000
01  PROFILE               PIC X(8)     VALUE 'PROFILE '.            00360000
                                                                    00370000
                                                                    00380000
*  THE NAME OF THE FILE MEMBER TO TAILOR:                           00390000
                                                                    00400000
01  SKELETON-NAME         PIC X(8)     VALUE 'WSKEL1  '.            00410000
                                                                    00420000
                                                                    00430000
*  THE NAME OF THE DATA ENTRY PANEL TO DISPLAY:                     00440000
                                                                    00450000
01  PANEL-NAME            PIC X(8)     VALUE 'WPAN2   '.            00460000
                                                                    00470000
                                                                    00480000
*  VARIABLES TO GET FROM THE PROFILE POOL:                          00490000
                                                                    00500000
01  VARLIST               PIC X(24)                                00510000
                          VALUE '(PROJECT ASSIGN CLOCKID)'.         00520000
                                                                    00530000
                                                                    00540000
*  VARIABLE TYPE FOR VARIABLE DEFINITION TO ISPF DIALOG MANAGER:    00550000
                                                                    00560000
01  CHAR                  PIC X(8)     VALUE 'CHAR    '.            00570000
                                                                    00580000
                                                                    00590000
*  OUTPUT FOR FILE TAILORING GOES TO SYSTEM TEMPORARY VARIABLE:     00600000
                                                                    00610000
01  TEMP                  PIC X(8)     VALUE 'TEMP    '.            00620000
                                                                    00630000
                                                                    00640000
*  A FLAG INDICATING WHETHER FILE TAILORING OCCURED:                00650000
                                                                    00660000
01  RETURN-STATUS         PIC 9(4)     VALUE  0.                    00670000
                                                                    00680000
                                                                    00690000
*  MESSAGES:                                                        00700000
                                                                    00710000
                                                                    00720000
01  ENTER-DATA-MSG            PIC X(8)     VALUE 'WDAR002E'.        00730000
01  REPORT-SUBMITTED-MSG      PIC X(8)     VALUE 'WDAR002F'.        00740000
01  PROCESSING-TERMINATED-MSG PIC X(8)     VALUE 'WDAR000A'.        00750000
                                                                    00760000
                                                                    00770000
*  DEFINE STORAGE SPACE FOR DIALOG VARIABLES:                       00780000
                                                                    00790000
                                                                    00800000
01  NAME                  PIC X(8)     VALUE  SPACES.               00810000
01  DIST                  PIC X(4)     VALUE  SPACES.               00820000
01  CLASS                 PIC X(1)     VALUE  SPACES.               00830000
01  FORMS                 PIC X(1)     VALUE  SPACES.               00840000
01  CDATE                 PIC X(8)     VALUE  SPACES.               00850000
01  SSTATUS               PIC X(1)     VALUE  SPACES.               00860000
                                                                    00870000
```

(continued)

Figure 6-4. (*Continued*)

```
*   DEFINE THE LENGTH OF EACH DIALOG VARIABLE:                      00880000
                                                                   00890000
                                                                   00900000
                                                                   00910000
    01   NAME-LENGTH        PIC 9(6)      VALUE  8   COMP.          00920000
    01   DIST-LENGTH        PIC 9(6)      VALUE  4   COMP.          00930000
    01   CLASS-LENGTH       PIC 9(6)      VALUE  1   COMP.          00940000
    01   FORMS-LENGTH       PIC 9(6)      VALUE  1   COMP.          00950000
    01   CDATE-LENGTH       PIC 9(6)      VALUE  8   COMP.          00960000
    01   STATUS-LENGTH      PIC 9(6)      VALUE  1   COMP.          00970000
                                                                   00980000
                                                                   00990000
*   DEFINE DIALOG VARIABLE NAMES FOR ISPF DIALOG MANAGER:          01000000
                                                                   01010000
                                                                   01020000
    01   NAME-NAME          PIC X(6)      VALUE  '(NAME)'.          01030000
    01   DIST-NAME          PIC X(6)      VALUE  '(DIST)'.          01040000
    01   CLASS-NAME         PIC X(7)      VALUE  '(CLASS)'.         01050000
    01   FORMS-NAME         PIC X(7)      VALUE  '(FORMS)'.         01060000
    01   CDATE-NAME         PIC X(7)      VALUE  '(CDATE)'.         01070000
    01   STATUS-NAME        PIC X(8)      VALUE  '(STATUS)'.        01080007
                                                                   01090000
                                                                   01100000
                                                                   01110000
    PROCEDURE DIVISION.                                            01120000
                                                                   01130000
                                                                   01140000
*                                                                  01150000
*   DEFINE ALL DIALOG FUNCTION VARIABLES TO ISPF DIALOG MANAGER:   01160000
*                                                                  01170000
                                                                   01180000
        PERFORM DEFINE-VARIABLES THRU DEFINE-VARIABLES-EXIT.       01190000
                                                                   01200000
                                                                   01210000
*                                                                  01220000
*   GET EMPLOYEE ACCOUNTING DATA FROM THE APPLICATION PROFILE:     01230000
*                                                                  01240000
                                                                   01250000
        CALL 'ISPLINK' USING  VGET                                 01260000
                              VARLIST                              01270000
                              PROFILE.                             01280000
                                                                   01290000
                                                                   01300000
                                                                   01310000
*                                                                  01320000
*   SET UP DEFAULT VARIABLES FOR SCREEN DISPLAY:                   01330000
*                                                                  01340000
                                                                   01350000
        MOVE SPACES TO NAME.                                       01360000
        MOVE SPACES TO DIST.                                       01370000
        MOVE 'A'    TO CLASS.                                      01380000
        MOVE '1'    TO FORMS.                                      01390000
        MOVE SPACES TO CDATE.                                      01400000
        MOVE 'W'    TO SSTATUS.                                    01410000
                                                                   01420000
                                                                   01430000
*                                                                  01440000
*   GET JOB AND REPORT CONTROL INFORMATION FROM THE USER:          01450000
*                                                                  01460000
                                                                   01470000
        CALL 'ISPLINK' USING  DISPLAY-PANEL                        01480000
                              PANEL-NAME                           01490000
                              ENTER-DATA-MSG.                      01500000
                                                                   01510000
                                                                   01520000
*                                                                  01530000
*   IF THE USER ENTERED THE CONTROL DATA, OPEN FILE                01540000
*   TAILORING SERVICES USING A TEMPORARY OUTPUT FILE:              01550000
*                                                                  01560000
                                                                   01570000
        IF RETURN-CODE = 0                                         01580000
                                                                   01590000
            CALL 'ISPLINK' USING  FTOPEN                           01600000
                                  TEMP                             01610000
                                                                   01620000
            CALL 'ISPLINK' USING  FTINCL                           01630000
                                  SKELETON-NAME                    01640000
                                                                   01650000
*                                                                  01660000
*   END FILE TAILORING, SET UP PROPER MESSAGE FOR USER             01670000
*   AND RETURN CODE SO THAT INVOKING CLIST WILL SUBMIT JOB:        01680000
*                                                                  01690000
                                                                   01700000
            CALL 'ISPLINK' USING  FTCLOSE                          01710000
                                                                   01720000
            CALL 'ISPLINK' USING  SETMSG                           01730000
                                  REPORT-SUBMITTED-MSG             01740000
                                                                   01750000
            MOVE 0 TO RETURN-STATUS                                01760000
```

```
                                                             01770000
                                                             01780000
                                                             01790000
*  IF THE USER HIT THE 'END' KEY, TERMINATE PROCESSING       01800000
*  WITH MESSAGE AND RETURN CODE OF 4 SO INVOKING CLIST WILL   01810000
*  NOT ATTEMPT SUBMISSION OF BATCH JOB:                       01820000
*                                                             01830000
                                                             01840000
    ELSE                                                      01850000
                                                             01860000
        CALL 'ISPLINK'  USING  SETMSG                         01870000
                               PROCESSING-TERMINATED-MSG      01880000
                                                             01890000
        MOVE 4 TO RETURN-STATUS.                              01900000
                                                             01910000
                                                             01920000
                                                             01930000
*                                                             01940000
*  DELETE ALL DIALOG FUNCTION VARIABLES RE ISPF DIALOG MANAGER:  01950000
*                                                             01960000
                                                             01970000
    PERFORM DELETE-VARIABLES THRU DELETE-VARIABLES-EXIT.      01980002
                                                             01990000
                                                             02000000
                                                             02010000
*  SET RETURN CODE TO 0 IF FILE TAILORING OCCURRED, 4 OTHERWISE:  02020000
*                                                             02030000
                                                             02040000
    IF  RETURN-STATUS = 0                                     02050000
                                                             02060000
        MOVE 0 TO RETURN-CODE                                 02070000
                                                             02080000
    ELSE                                                      02090000
                                                             02100000
        MOVE 4 TO RETURN-CODE.                                02110000
                                                             02120000
    GOBACK.                                                   02130000
                                                             02140000
MAIN-LINE-EXIT.                                               02150000
                                                             02160000
                                                             02170000
                                                             02180000
                                                             02190000
DEFINE-VARIABLES.                                             02200000
                                                             02210000
*                                                             02220000
*  THIS PARAGRAPH DEFINES DIALOG VARIABLES TO THE DIALOG MANAGER:  02230000
*                                                             02240000
                                                             02250000
    CALL 'ISPLINK'  USING  VDEFINE                            02260000
                           NAME-NAME                          02270000
                           NAME                               02280000
                           CHAR                               02290000
                           NAME-LENGTH.                       02300000
    CALL 'ISPLINK'  USING  VDEFINE                            02310000
                           DIST-NAME                          02320000
                           DIST                               02330000
                           CHAR                               02340000
                           DIST-LENGTH.                       02350000
    CALL 'ISPLINK'  USING  VDEFINE                            02360000
                           CLASS-NAME                         02370000
                           CLASS                              02380000
                           CHAR                               02390000
                           CLASS-LENGTH.                      02400000
    CALL 'ISPLINK'  USING  VDEFINE                            02410000
                           FORMS-NAME                         02420000
                           FORMS                              02430000
                           CHAR                               02440000
                           FORMS-LENGTH.                      02450000
    CALL 'ISPLINK'  USING  VDEFINE                            02460000
                           CDATE-NAME                         02470000
                           CDATE                              02480000
                           CHAR                               02490000
                           CDATE-LENGTH.                      02500000
    CALL 'ISPLINK'  USING  VDEFINE                            02510000
                           STATUS-NAME                        02520000
                           SSTATUS                            02530000
                           CHAR                               02540000
                           STATUS-LENGTH.                     02550000
                                                             02560000
DEFINE-VARIABLES-EXIT.                                        02570000
    EXIT.                                                     02580000
                                                             02590000
                                                             02600000
                                                             02610000
DELETE-VARIABLES.                                             02620000
                                                             02630000
```

(continued)

Figure 6-4. (*Continued*)

```
*                                                                    02640000
*    THIS PARAGRAPH DELETES DIALOG VARIABLES RE THE DIALOG MANAGER:  02650000
*                                                                    02660000
                                                                     02670000
     CALL 'ISPLINK'  USING  VDELETE                                  02680000
                            NAME-NAME.                               02690000
     CALL 'ISPLINK'  USING  VDELETE                                  02700000
                            DIST-NAME.                               02710000
     CALL 'ISPLINK'  USING  VDELETE                                  02720000
                            CLASS-NAME.                              02730000
     CALL 'ISPLINK'  USING  VDELETE                                  02740000
                            FORMS-NAME.                              02750000
     CALL 'ISPLINK'  USING  VDELETE                                  02760000
                            CDATE-NAME.                              02770000
     CALL 'ISPLINK'  USING  VDELETE                                  02780000
                            STATUS-NAME.                             02790000
                                                                     02800000
 DELETE-VARIABLES-EXIT.                                              02810000
     EXIT.                                                           02820000
                                                                     02830000
```

Figure 6-5. WSKEL1 file tailoring skeleton.

```
//&ZUSER.A      JOB (&PROJECT.&CLOCKID.,&ASSIGN.,,20,B),
//             '&NAME.,BN&DIST.',
//             MSGLEVEL=1,MSGCLASS=&CLASS.,CLASS=A,
//             PRTY=07,NOTIFY=&ZUSER.
)CM ********************************************************************
)CM *   NAME: WSKEL1                            BY: H. FOSDICK     *
)CM *                                                             *
)CM *   PURPOSE: THIS SKELETON JCL IS PROCESSED BY THE DIALOG MANAGER *
)CM *   FILE TAILORING SERVICES TO SET UP AN APPROPRIATE BATCH JOB    *
)CM *   TO PRODUCE THE ACCOUNTS RECEIVABLE SIMPLE REPORT.         *
)CM *                                                             *
)CM ********************************************************************
//*MAIN ORG=ANYLOCAL
//STEP1     EXEC PGM=WACCT
//STEPLIB   DD DSN=&ZUSER..W.LOAD,DISP=SHR
)CM
)CM   SELECT THE PROPER 'SYSPRINT' STATEMENT BASED ON CONTENTS OF 'FORMS'
)CM
)SEL    &FORMS = 1
//SYSPRINT DD SYSOUT=A,DCB=BLKSIZE=133
)ENDSEL
)SEL    &FORMS = 2
//SYSPRINT DD SYSOUT=A,FLASH=NONE,DCB=BLKSIZE=133
)ENDSEL
//SYSOUT    DD SYSOUT=*,DCB=BLKSIZE=133
//SYSIN     DD DSN=&ZUSER..ACCT.OUT,DISP=SHR
//CONTROL   DD *
NAME      = &NAME.
ACCT      = &PROJECT.&CLOCKID.
STATUS    = &STATUS.
DIST      = &DIST.
CONTDATE  = &CDATE.
JOBNAME   = &ZUSER.A
/*
//
```

Figure 6-6. Results of file tailoring on **WSKEL1** skeleton.

```
//ZHMF01A      JOB (111222211504,C137,14AA,,20,B),
//             'FOSDICK,BN6127',
//             MSGLEVEL=1,MSGCLASS=A,CLASS=A,
//             PRTY=07,NOTIFY=ZHMF01
//*MAIN ORG=ANYLOCAL
//STEP1     EXEC PGM=WACCT
//STEPLIB   DD DSN=ZHMF01.W.LOAD,DISP=SHR
//SYSPRINT  DD SYSOUT=A,FLASH=NONE,DCB=BLKSIZE=133
//SYSOUT    DD SYSOUT=*,DCB=BLKSIZE=133
//SYSIN     DD DSN=ZHMF01.ACCT.OUT,DISP=SHR
//CONTROL   DD *
NAME     = FOSDICK
ACCT     = 111222211504
STATUS   = E
DIST     = 6127
CONDATE  = 01/01/85
JOBNAME  = ZHMF01A
/*
//
```

Figure 6-7. Values entered via screen **WPAN2** for file tailoring.

```
-------------- WEST DEPARTMENT ACCOUNTS RECEIVABLE ---- ENTER JOB CONTROL DATA


RUN BATCH ACCOUNTS RECEIVABLE SIMPLE REPORT:


   FOR  LOGON ID:  ZHMF01


   YOUR LAST  NAME    ===> FOSDICK
   DISTRIBUTION CODE ===> 6127
   OUTPUT  CLASS      ===> A          (EITHER 'T' OR 'A')
   FORMS SELECTION    ===> 2          (EITHER '1' OR '2')

   REPORT CONTROL DATE   ===> 01/01/85 (IN FORM 'MM/DD/YY')
   REPORT CONTROL STATUS ===> E        (EITHER 'W', 'E' OR 'S')
```

Figure 6-8. XREPTS CLIST Function

```
00010000  PROC 0
00020000  CONTROL MSG NOFLUSH
00030000  /************************************************************/
00040000  /* NAME: XREPTS                             BY: H. FOSDICK  */
00050000  /*                                                          */
00060000  /* PURPOSE: THIS CLIST ILLUSTRATES THE FILE TAILORING       */
00070000  /* SERVICES.  AFTER RECEIVING USER-ENTERED DATA THROUGH ITS */
00080000  /* DATA ENTRY PANEL, THE CLIST RUNS FILE TAILORING SERVICES */
00090000  /* AGAINST A SKELETON JCL FILE FOR RUNNING THE ACCOUNTS     */
00100000  /* RECEIVABLE BATCH SIMPLE REPORT PROGRAM.                  */
00110000  /*                                                          */
00120000  /* NOTE: THIS ROUTINE ASSUMES THE PROFILE VARIABLES ARE     */
00130000  /* VALID.                                                   */
00140000  /*                                                          */
00150000  /************************************************************/
00160000
00170000  /*                                                          */
00180000  /*   SET UP THE ENVIRONMENT FOR THE CLIST:                  */
00190000  /*                                                          */
00200000
00210000  ISPEXEC  CONTROL  ERRORS  CANCEL
00220000
00230000
00240000  /*                                                          */
00250000  /*   GET EMPLOYEE ACCOUNTING DATA FROM APPLICATION PROFILE:  */
00260000  /*                                                          */
00270000
00280000  ISPEXEC  VGET  (PROJECT ASSIGN CLOCKID) PROFILE
00290000
00300000
00310000  /*                                                          */
00320000  /*   SET UP DEFAULT VARIABLES FOR SCREEN DISPLAY:           */
00330000  /*                                                          */
00340000
00350000  SET NAME   =
00360000  SET DIST   =
00370000  SET CLASS  = A
00380000  SET FORMS  = 1
00390000  SET CDATE  =
00400000  SET STATUS = W
00410000
00420000
00430000  /*                                                          */
00440000  /*   GET JOB AND REPORT CONTROL INFORMATION FROM THE USER:   */
00450000  /*                                                          */
00460000
00470000  ISPEXEC  DISPLAY PANEL(WPAN2)  MSG(WDAR002E)
00480000
00490000
00500000  /*                                                          */
00510000  /*   IF THE USER ENTERED THE CONTROL DATA, OPEN FILE         */
00520000  /*   TAILORING SERVICES USING A TEMPORARY OUTPUT FILE:       */
00530000  /*                                                          */
00540000
00550000  IF &LASTCC = 0 THEN DO
00560000
00570000       ISPEXEC FTOPEN TEMP
00580000
00590000
00600000       /*                                                     */
00610000       /*   TAILOR THE JCL SKELETON FILE 'WSKEL1':             */
00620000       /*                                                     */
00630000
00640000       ISPEXEC FTINCL WSKEL1
00650000
00660000
00670000       /*                                                     */
00680000       /*   END FILE TAILORING, GET TEMPORARY FILE NAME FROM THE */
00690000       /*   SHARED VARIABLE POOL, AND SUBMIT THE BACKGROUND JOB: */
00700000       /*                                                     */
00710000
00720000       ISPEXEC FTCLOSE
00730000       ISPEXEC VGET ZTEMPF SHARED
00740000       SUBMIT '&ZTEMPF'
00750000
00760000       ISPEXEC  SETMSG MSG(WDAR002F)
00770000
00780000       END
00790000
00800000  /*                                                          */
00810000  /*   IF THE USER HIT THE 'END' KEY, TERMINATE PROCESSING:   */
00820000  /*                                                          */
00830000
00840000  ELSE +
00850000       ISPEXEC SETMSG MSG(WDAR000A)
00860000
00870000
00880000  EXIT CODE(0)
```

7
More on File Tailoring

This chapter describes the functions that implement the Distribution Report option, selectable as option 5 from either version of the dialog's master menus. Selection of option 5 results in processing that is highly similar to that discussed in the previous chapter, except that the Distribution Report requires an additional input file in the file tailoring skeleton. This in-stream input file contains control date information for a number of users, thereby allowing the batch job to print a Distribution Report listing. This additional information is included from a table created and maintained by the dialog through the Dialog Manager's table services. How this permanent table is maintained is the subject of chapters 9, 10, and 11. In this chapter, it is assumed that the table exists and that it contains at least one record (or "row") of valid data.

DATA ENTRY PANEL

The data entry panel for the Distribution Report option of the master menu is contained in figure 7-1. This file, **WPAN3**, displays a screen that looks the same to the user as the panel definition of **WPAN2** did in the previous chapter. Close inspection of these two panels shows, however, that although the user may not recognize any differences, the encoding varies. This was done in order to introduce several aspects of panel design that result in more sophisticated definitions.

In figure 6-2, the allowable input lengths for the variables in the **)BODY** section of the panel definition are defined by the number of character positions between the attribute character preceding an input field and the attribute character immediately following that field. For example, in this line:

```
+    FORMS SELECTION % = = = > _ FORMS +      (EITHER '1' OR '2')
```

there are five character positions between the attribute character preceding the variable **&FORMS** and the next attribute byte. In other words, five character positions occur between the underscore preceding the word **FORMS** and the + following it. The user can enter up to five characters after the input arrow. If he or she attempts to enter a sixth character, the keyboard physically jams because the + attribute character indicates a protected field.

This verification function in the processing section of the panel definition

VER (&FORMS,NONBLANK, LIST, 1, 2, MSG = WDAR002B)

then edits user-input data to ensure that it has been entered (the **NONBLANK** keyword specifies this) and that it is either a **1** or a **2**. The latter criterion is enforced as part of the **LIST** keyword. A group of acceptable values follow the **LIST** keyword, and the edit fails unless the input data matches a value in this list. The **MSG** parameter cites the message ID of the message to display on the data entry panel if it is redisplayed as a result of a failed edit. This message overrides any default message of the Dialog Manager.

Figure 6-2 shows one method used to verify values entered by the user in panel input fields: edit them via the **LIST** keyword in a verify statement. The panel definition shows another way to edit user input in the instance of the **&STATUS** variable. This field, too, should be only a single character long. The user can physically enter up to six characters into the field before the keyboard jams (because of the position of the + attribute character following the input field). However, this processing section statement

&STATUS = TRUNC (&STATUS, 1)

truncates anything entered beyond a single character. The **&STATUS** variable is then tested by a verify function that includes the **LIST** keyword, restricting it to the valid values of **W**, **E**, and **S**. The keyword **NB** is an abbreviation for the **NONBLANK** keyword.

In figure 7-1, **WPAN3** shows a more sophisticated way to edit short user input fields. In the panel initialization section, the control variable **.ZVARS** is set to a name-list of all the variables appearing on the screen whose variable name length exceeds the desired input data length. This is the case for the variables **&CLASS**, **&FORMS**, and **&STATUS**. Wherever the system variable **Z** occurs in the **)BODY** section of the panel definition, it represents one of the variables in the **.ZVARS** name-list. Each occurrence of **Z** represents the next variable in the **.ZVARS** name-list according to the specification order of that list. Thus, the three occurrences of the **Z** variable in the **)BODY** section of the panel definition stand for the variables **&CLASS**, **&FORMS**, and **&STATUS**, in that order.

The effect is to jam the keyboard physically if the user attempts entry of more than a single character in any of these three input fields, informing the user in the most direct fashion of the expected maximum input length for each of the input fields. It is a better approach than allowing the user to enter too many characters and then truncating overly long inputs through the truncation function in the processing section of the panel definition.

The **Z** system variable in this role is referred to as the *placeholder* variable. Its use provides much greater flexibility in the location of variables during panel design.

The panel definitions of figures 6-2 and 7-1 show several other ways to validate user inputs. In figure 6-2, this statement

    VER (&NAME, NONBLANK, ALPHA)

ensures that **&NAME** will consist of letters of the alphabet and the national characters (#, $, and @).

Picture verification is illustrated in these three statements:

    VER (&DIST, NONBLANK, PICT, 'NNNN')
    VER (&DIST, NONBLANK, NUM)
    VER (&CDATE,NONBLANK, PICT, '99/99/99', MSG = WDAR002C)

The first two statements are equivalent; each requires that all characters entered be digits, **0** through **9**. The statements result in slightly different ISPF default error messages since the first verification indicates a **PICT** character string that happens to consist solely of digits, whereas the use of the **NUM** keyword specifies a numeric value. The last statement is useful for verifying a date. The date string consists of two digits, followed by a literal slash, followed by two more digits, a slash, and two final digits. Notice that the picture character **9** is synonymous with the **N** used in the first statement.

COBOL IMPLEMENTATION OF MENU OPTION 5

To continue discussion of the function of master menu option 5, figure 7-2 shows the COBOL program code for this function. As in the instance of master menu option 4, the COBOL function is executed as a lower level function by a CLIST through the **SELECT** service. The purpose of this CLIST is to submit the batch job generated by the file tailoring process of the COBOL program. The code for the CLIST is in figure 7-3. It requires no explanation beyond what was said in the preceding chapter because its code is almost an exact duplicate of that of the CLIST of the previous chapter.

The COBOL program, too, is similar to that discussed in the previous chapter for menu option 4; however, there are two differences worth mentioning. First, this program does not issue any **VDEFINE** (or corresponding **VDELETE**) service calls because it does not attempt to manipulate any dialog variables directly. The function of the last chapter initialized the screen variables through the code of the COBOL program. This program does not attempt to alter variables directly.

The COBOL program of option 4 worked with what are referred to as *explicit* variables. That is, it invoked the **VDEFINE** service to create the necessary link between the program variables and the dialog variables such that the program code could update these variables directly.

The program of this chapter works with the dialog variables *implicitly*. It invokes ISPF services that display variables on the user's screen and ISPF services that process variables against file tailoring skeletons. But never does the program issue a **VDEFINE** call nor does it directly alter a variable through COBOL assignment statements in the code.

The other respect in which this COBOL program differs from that of option 4 is that it processes a different skeleton file via the Dialog Manager's file tailoring services. This program processes the sequential file **WSKEL2**. **WSKEL2** is listed in figure 7-4.

In looking at the skeleton JCL of member **WSKEL2**, the first control record in the file is the first line:

```
)IM WSKEL3
```

This control statement contains the "imbed" command. It imbeds the complete contents of another skeleton file at this point in this file. In this sense, it is analogous to use of the COBOL **COPY** compiler directive or the preprocessor %**INCLUDE** in PL/I. The purpose of the imbed command is to replicate some other skeleton at this position in this file. Figure 7-5 shows the contents of the imbedded skeleton file. This skeleton file must also reside in the library of file tailoring input files defined to the Dialog Manager. In this case, the member name is **WSKEL3**.

WSKEL3 contains the Job Card portion of the background job that is created as a result of the file tailoring process. The value of creating only a single Job Card skeleton, and then referring to this skeleton file from many other skeleton files by the)**IM** statement, should be obvious. This localizes any potential maintenance tasks associated with enhancing skeleton files. In effect, the)**IM** command lends the advantages of modular design to development of skeleton JCL files.

The general format of the)**IM** command is:

```
)IM skeleton-name NT OPT
```

In the example of figure 7-5, the Dialog Manager performs symbolic substitution on the dialog variables in the file **WSKEL3**, the imbedded skeleton file, as well as on **WSKEL2**. The **NT**, or "no tailoring," option could be specified to prevent variable substitution on an imbedded file. The **OPT** keyword informs the Dialog Manager that the skeleton to be imbedded may not exist. If **OPT** is not specified and the file to imbed does not exist, a severe error results.

These lines in the file **WSKEL2** serve to select and generate a **SYS-PRINT DD** statement in the output file, depending on the value of the variable **&FORMS**:

```
)SEL       &FORMS = &Z
//SYSPRINT DD SYSOUT=A,FLASH=NONE,
               FCB=847Z,CHARS=CRR0,DCB=BLKSIZE=133
)ENDSEL
)SEL       &FORMS = 1
//SYSPRINT DD SYSOUT=A,DCB=BLKSIZE=133
)ENDSEL
)SEL       &FORMS = 2
//SYSPRINT DD SYSOUT=A,FLASH=NONE,DCB=BLKSIZE=133
)ENDSEL
```

The selection tests compare the value entered by the terminal user
for the variable **&FORMS**. If the user did not enter anything or entered
blanks, **&FORMS** compares equally to the system variable **Z**, also
known as the *null variable*. In this case, a **SYSPRINT DD** is generated
for the Distribution Report that prints the report listing on plain white
paper with a special forms control block and character set. These parameters are indicated by the **FLASH**, **FCB**, and **CHARS** keywords in
the generated JCL statement. If the user entered a **1** for the **&FORMS**
variable, a standard report listing results; for a **2**, a standard report
listing prints on plain white paper. This series of **)SEL** and corresponding **)ENDSEL** control commands shows how various skeleton output
lines are generated depending on a variable's value.

The selection control record can be nested up to eight levels deep. It
can test simple compound conditions, such as in:

```
)SEL       &FORMS = 1   |   & FORMS = 2
```

where the allowable logical connectors are | **(OR)** and **&& (AND)**. The
selection control statement does not support an **ELSE** clause.

The final difference between **WSKEL2** and **WSKEL1** is seen in the
last few lines of **WSKEL2**:

```
//CONTRL2     DD *
)TB 15 30 45 60
)DOT CONTDATA
&CONTACT &COSCTR &SUBCTR &DISTRIB &INVDATE
)ENDDOT
```

The intent of these lines is to generate the **DD** statement data for the
additional input file used by the Distribution Report program. Recall
that this additional input file distinguishes the Distribution Report program from the Simple Report illustrated in the previous chapter. Each
record of information in this file contains a user contact name (**&CON-
TACT**), the user cost center and sub-cost center (**&COSCTR** and
&SUBCTR), the user routing code (**&DISTRIB**), and the user's control
date (**&INVDATE**).

These data items are stored by this dialog in a permanent table created and maintained through the Dialog Manager's table services. The
programs of option 6 of the master menu of figures 3-1 and 3-2 perform table creation and maintenance. At this point, it is assumed that
the table exists and that it contains at least one row of valid data.

Note: In the example code at the top of the page, line 3 represents a continuation of line 2.

This file skeleton uses the **)DOT** and **)ENDDOT** control keywords to specify that the Dialog Manager process the variables occurring between them against the table named in the **)DOT** control record. In this case, the table name is **CONTDATA**. This table is a member of the table library defined to the Dialog Manager.

The records between the **)DOT** and **)ENDDOT** keywords are iteratively processed, one time for each row in the table. An output record results for each row processed against the variables. Thus, for a table containing seven rows of these five variables, seven lines of information would be generated as the in-stream data for the **CONTRL2 DD** statement.

The function of the **)TB** control record is to specify tab stops for each data element. Each tab stop specifies a columnar position in the output record and must be less than the logical record length of the output record.

A sample result of file tailoring with the skeleton of figure 7-4 is shown in figure 7-6. The data entered for the tailoring process are contained in the screen reproduction of figure 7-7, and the user's employee accounting parameters are as entered via figure 5-2.

The output shows the imbedding of skeleton **WSKEL3**, the substitution of variables in both **WSKEL2** and **WSKEL3**, the selection of an appropriate **SYSPRINT DD** statement based on user **&FORMS** input, and the results of table processing via the **)DOT** and **)ENDDOT** commands. The table processing result was obtained for a table containing seven rows of data with the values shown.

CLIST IMPLEMENTATION
OF MENU OPTION 5

The CLIST version of the function selected from master menu option 5 is shown in figure 7-8. Similar to the function **XREPTS** in the previous chapter, the CLIST version of this menu option is encoded as one member.

The CLIST function utilizes the same data entry panel and two file skeletons as the COBOL program. The CLIST also performs file tailoring in the same manner, producing identical output.

Notice that the CLIST of figure 7-8 is highly similar to the CLIST of menu option 4 (figure 6-8). Unlike compiled program functions, command procedure functions do not issue **VDEFINE**s in order to gain direct access to dialog variables. With command procedures, no coding differences are required, whether the function works *explicitly* or *implicitly* with dialog variables. Remember that compiled programs must issue **VDEFINE**s to manipulate *explicit* variables.

MORE ON PANEL DEFINITIONS

The Dialog Manager documentation suggests a default panel layout, or template, for panel design. The basic panel arrangement looks like this:

LINE 1:	**Panel Title**	**Short Message**
LINE 2:	**Command Input**	**Scroll Amount**
LINE 3:	**Long Message**	

The Panel Title is encoded as a literal by the panel designer and serves to identify the panel.

The "Short" and "Long" Messages have already been discussed. Although the positions where these messages appear are system defaults, they can be overridden.

The Command Input corresponds to the option selected by a terminal user from a menu panel. The vendor's reference manuals indicate that all panel definitions should have a command input field. Actually this field is not required other than on menus and table display panels. Some dialog developers adopt a closed system approach, excluding a command input field from all other panel definitions. Other developers place a command line on every panel to give users maximum flexibility in entering commands.

The Scroll Amount field is present on panels that display scrollable data. An example is the data display panel brought up through master menu option 2 via the ISPF **BROWSE** service. Use of the **EDIT** service similarly displays a scroll amount. *Table display panels*, discussed in later chapters, are among the few other panels that require this field.

The principles of good panel design dictate several informal standards. First, *consistency* is a major virtue in panel layout. Users are confused by panels that arrange data differently within the same dialog. Care should be taken to make sure that attribute bytes are used consistently, that the kind of panel template described in this section is employed throughout a system, and that the dialog responds to the user in the same manner in similar situations. The panels defined in the sample system in this book were designed in a consistent manner. For example, the dialog error messages of figure 5-5 show that all informational messages to the user specify **.ALARM = NO,** and those that denote errors of some kind sound the alarm to gain the user's attention. Consistent application of this design choice throughout the message definitions makes the intent of the messages clear to users. This is just one example of the virtue of consistency in creating professional dialogs.

Good panel design also dictates that developers use the message facility to the fullest extent possible. Each message definition should include a long message and a short message. The dialog should take complete advantage of the tutorial system services. It should include an index "help" panel, a table of contents "help" panel, and "help" panels for each function in the dialog. The Dialog Manager's tutorial services are covered in detail in the next chapter.

Dialog designers should take care that their panel definitions do not result in overly busy panels. Panels that look cluttered appear complicated or intimidating to users. It is better to have a function present two data entry panels with well-spaced input items to the user than one cluttered panel requesting too much information.

Panels can also be made more appealing by judiciously mixing upper- and lower-case literals. If the designer knows that all hardware in the environment can handle lower case alphabetics, screen designs that include lower-case make much more attractive displays than all upper-case monochrome green screens. (The sample dialog in this book uses only upper-case alphabetics in screens because of hardware constraints.)

Panel designers should not overuse highlighting. Highlighting is best used to draw the terminal user's attention to important items, and this will be effective only if few fields on the screen are highlighted.

Finally, input fields should be vertically aligned whenever possible. This makes for a much more attractive screen display. In the example dialog, the aligned input fields are preceded by input arrows (= = = >).

Whatever choices are made in panel design decisions, consistent application of those choices is one of the highest virtues. Users find dialogs that look and respond in the most consistent manner the easiest to use.*

_____

*For further information on panel design, see the publications of the GUIDE ISPF Project.

Figure 7-1. WPAN3 panel definition.

```
)BODY
%-------------- WEST DEPARTMENT ACCOUNTS RECEIVABLE -------------------------
+
+
%RUN BATCH ACCOUNTS RECEIVABLE DISTRIBUTION REPORT:
+
+
+   FOR  LOGON ID: %%ZUSER
+
+
+   YOUR LAST  NAME  %===>_NAME    +
+   DISTRIBUTION CODE%===>_DIST+
+   OUTPUT  CLASS    %===>_Z+          (EITHER 'T' OR 'A')
+   FORMS SELECTION  %===>_Z+          (EITHER '1', '2' OR BLANK)
+
+   REPORT CONTROL DATE  %===>_CDATE   +(IN FORM 'MM/DD/YY')
+   REPORT CONTROL STATUS%===>_Z+      (EITHER 'W', 'E' OR 'S')
+
+
)INIT
   .HELP = WH006
   .ZVARS = '(CLASS FORMS STATUS)'
)PROC
   &NAME = TRUNC (&NAME, 8)
   VER (&NAME, NONBLANK, ALPHA)
   &DIST = TRUNC (&DIST, 4)
   VER (&DIST, NONBLANK, NUM)
   VER (&CLASS,NONBLANK, LIST, T, A, MSG=WDAR002A)
   VER (&FORMS, LIST, 1, 2, MSG=WDAR003A)
   VER (&CDATE,NONBLANK, PICT, '99/99/99', MSG=WDAR002C)
   &STATUS = TRUNC (&STATUS, 1)
   VER (&STATUS,NB, LIST, W, E, S, MSG=WDAR002D)
)END
```

Figure 7-2. CREPTC COBOL function.

```
       IDENTIFICATION DIVISION.                                        00010000
       PROGRAM-ID. CREPTC.                                             00020000
      ****************************************************************00030000
      *  NAME: CREPTC                                 BY: H. FOSDICK *00040000
      *                                                              *00050000
      *  PURPOSE: THIS ROUTINE ILLUSTRATES ADVANCED FILE TAILORING.  *00060000
      *  IT IS SIMILAR TO THE 'CREPTS' PROGRAM.  IT SETS UP THE      *00070000
      *  ACCOUNTS RECEIVABLE BATCH DISTRIBUTION REPORT PROGRAM.      *00080000
      *                                                              *00090000
      *  NOTE: THIS PROGRAM ASSUMES THAT TABLE 'CONTDATA' EXISTS,    *00100000
      *  AND THAT IT CONTAINS AT LEAST ONE ROW.  IT ALSO ASSUMES THE *00110000
      *  PROFILE VARIABLES ARE VALID.                                *00120000
      *                                                              *00130000
      ****************************************************************00140000
       ENVIRONMENT DIVISION.                                           00150000
       DATA DIVISION.                                                  00160000
                                                                       00170000
                                                                       00180000
       WORKING-STORAGE SECTION.                                        00190000
                                                                       00200000
                                                                       00210000
      *  SERVICE CALL TYPES:                                           00220000
                                                                       00230000
       01  VGET            PIC X(8)     VALUE 'VGET    '.              00240000
       01  DISPLAY-PANEL   PIC X(8)     VALUE 'DISPLAY '.              00250000
       01  FTOPEN          PIC X(8)     VALUE 'FTOPEN  '.              00260000
       01  FTINCL          PIC X(8)     VALUE 'FTINCL  '.              00270000
       01  FTCLOSE         PIC X(8)     VALUE 'FTCLOSE '.              00280000
       01  SETMSG          PIC X(8)     VALUE 'SETMSG  '.              00290000
                                                                       00300000
                                                                       00310000
      *  REFER TO THE PROFILE POOL IN THE 'VGET' CALL:                 00320000
                                                                       00330000
       01  PROFILE         PIC X(8)     VALUE 'PROFILE '.              00340000
                                                                       00350000
                                                                       00360000
      *  THE NAME OF THE FILE MEMBER TO TAILOR:                        00370000
                                                                       00380000
       01  SKELETON-NAME   PIC X(8)     VALUE 'WSKEL2  '.              00390000
                                                                       00400000
                                                                       00410000
      *  THE NAME OF THE DATA ENTRY PANEL TO DISPLAY:                  00420000
                                                                       00430000
       01  PANEL-NAME      PIC X(8)     VALUE 'WPAN3   '.              00440000
                                                                       00450000
                                                                       00460000
      *  VARIABLES TO GET FROM THE PROFILE POOL:                       00470000
                                                                       00480000
       01  VARLIST         PIC X(24)                                   00490000
                           VALUE '(PROJECT ASSIGN CLOCKID)'.           00500000
                                                                       00510000
                                                                       00520000
      *  OUTPUT FOR FILE TAILORING GOES TO SYSTEM TEMPORARY VARIABLE:  00530000
                                                                       00540000
       01  TEMP            PIC X(8)     VALUE 'TEMP    '.              00550000
                                                                       00560000
                                                                       00570000
      *  MESSAGES:                                                     00580000
                                                                       00590000
                                                                       00600000
       01  ENTER-DATA-MSG           PIC X(8)   VALUE 'WDAR002E'.       00610000
       01  REPORT-SUBMITTED-MSG     PIC X(8)   VALUE 'WDAR002F'.       00620000
       01  PROCESSING-TERMINATED-MSG PIC X(8)  VALUE 'WDAR000A'.       00630000
                                                                       00640000
                                                                       00650000
                                                                       00660000
       PROCEDURE DIVISION.                                             00670000
                                                                       00680000
                                                                       00690000
      *                                                                00700000
      *  GET EMPLOYEE ACCOUNTING DATA FROM THE APPLICATION PROFILE:    00710000
      *                                                                00720000
                                                                       00730000
           CALL 'ISPLINK' USING  VGET                                  00740000
                                 VARLIST                               00750000
                                 PROFILE.                              00760000
                                                                       00770000
                                                                       00780000
      *                                                                00790000
      *  GET JOB AND REPORT CONTROL INFORMATION FROM THE USER:         00800000
      *                                                                00810000
                                                                       00820000
           CALL 'ISPLINK' USING  DISPLAY-PANEL                         00830000
                                 PANEL-NAME                            00840000
                                 ENTER-DATA-MSG.                       00850000
                                                                       00860000
                                                                       00870000
```

(continued)

Figure 7-2. (*Continued*)

```
*                                                                00880000
*    IF THE USER ENTERED THE CONTROL DATA, OPEN FILE              00890000
*    TAILORING SERVICES USING A TEMPORARY OUTPUT FILE:            00900000
*                                                                00910000
                                                                 00920000
      IF RETURN-CODE = 0                                         00930000
                                                                 00940000
          CALL 'ISPLINK' USING    FTOPEN                         00950000
                                  TEMP                           00960000
                                                                 00970000
          CALL 'ISPLINK' USING    FTINCL                         00980000
                                  SKELETON-NAME                  00990000
                                                                 01000000
*                                                                01010000
*    END FILE TAILORING, SET UP PROPER MESSAGE FOR USER          01020000
*    AND RETURN CODE SO THAT INVOKING CLIST WILL SUBMIT JOB:     01030000
*                                                                01040000
                                                                 01050000
          CALL 'ISPLINK' USING    FTCLOSE                        01060000
                                                                 01070000
          CALL 'ISPLINK' USING    SETMSG                         01080000
                                  REPORT-SUBMITTED-MSG           01090000
                                                                 01100000
          MOVE 0 TO RETURN-CODE                                  01110000
                                                                 01120000
                                                                 01130000
*                                                                01140000
*    IF THE USER HIT THE 'END' KEY, TERMINATE PROCESSING         01150000
*    WITH MESSAGE AND RETURN CODE OF 4 SO INVOKING CLIST WILL    01160000
*    NOT ATTEMPT SUBMISSION OF BATCH JOB:                        01170000
*                                                                01180000
                                                                 01190000
      ELSE                                                       01200000
                                                                 01210000
          CALL 'ISPLINK'  USING   SETMSG                         01220000
                                  PROCESSING-TERMINATED-MSG      01230000
                                                                 01240000
          MOVE 4 TO RETURN-CODE.                                 01250000
                                                                 01260000
                                                                 01270000
      GOBACK.                                                    01280000
                                                                 01290000
  MAIN-LINE-EXIT.                                                01300000
```

Figure 7-3. SUBREPTC CLIST function.

```
00010000   PROC 0
00020000   CONTROL MSG NOFLUSH
00030000   /*****************************************************************/
00040000   /* NAME: SUBREPTC                           BY: H. FOSDICK     */
00050000   /*                                                             */
00060000   /* PURPOSE: THIS CLIST RUNS A COBOL PROGRAM TO PERFORM         */
00070000   /* FILE TAILORING ON A SKELETON TO SET UP A BATCH JOB.         */
00080000   /* THIS CLIST CHECKS THE RETURN CODE FROM THAT PROGRAM,        */
00090000   /* AND SUBMITS THE BATCH JOB IF THAT RETURN CODE WAS ZERO.     */
00100000   /*                                                             */
00110000   /*****************************************************************/
00120000
00130000
00140000   /*                                                             */
00150000   /*    RUN THE COBOL PROGRAM VIA THE ISPF 'SELECT' SERVICE:     */
00160000   /*                                                             */
00170000
00180000   ISPEXEC   SELECT   PGM(CREPTC)
00190000
00200000
00210000   /*                                                             */
00220000   /*    IF RETURN CODE FROM PROGRAM WAS 0, SUBMIT THE BATCH JOB:*/
00230000   /*                                                             */
00240000
00250000   IF &LASTCC = 0 THEN DO
00260000
00270000        ISPEXEC  VGET  ZTEMPF   SHARED
00280000        SUBMIT '&ZTEMPF'
00290000        END
00300000
00310000
00320000   EXIT CODE(0)
```

Figure 7-4. **WSKEL2** file tailoring skeleton.

```
)IM WSKEL3
)CM ********************************************************************
)CM *   NAME: WSKEL2                              BY: H. FOSDICK   *
)CM *                                                              *
)CM *   PURPOSE: THIS SKELETON JCL IS PROCESSED BY THE DIALOG MANAGER *
)CM *   FILE TAILORING SERVICES TO SET UP AN APPROPRIATE BATCH JOB   *
)CM *   TO PRODUCE THE ACCOUNTS RECEIVABLE DISTRIBUTION REPORT.  IT  *
)CM *   ILLUSTRATES IMBEDDING A SECOND SKELETON INTO THIS ONE AND THE *
)CM *   )DOT AND )ENDDOT COMMANDS.                                  *
)CM *                                                              *
)CM ********************************************************************
//*MAIN ORG=ANYLOCAL
//STEP1    EXEC PGM=WACCT2
//STEPLIB  DD DSN=&ZUSER..W.LOAD,DISP=SHR
)CM
)CM  SELECT THE PROPER 'SYSPRINT' STATEMENT BASED ON CONTENTS OF 'FORMS'
)CM
)SEL    &FORMS = &Z
//SYSPRINT DD SYSOUT=A,FLASH=NONE,FCB=847Z,CHARS=CRR0,DCB=BLKSIZE=133
)ENDSEL
)SEL    &FORMS = 1
//SYSPRINT DD SYSOUT=A,DCB=BLKSIZE=133
)ENDSEL
)SEL    &FORMS = 2
//SYSPRINT DD SYSOUT=A,FLASH=NONE,DCB=BLKSIZE=133
)ENDSEL
//SYSOUT   DD SYSOUT=*
//SYSIN    DD DSN=&ZUSER..ACCT.OUT,DISP=SHR
//CONTROL  DD *
NAME     = &NAME.
ACCT     = &PROJECT.&CLOCKID.
STATUS   = &STATUS.
DIST     = &DIST.
CONTDATE = &CDATE.
JOBNAME  = &ZUSER.B
/*
//CONTRL2  DD *
)TB 15 30 45 60
)DOT CONTDATA
&CONTACT &COSCTR &SUBCTR &DISTRIB &INVDATE
)ENDDOT
/*
//
```

Figure 7-5. WSKEL3 file tailoring skeleton.

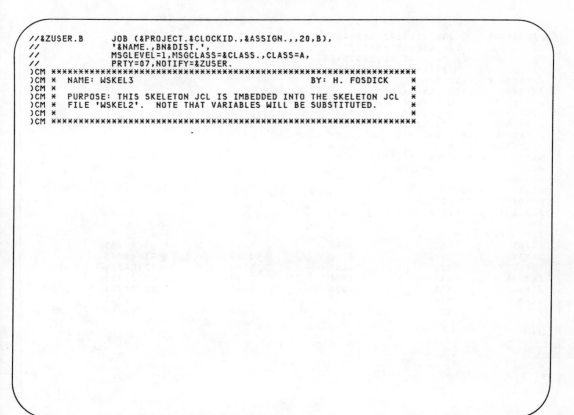

```
//&ZUSER.B       JOB (&PROJECT.&CLOCKID.,&ASSIGN.,,20,B),
//               '&NAME.,BN&DIST.',
//               MSGLEVEL=1,MSGCLASS=&CLASS.,CLASS=A,
//               PRTY=07,NOTIFY=&ZUSER.
)CM **************************************************************
)CM *  NAME: WSKEL3                               BY: H. FOSDICK   *
)CM *                                                              *
)CM *  PURPOSE: THIS SKELETON JCL IS IMBEDDED INTO THE SKELETON JCL *
)CM *  FILE 'WSKEL2'.  NOTE THAT VARIABLES WILL BE SUBSTITUTED.     *
)CM *                                                              *
)CM **************************************************************
```

Figure 7-6. Results of file tailoring on **WSKEL2** skeleton.

```
//ZHMF01B     JOB (111222211504,C137,14AA,,20,B),
//            'FOSDICK,BN6127',
//            MSGLEVEL=1,MSGCLASS=A,CLASS=A,
//            PRTY=07,NOTIFY=ZHMF01
//*MAIN ORG=ANYLOCAL
//STEP1     EXEC PGM=WACCT2
//STEPLIB   DD DSN=ZHMF01.W.LOAD,DISP=SHR
//SYSPRINT  DD SYSOUT=A,FLASH=NONE,FCB=847Z,CHARS=CRRO,DCB=BLKSIZE=133
//SYSOUT    DD SYSOUT=*
//SYSIN     DD DSN=ZHMF01.ACCT.OUT,DISP=SHR
//CONTROL   DD *
NAME     = FOSDICK
ACCT     = 111222211504
STATUS   = S
DIST     = 6127
CONDATE  = 02/12/85
JOBNAME  = ZHMF01B
/*
//CONTRL2 DD *
FLINT        1100          1000          2022          03/02/85
DAMIEN       2260          8600          3343          01/06/85
BECKLEY      2260          8400          6140          11/04/84
FREDERIK     1242          2000          1010          01/01/85
MURRAY       1242          1010          3343          12/01/84
PLUM         1242          1000          3343          11/11/84
POLK         1242          1222          6424          11/11/84
/*
//
```

Figure 7-7. Values entered via screen **WPAN3** for file tailoring.

```
-------------- WEST DEPARTMENT ACCOUNTS RECEIVABLE ---- ENTER JOB CONTROL DATA


RUN BATCH ACCOUNTS RECEIVABLE DISTRIBUTION REPORT:


   FOR  LOGON ID:  ZHMF01


   YOUR LAST  NAME    ===> FOSDICK
   DISTRIBUTION CODE ===> 6127
   OUTPUT  CLASS      ===> A            (EITHER 'T' OR 'A')
   FORMS SELECTION    ===>              (EITHER '1', '2' OR BLANK)

   REPORT CONTROL DATE   ===> 02/12/85 (IN FORM 'MM/DD/YY')
   REPORT CONTROL STATUS ===> S         (EITHER 'W', 'E' OR 'S')
```

Figure 7-8. XREPTC CLIST function.

```
00010000   PROC 0
00020000   CONTROL MSG NOFLUSH
00030000   /*******************************************************************/
00040000   /* NAME: XREPTC                          BY: H. FOSDICK       */
00050000   /*                                                           */
00060000   /* PURPOSE: THIS CLIST ILLUSTRATES ADVANCED FILE TAILORING.  */
00070000   /* IT IS SIMILAR TO THE 'XREPTS' CLIST.  IT SETS UP THE       */
00080000   /* ACCOUNTS RECEIVABLE BATCH DISTRIBUTION REPORT PROGRAM.     */
00090000   /*                                                           */
00100000   /* NOTE: THIS CLIST ASSUMES THAT TABLE 'CONTDATA' EXISTS,    */
00110000   /* AND THAT IT CONTAINS AT LEAST ONE ROW.  IT ALSO ASSUMES   */
00120000   /* THE PROFILE VARIABLES ARE VALID.                          */
00130000   /*                                                           */
00140000   /*******************************************************************/
00150000
00160000   /*                                                           */
00170000   /*   SET UP THE ENVIRONMENT FOR THE CLIST:                    */
00180000   /*                                                           */
00190000
00200000   ISPEXEC   CONTROL   ERRORS   CANCEL
00210000
00220000
00230000   /*                                                           */
00240000   /*   GET EMPLOYEE ACCOUNTING DATA FROM APPLICATION PROFILE:   */
00250000   /*                                                           */
00260000
00270000   ISPEXEC   VGET  (PROJECT ASSIGN CLOCKID) PROFILE
00280000
00290000
00300000   /*                                                           */
00310000   /*   GET JOB AND REPORT CONTROL INFORMATION FROM THE USER:    */
00320000   /*                                                           */
00330000
00340000   ISPEXEC   DISPLAY PANEL(WPAN3)  MSG(WDAR002E)
00350000
00360000
00370000   /*                                                           */
00380000   /*   IF THE USER ENTERED THE CONTROL DATA, OPEN FILE          */
00390000   /*   TAILORING SERVICES USING A TEMPORARY OUTPUT FILE:        */
00400000   /*                                                           */
00410000
00420000   IF &LASTCC = 0 THEN DO
00430000
00440000       ISPEXEC FTOPEN TEMP
00450000
00460000
00470000       /*                                                         */
00480000       /*   TAILOR THE JCL SKELETON FILE 'WSKEL2':                 */
00490000       /*                                                         */
00500000
00510000       ISPEXEC FTINCL WSKEL2
00520000
00530000
00540000       /*                                                         */
00550000       /*   END FILE TAILORING, GET THE TEMPORARY FILE NAME FROM   */
00560000       /*   THE SHARED VARIABLE POOL, AND SUBMIT THE BACKGROUND JOB:*/
00570000       /*                                                         */
00580000
00590000       ISPEXEC FTCLOSE
00600000       ISPEXEC VGET  ZTEMPF   SHARED
00610000       SUBMIT '&ZTEMPF'
00620000
00630000       ISPEXEC  SETMSG MSG(WDAR002F)
00640000
00650000       END
00660000
00670000   /*                                                           */
00680000   /*   IF THE USER HIT THE 'END' KEY, TERMINATE PROCESSING:     */
00690000   /*                                                           */
00700000
00710000   ELSE +
00720000       ISPEXEC SETMSG MSG(WDAR000A)
00730000
00740000
00750000   EXIT CODE(0)
```

⑧
Dialog Test and the Tutorial System

This chapter digresses from the progressive discussion of the sample dialog in order to treat three important topics in depth. First, it explores the facilities provided by ISPF/PDF for the development and testing of dialogs. Then the chapter describes the Dialog Manager's complete tutorial system. These tutorial services enable developers to implement quickly both "help" panels and an online instructional system for their dialogs. Finally, this chapter discusses the ISPF/PDF Editor **MODEL** primary command. This Editor feature provides coding templates for use in developing dialog functions, panels, skeletons, and messages. Many programmers find that this productivity aid increases both coding speed and accuracy.

DIALOG TEST

Dialog Test is a component of ISPF/PDF designed to aid dialog developers in designing and testing their applications. Since Dialog Test is a component in a separately purchased product, you must have the PDF program product installed at your site in order to use it. Most installations that develop applications with the Dialog Manager also have PDF and Dialog Test.

One normally enters the ISPF/PDF facility by typing the letters **ISPF** when interacting with the teleprocessing monitor (**TSO** for MVS sites, **CMS** for VM machines).* The PDF *Primary Option Menu*, or application master menu, is then displayed for the PDF system. This master menu appears similar to that depicted in figure 8-1. To access Dialog Test from this menu, the user selects option 7. The menu thus retrieved is the Dialog Test primary option menu shown in figure 8-2.

Once in the Dialog Test subsystem, the user has at his or her command a wide array of services designed to support the development of

---

*This varies at some installations.

dialogs. These facilities enable the user to view and test individual panel and message definitions, skeletons, command procedure and program functions; create, maintain, and alter Dialog Manager tables; inspect and write to the ISPF log; turn on trace facilities when testing dialogs; and halt dialog execution at relevant points to examine variables and execution status. The following material describes these features in the order in which they appear on the Dialog Test menu of figure 8-2.

DIALOG TEST FEATURES

The *Functions* option of Dialog Test aids developers in testing menu panel definitions and functions. Users can do this without developing throw-away test code used only for the purposes of dialog testing.

In testing menu panels, the developer enters the panel name, and this prompts the test facility to display that panel. The designer can enter options from the menu panel and execute the selectable functions if they have been developed.

Users can run and test either command procedure or program functions using this Dialog Test option. During the execution of these functions, the programmer can use *breakpoints* if desired and can also enable the *trace* feature. *Breakpoints* allow users to halt function execution at predetermined points. They can then inspect the values of variables, the status of dialog service return codes, and other aspects of function execution. The *trace* feature helps in tracking Dialog Manager service calls and variable usage by automatically writing messages to the ISPF log file. Both capabilities are described further when their respective Dialog Test menu options are discussed below.

The Dialog Test option for testing *Panels* makes it easy to display panel definitions. Programmers can review panel appearance, test input validation criteria and messages, and ensure that panels are properly linked to their "help" panels. A major advantage of the panel test option is that the developer can easily split the screen into two logical screens by the **SPLIT** screen program function key. Then the designer can quickly alter the original panel definition and display the results on the other logical screen. The user thus has a convenient way to make rapid changes in the panel definition and view the impact of those alterations. Imagine the utility of this approach when designing screens in cooperation with application end users, for example. The developer can provide real-time response to user requests for panel alterations, and together programmer and end user can view the effects of the proposed design updates.

The *Variables* option of Dialog Test lets the user inspect and modify the values of dialog variables. These variables include those in the function, shared, and application profile pools. New variables can also be created. Variables are displayed in alphabetical name order. Recall that many of the system variables are resident in the shared pool; these are viewed through this option also.

The *Tables* option of Dialog Test allows developers to view and alter the contents of tables maintained through the Dialog Manager's table services. The user can display, modify, or delete the contents of table variables for specified rows and also list information about the variables and the table's structure. For example, the programmer can view and change variable names and values for key and name fields. He or she can find out such information as the number and names of key fields defined for the table, the number and names of name fields, the value of the current row pointer, and the number of rows in the table. A final facility, the *Display Status* option, provides statistics on table usage. This tells whether the table is temporary or permanent; whether the table is open or closed; whether access is for update or read-only; the dates of table creation and last update; the original, current, and modified row counts; and an update count indicating the number of times the table has been modified. Such information aids developers in understanding the excution patterns of their dialogs and in designing efficient applications.

The *Log* option of Dialog Test allows developers to browse the contents of the ISPF transaction log. The trace facility writes messages to this log based on user-defined criteria. This feature is especially useful in discerning the pattern of Dialog Manager service call usage within a function. It presents a complementary tool to the *breakpoint* option detailed below.

Dialog Test's *Dialog Services* option permits programmers to directly enter and immediately execute dialog services. The service commands are entered either in command procedure format or in command procedure format without the **ISPEXEC** keyword. For example, these two commands are both valid:

```
ISPEXEC DISPLAY PANEL(WPAN3)
DISPLAY PANEL(WPAN3)
```

All Dialog Manager services except **CONTROL** can be entered through this facility. This feature is useful in a wide variety of ways. For example, many of the features of Dialog Test's *Tables* option work only with tables that are open. One can easily open any table by using this option and a **TBOPEN** command.

The *Traces* option of Dialog Test has been mentioned already. Through this option one can direct the facility to write output automatically to the ISPF log file. Developers can create trace definitions that monitor dialog service calls and variable usage within their functions. A common example is for dialog trace to write a log message whenever a function issues an ISPF service call. This log message provides a complete execution profile of the function's use of Dialog Manager services.

Finally, the *Breakpoints* option of Dialog Test supplies the dialog developer with a mechanism to halt dialog execution at prespecified points. With dialog execution suspended, the programmer utilizes the facilities of the Dialog Test environment to inspect and/or alter the various dialog elements. The developer resumes dialog execution by a simple command. A sophisticated feature of this breakpoint facility allows programmers to specify the conditions under which breakpoints will occur. A definitional panel called the *Qualification Panel* aids in enumerating breakpoint criteria.

The breakpoint feature is the ISPF equivalent to the step-execution tools used with many programming languages. For example, it is analogous to the MVS/TSO **TEST** command for Assembler language or the **TESTCOB** command for COBOL. Programmers familiar with this interactive approach to debugging will agree that it speeds application testing and proves invaluable to tracking down subtle program bugs.

TUTORIAL SYSTEM

The Dialog Manager provides a complete tutorial or "help" system. This system consists of a group of hierarchically arranged information panels designed by the dialog developers.

The terminal user can use the tutorial system in several ways. First, by pressing the **HELP** program function key, the user views the "short form" message associated with his or her present position in the dialog. Pressing this program function key again shows the "long form" of that same message. The third time the user presses the **HELP** program function key, he or she gains access to the "help" panel associated with the current value of the control variable **.HELP**. The control variable **.HELP** is usually initialized by the initialization section of the panel the user was viewing when he or she pressed the **HELP** program function key. As an example, figure 7-1 illustrated the panel definition for panel **WPAN3**. Should the user enter the tutorial system from panel **WPAN3**, control variable **.HELP** was set to **WH006** in the initialization section of that panel. The user would view panel **WH006** from the tutorial system.

.HELP can also be assigned a value from within a message definition, as discussed in chapter 5. If **.HELP** is assigned a value by a message definition, this value overrides that set in a panel definition's initialization section when the message displays.

As well as a system of "help" panels accessible to the user through the **HELP** program function key, the "help" panels can be considered an online tutorial system. The panels are connected together such that the user can read them in logical sequential order. From this viewpoint, dialog designers often list the tutorial subsystem as an option selectable from the application master menu. In order to do this in the sample dialog, the option **T** would be added to the master menus of figures 3-1 and 3-2. Addition of option **T** to those master menus results in processing sections that look similar to this:

```
)PROC
&ZSEL = TRANS ( TRUNC (&ZCMD,'.')
              1,'CMD(XEXTRACT)'
              2,'PGM(CBROWSE)'
                    .
                    .
                    .
              T,'PGM(ISPTUTOR) PARM(WH001)'
```

The user's selection of option **T** starts the ISPF tutorial program, named **ISPTUTOR**, and passes it the parameter **WH001**. This parameter is the name of the first panel to display in the tutorial system. **WH001** is the member name of the topmost "help" panel defined in the panel library. The tutorial or "help" panels are defined using the same notation as data entry, output display, and menu panels, and all these panel definitions reside in the same panel library. Notice that the master menus of figures 3-1 and 3-2 also refer to panel **WH001** as their context-sensitive "help" panel. In the sample dialog, option **T** was not explicitly listed on the master menu because the users know to access it through pressing the **HELP** program function key. Dialog designers can list the tutorial system as an option selectable from their application master menu or not. However the designers intend users to access the tutorial system, it is strongly recommended that any dialog include a complete complement of "help" panels. The tutorial system represents a major advantage to the Dialog Manager as a supporting tool for application design. Certainly the tutorial system provides users a highly convenient overview of any dialog, used in its role as an online tutorial system, and a vitally important problem-assistance aid when used as a context-sensitive "help" function.

Similar to the Dialog Manager's hierarchical arrangement of functions and panel definitions, one can diagram any dialog's scheme of "help" panels. Diagram 8-1 describes the tutorial system for the sample dialog. It indicates that several tutorial panels have special functions in the tutorial system. First, there is the "Table of Contents" panel for the tutorial system, embodied in the panel named **WH001**. This panel definition is contained in figure 8-3. Remember that this panel is referred to from the master menus of figures 3-1 and 3-2 in two places in their initialization sections. These master menus set the control variable **.HELP** to **WH001** so that the tutorial "Table of Contents" is accessible through the **HELP** program function key from the master menus. The master menus also set the value of system variable **ZHTOP** to **WH001**. **ZHTOP** defines the topmost or first panel of the tutorial hierarchy to the Dialog Manager.

Figure 8-3 shows that this topmost panel is in fact a master menu panel for the dialog's tutorial system. The terminal user can select topics directly for viewing by entering the proper option number. This leads directly to the tutorial panel he or she wishes to view. In the sample dialog, the options of panel **WH001** correspond on a one-to-one basis with functions selectable from the dialog master menus.

From the tutorial "Table of Contents," the user may also press the **ENTER** key. Repeatedly doing so displays all the tutorial panels in sequential order, wrapping back to the top panel at the end. In the sample

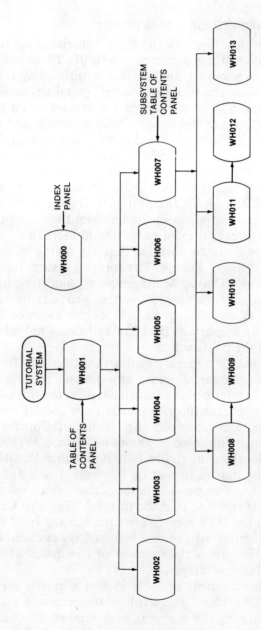

Diagram 8-1. Sample dialog tutorial system.

dialog, the first three panels displayed in this manner are defined in figures 8-4, 8-5, and 8-6. These panels are the "help"s for master menu options 1, 2, and 3, respectively. Notice that these tutorial panels consist of literal text. These are not data entry panels so only one input field, the command field, is present in each. This field allows the user to enter one of these commands:

B or **BACK**	returns to previously displayed tutorial panel
S or **SKIP**	skips forward to next topic
U or **UP**	displays the parent panel to this tutorial panel
T or **TOP**	displays the top panel in the tutorial hierarchy
I or **INDEX**	displays the tutorial index panel

What happens when the user enters **UP** in the command field is defined in the processing section of each tutorial panel definition. For example, in figures 8-4, 8-5, and 8-6, the *parent* (or next-higher-level panel) is specified by this statement:

&ZUP = WH001

Should the user enter **TOP** in the command input field, he or she views panel **WH001**. This was determined by this initialization statement in the dialog master menus of figures 3-1 and 3-2:

&ZHTOP = WH001

The definition of which panel is the tutorial index panel was accomplished by this statement of figures 3-1 and 3-2:

&ZHINDEX = WH000

The tutorial "index panel" definition is contained in figure 8-7. The index panel refers to selectable topics, like any menu panel. Users reach it by entering the command **INDEX**, or **I**, into the command input field of any "help" panel in the tutorial system due to the system variable value of **ZHINDEX**. Notice that the index panel definition declares itself as such by this statement in its processing section:

&ZIND = YES

There is one last system variable of importance to the tutorial system: **ZCONT** can be used to explicitly link one panel definition to another as a *continuation panel*. For example, what if in the panel definition of figure 8-6 the dialog designer needed to specify a second page of tutorial information? The solution is to encode

&ZCONT = CONTPANL

in the processing section of the panel definition, where **CONTPANL** is the member name of the second page of the "help" information. The terminal user passes from the first tutorial panel to its continuation panel by pressing the **ENTER** key.

Finally, a tutorial system can contain more than a single menu panel. In the example dialog, option 6 of the master menu displays a menu panel definition that is a subsystem menu for the Accounting Control Administration Subsystem. The corresponding tutorial panel for this subsystem menu is a tutorial "Table of Contents" panel definition, shown in figure 8-8. This menu permits selectable "help" topics in the same manner as the topmost "Table of Contents" panel **WH001**. All tutorial panels selectable from menu **WH007** specify **&ZUP = WH007**. Throughout the sample dialog's tutorial system, **ZHTOP** remains **WH001**, and **ZHINDEX** remains **WH000**.

ISPF/PDF EDITOR MODEL
PRIMARY COMMAND

The ISPF/PDF Editor provides the **MODEL** command to aid programmers in rapid development of dialogs. **MODEL** is an Editor *primary command*, meaning that one enters it on the command line at the top of the Editor screen. The **MODEL** command copies ISPF-provided source code statements into the file being edited at a location indicated by the user. The **MODEL** command optionally provides explanatory notes concerning the usage of the copied code.

The code accessible through the **MODEL** command can be used as a coding template or model for building dialogs. The **MODEL** command provides this skeletal code for developing dialog panels, functions, skeletons, and messages. The command generates code appropriate to the type or *class* of file being edited; however, users can override the default class specification and indicate the model class if desired. The classes of files include the following:

CLIST	ISPF service invocations for developing CLIST functions
COBOL	ISPF service invocations for developing COBOL functions
EXEC	ISPF service invocations for developing EXEC functions
FORTRAN	ISPF service invocations for developing FORTRAN functions
MSGS	format model for creating dialog messages
PANELS	models for designing dialog panels
PASCAL	ISPF service invocations for developing Pascal functions
PLI	ISPF service invocations for developing PL/I functions
SKELS	models for developing dialog file tailoring skeletons

Thus, if the user enters the word **MODEL** as an Editor primary command, the Editor displays a menu for selecting the model code to include in the file. This selectable code relates to all aspects of the development of dialog code for panels, functions, skeletons, and messages. The Editor determines the syntax of the code to copy into the file from the coding class of that file.

For example, in developing a COBOL function, one enters the **MODEL** command in the primary command area. ISPF/PDF will display a menu listing the kinds of model code statements one might wish to copy into a COBOL dialog function. This menu appears similar to the illustration in figure 8-9. From this menu, the user selects the ISPF service invocation he or she wishes to encode. For instance, entering option **D1** copies generic COBOL code for invocation of the Dialog Manager **DISPLAY** service into the user's editable file, as shown in figure 8-10. ISPF/PDF knows from the class of the file being edited that it is to provide service invocation code in the COBOL language. Notice that the lines indicated by the phrase = **NOTE** = are *not* actually part of the file. These are explanatory comments designed to aid the programmer. They can be removed from the display by entering the ISPF Editor **RESET** command on the primary command line. Entry of the **RESET** command results in the **DISPLAY** service model code shown in figure 8-11.

Use of the **MODEL** command in the Editor speeds the application development process by providing skeletal code. It increases the ease and accuracy of coding through the code it provides and the explanatory notes it offers. It standardizes an installation's code, and installations can add their own models too.

You should access the ISPF/PDF Editor and enter the **MODEL** command in the primary command area. Based on the discussion, you should try selecting several of the model code options for a programming language with which you are familiar and look at the coding options for panel, skeleton, and message development as well. Remember that the ISPF/PDF tutorial system is accessible for further information by pressing the **HELP** key, program function key 1.

Figure 8-1. ISPF/PDF primary option menu.

```
----------------------- ISPF/PDF PRIMARY OPTION MENU -------------< 02/26/83 >
SELECT OPTION ===>
    0   ISPF PARMS  - TERMINAL AND ISPF PARAMETERS       -------------------------
    1   BROWSE      - DISPLAY SOURCE/OUTPUT/DATA         ! USERID    - POLK01    !
    2   EDIT        - CREATE OR CHANGE SOURCE DATA       ! PREFIX    - POLK01    !
    3   UTILITIES   - PERFORM ISPF UTILITY FUNCTIONS     !           -           !
    4   FOREGROUND  - COMPILE/LINK OR DEBUG              ! TERMINAL  - 3278      !
    5   BACKGROUND  - COMPILE, OR LINK EDIT              ! PF KEYS   - 24        !
    6   COMMAND     - ENTER TSO COMMAND OR CLIST         ! PROCEDURE - TSOPRC01  !
    7   DIALOG TEST - PERFORM DIALOG TESTING             ! DATE      - 84/12/15  !
    C   CHANGES     - CHANGE SUMMARY FOR THIS RELEASE    !           -           !
    T   TUTORIAL    - DISPLAY INFORMATION ABOUT ISPF     ! TIME      - 16:34     !
    X   EXIT        - EXIT ISPF-USE LIST/LOG DEFAULTS    -------------------------

PRESS END KEY TO TERMINATE ISPF
```

Figure 8-2. Dialog Test primary option menu.

```
-------------------- DIALOG TEST PRIMARY OPTION MENU --------------------
OPTION  ===>

     1  FUNCTIONS        - Invoke dialog functions/selection menus
     2  PANELS           - Display panels
     3  VARIABLES        - Display/set variable information
     4  TABLES           - Display/modify table information
     5  LOG              - Browse ISPF log
     6  DIALOG SERVICES  - Invoke dialog services
     7  TRACES           - Specify trace definitions
     8  BREAKPOINTS      - Specify breakpoint definitions
     T  TUTORIAL         - Display information about Dialog Test
     X  EXIT             - Terminate dialog testing

Enter END command to terminate dialog testing.
```

Figure 8-3. **WH001** tutorial panel definition for a table of contents.

```
)BODY
%TUTORIAL------ WEST DEPARTMENT ACCOUNTS RECEIVABLE ----------------------------
%                   APPLICATION MASTER MENU HELP PANEL
%
%NEXT SELECTION ===>_ZCMD                                    +
%
+        THE WEST DEPARTMENT ACCOUNTS RECEIVABLE SYSTEM ENABLES
         YOU TO REQUEST SIMPLE AND DISTRIBUTION ACCOUNTS RECEIVABLE
         REPORTS.  IT ALSO ENABLES YOU TO ENTER AND UPDATE CONTROL
         INFORMATION REQUIRED TO GENERATE THESE REPORTS.

         THE FOLLOWING TOPICS ARE PRESENTED BY SEQUENCE, OR MAY BE
         SELECTED BY NUMBER:

         %1 +EXTRACT DATA FROM MASTER FILES
         %2 +VIEW EXTRACTED DATA FILE
         %3 +ADD / UPDATE YOUR EMPLOYEE ACCOUNTING PARAMETERS
         %4 +RUN BATCH RECEIVABLES SIMPLE REPORT
         %5 +RUN BATCH RECEIVABLES DISTRIBUTION REPORT
         %6 +ACCOUNTING CONTROL ADMINISTRATION SUBSYSTEM


)PROC
   &ZSEL = TRANS(&ZCMD  1,WH002   2,WH003   3,WH004,   4,WH005
                        5,WH006   6,WH007   *,'?')
)END
```

Figure 8-4. WH002 tutorial panel definition.

```
)BODY
%TUTORIAL------ WEST DEPARTMENT ACCOUNTS RECEIVABLE ---------------------------
%                  DATA EXTRACTION HELP PANEL
%
%COMMAND ===>_ZCMD                                       +
%
+     SELECTING OPTION 1 FROM THE WEST DEPARTMENT ACCOUNTS RECEIVABLE
      SYSTEM ALLOWS YOU TO EXTRACT DATA FROM THE MASTER FILES OF
      ANOTHER PROGRAMMING SYSTEM, AND TO BUILD THE ACCOUNTING MASTER
      FILE FOR THIS SYSTEM.  IF YOU WISH TO SEE THE GENERATED ACCOUNTS
      RECEIVABLE MASTER FILE, SELECT OPTION 2 FROM THE MASTER MENU
      (AFTER USING OPTION 1).  THIS WILL ALLOW YOU TO BROWSE THE
      DEPARTMENTAL MASTER FILE.

)PROC
   &ZUP = WH001
)END
```

Figure 8-5. WH003 tutorial panel definition.

```
)BODY
%TUTORIAL------ WEST DEPARTMENT ACCOUNTS RECEIVABLE ----------------------------
%                 VIEWING EXTRACTED DATA HELP PANEL
%
%COMMAND ===>_ZCMD                                     +
%
+      SELECTING OPTION 2 FROM THE WEST DEPARTMENT ACCOUNTS RECEIVABLE
       SYSTEM ALLOWS YOU TO VIEW THIS SYSTEM'S ACCOUNTING MASTER FILE.
       IF YOU WISH TO CREATE (OR "REFRESH") THIS MASTER FILE, ENTER
       OPTION 1 FROM THIS SYSTEM'S MASTER MENU.

)PROC
   &ZUP = WH001
)END
```

Figure 8-6. WH004 tutorial panel definition.

```
)BODY
%TUTORIAL------ WEST DEPARTMENT ACCOUNTS RECEIVABLE ----------------------------
%                    EMPLOYEE ACCOUNTING HELP PANEL
%
%COMMAND ===>_ZCMD                                       +
%
+       ON THIS PANEL, ENTER YOUR PROJECT NUMBER, CLOCK ID AND
        ASSIGNMENT.  THE EDIT RULES FOR THESE INPUTS ARE:

             PROJECT NUMBER = UP TO EIGHT CHARACTERS LONG
             CLOCK ID       = UP TO EIGHT DIGITS LONG
             ASSIGNMENT     = NINE CHARACTERS LONG IN THE
                              REQUIRED FORMAT OF:
                              %A999,99AA
+                               WHERE %A+'S ARE LETTERS AND %9+'S ARE DIGITS

)PROC
   &ZUP = WH001
)END
```

Figure 8-7. WH000 tutorial panel definition for an index panel.

```
)BODY
%TUTORIAL------ WEST DEPARTMENT ACCOUNTS RECEIVABLE -----------------------------
%                         INDEX HELP PANEL
%
%NEXT SELECTION ===>_ZCMD                                    +
%
+       SELECT ONE OF THE FOLLOWING TOPICS:

        %0 +EXTRACT DATA FROM MASTER FILES
        %1 +VIEW EXTRACTED DATA FILE
        %2 +ADD / UPDATE YOUR EMPLOYEE ACCOUNTING PARAMETERS
        %3 +RUN BATCH RECEIVABLES SIMPLE REPORT
        %4 +RUN BATCH RECEIVABLES DISTRIBUTION REPORT
        %5 +ACCOUNTING CONTROL ADMINISTRATION SUBSYSTEM
        %6 +VIEW ACCOUNTING CONTROL PARAMETERS FOR A SPECIFIED CENTER
        %7 +VIEW ALL ACCOUNTING CONTROL PARAMETERS
        %8 +ADD, UPDATE OR DELETE ACCOUNTING PARAMETERS FOR A SPECIFIED CENTER
        %9 +SCAN ACCOUNTING CONTROL PARAMETERS

)PROC
    &ZIND = YES
    &ZSEL = TRANS(&ZCMD   0,WH002   1,WH003   2,WH004,   3,WH005
                          4,WH006   5,WH007   6,WH008    7,WH010
                          8,WH011   9,WH013   *,'?')
)END
```

Figure 8-8. WH007 tutorial panel definition for a subtable of contents.

```
)BODY
%TUTORIAL------ WEST DEPARTMENT ACCOUNTS RECEIVABLE ---------------------------
%              ACCOUNTING CONTROL ADMINISTRATION
%
%NEXT SELECTION ===>_ZCMD                              +
%
+        THE WEST DEPARTMENT ACCOUNTING CONTROL ADMINISTRATION SUBSYSTEM
         ALLOWS YOU TO VIEW, ADD, UPDATE, AND DELETE ACCOUNTING CONTROL
         DATA USED AS INPUT TO THE DISTRIBUTION REPORT (RUN BY SELECTING
         OPTION 5 FROM THE MASTER APPLICATION MENU).

         THE FOLLOWING TOPICS ARE PRESENTED BY SEQUENCE, OR MAY BE
         SELECTED BY NUMBER:

         %1 +VIEW ACCOUNTING CONTROL PARAMETERS FOR A SPECIFIED CENTER
         %2 +VIEW ALL ACCOUNTING CONTROL PARAMETERS
         %3 +ADD, UPDATE OR DELETE ACCOUNTING PARAMETERS FOR A SPECIFIED CENTER
         %4 +SCAN ACCOUNTING CONTROL PARAMETERS

)PROC
   &ZUP  = WH001
   &ZSEL = TRANS(&ZCMD   1,WH008   2,WH010   3,WH011,   4,WH013
                         *,'?')
)END
```

Figure 8-9. MODEL for COBOL functions.

```
--------------------------- COBOL MODELS ------------------------------------
OPTION  ===>

VARIABLES            WORKING-STORAGE        TABLES (Row)       LIBRARY ACCESS
V1   VGET            W1   WORKSTOR          R1   TBADD         L1   LMCLOSE
V2   VPUT                                   R2   TBDELETE      L2   LMERASE
V3   VDEFINE         TABLES (General)       R3   TBGET         L3   LMFREE
V4   VDELETE         G1   TBCREATE          R4   TBPUT         L4   LMGET
V5   VCOPY           G2   TBOPEN            R5   TBMOD         L5   LMINIT
V6   VREPLACE        G3   TBQUERY           R6   TBEXIST       L6   LMMADD
V7   VRESET          G4   TBSAVE            R7   TBSARG        L7   LMMDEL
                     G5   TBCLOSE           R8   TBSCAN        L8   LMMFIND
FILE TAILORING       G6   TBEND             R9   TBTOP         L9   LMMLIST
F1   FTOPEN          G7   TBERASE           R10  TBBOTTOM      L10  LMMREN
F2   FTINCL          G8   TBSTATS           R11  TBSKIP        L11  LMMREP
F3   FTCLOSE                                R12  TBVCLEAR      L12  LMOPEN
F4   FTERASE         MISCELLANEOUS          R13  TBSORT        L13  LMPROM
                     M1   SELECT                               L14  LMPUT
GRAPHICS             M2   CONTROL           DISPLAY            L15  LMQUERY
S1   GRINIT          M3   BROWSE            D1   DISPLAY       L16  LMRENAME
S2   GRTERM          M4   EDIT              D2   TBDISPL
S3   GRERROR         M5   LOG               D3   SETMSG
                     M6   GETMSG            D4   PQUERY
Enter END command to cancel MODEL command.
```

Figure 8-10. Copying model code for the COBOL **DISPLAY** service.

```
EDIT --- ZPOLK1.CONTROL.DATA(MODEL) - 01.02 ----------------- COLUMNS 001 072
COMMAND ===>                                                  SCROLL ===> HALF
****** ************************** TOP OF DATA **********************************
000100           MOVE "DISPLAY"  TO ISPF-SERVICE.
000200           MOVE "       "  TO ISPF-PANEL-NAME.
=NOTE=                                   MOVE NAME OF THE PANEL DISPLAYED
000300           MOVE "      "  TO ISPF-MSG-ID.
=NOTE=                                   MOVE IDENTIFIER OF MESSAGE TO BE
=NOTE=                                   DISPLAYED ON PANEL, IF ANY
000400           MOVE "        "  TO ISPF-FIELD-NAME.
=NOTE=                                   MOVE NAME OF FIELD WHERE THE CURSOR
=NOTE=                                   IS TO BE POSITIONED, IF ANY
000500           MOVE 00        TO ISPF-CSRPOS.
=NOTE=                                   MOVE THE FIELD POSITION WHERE THE
=NOTE=                                   CURSOR IS TO BE PLACED, THE
=NOTE=                                   DEFAULT IS 1
000600           CALL "ISPLINK" USING  ISPF-SERVICE   ISPF-PANEL-NAME
000700                                 ISPF-MSG-ID  ISPF-FIELD-NAME
000800                                 ISPF-CSRPOS.
=NOTE=
=NOTE=              NOTE: ALL NAMES EXCEPT SERVICE NAMES AND KEYWORDS
=NOTE=                    MUST BE PADDED WITH A BLANK IF LESS THAN EIGHT
=NOTE=                    CHARACTERS LONG.
=NOTE=
000900           IF RETURN-CODE NOT = 0
001000      *                              8  - END OR RETURN COMMAND ENTERED
001100      *                             12 - PANEL, MESSAGE OR CURSOR
001200      *                                   FIELD COULD NOT BE FOUND
001300      *                             16 - DATA TRUNCATION OR TRANSLATION
001400      *                                   ERROR
001500      *                             20 - SEVERE ERROR
****** ************************** BOTTOM OF DATA *******************************
```

Figure 8-11. Model code after editor **RESET** command.

```
EDIT --- ZPOLK1.CONTROL.DATA(MODEL) - 01.02 ----------------- COLUMNS 001 072
COMMAND ===>                                                  SCROLL ===> HALF
****** **************************** TOP OF DATA ********************************
000100              MOVE "DISPLAY"  TO ISPF-SERVICE.
000200              MOVE "        " TO ISPF-PANEL-NAME.
000300              MOVE "        " TO ISPF-MSG-ID.
000400              MOVE "        " TO ISPF-FIELD-NAME.
000500              MOVE 00         TO ISPF-CSRPOS.
000600              CALL "ISPLINK" USING  ISPF-SERVICE  ISPF-PANEL-NAME
000700                                    ISPF-MSG-ID  ISPF-FIELD-NAME
000800                                    ISPF-CSRPOS.
000900              IF RETURN-CODE NOT = 0
001000      *                                 8  - END OR RETURN COMMAND ENTERED
001100      *                                12  - PANEL, MESSAGE OR CURSOR
001200      *                                     FIELD COULD NOT BE FOUND
001300      *                                16  - DATA TRUNCATION OR TRANSLATION
001400      *                                     ERROR
001500      *                                20  - SEVERE ERROR
****** **************************** BOTTOM OF DATA *****************************
```

⑨

Functions That Use Table Services

The previous chapters have analyzed the functions associated with the first five options of the master menu of the West Department Accounts Receivable system. Through these options, terminal users can refresh the master file of this system from its external sources. They view that file through option 2. They can also enter their employee accounting information, which is used as the job accounting control information when they generate batch jobs through master menu options 4 and 5. Options 4 and 5, of course, allow users to run accounts receivable report programs. Option 4 lets the user run a Simple Report, which prints an accounts receivable report based on the single input control date specified by the user. Option 5 produces the more complicated Distribution Report, which prints a multipart listing. Each section of this report is based on a different control date and is produced for a different cost center. These control dates (and the related cost center information for each) were brought into the file skeleton by the Dialog Manager's file tailoring services from an ISPF permanent table. This table is created and maintained on disk by the functions of the example dialog, selectable as option 6 from the application master menu. Option 6 itself presents a lower-level menu, which might be referred to as a subsystem menu. This menu represents the user's entry point to the Accounting Control Administration Subsystem, the group of functions that display and update the control date table information used by the report program of master menu option 5.

The Accounting Control Administration Subsystem menu for the maintenance of the control date table is shown in figure 9-1. Because menu options must distinguish between compiled functions and those written as command procedures, a separate menu is required for the CLIST version of this system. It is presented in figure 9-2.

The COBOL version menu of figure 9-1 shows that there are four options selectable from this menu. The first option allows the user to view accounting control parameters for a specific cost center. This option allows the user to view a particular "row" or "record" in the control date table based on the key entered.

Option 2 permits the user to view all the accounting control information in the table. The user can thus see all the accounting parameters input to the Distribution Report at a glance. This option is somewhat similar to the browsing of the master file selectable from option 2 of the master menu of figures 3-1 and 3-2, except that here the user views a table of information maintained through Dialog Manager's table services.

Option 3 is the most complex. It allows the user to add, change, or delete accounting control date information in the table. The add, update, and delete actions operate on the basic unit of information in the table, the "row" or "record."

Finally, option 4 aids the user in scanning the table for specific data elements. This is conceptually analogous to scanning a table for specific attribute values in a relational database system. As in the first option, a successful retrieval displays a single row of accounting control date information to the user.

THE NATURE OF TABLES

Tables are two-dimensional collections of data. Diagram 9-1 shows that the basic unit of data manipulation in the table is called a *row*. This can also be considered the logical *record* of the table. In the table of the sample dialog, each row contains the information: **COSCTR** (Cost center code); **SUBCTR** (Sub-cost center code); **CONTACT** (User representative for this center); **DISTRIB** (Distribution code for this center); and **INVDATE** (Associated control date for this center).

Thus, each row contains five data elements, all of which concern an invoice control date for a particular cost/sub-cost center. Diagram 9-2 illustrates the table used by the example functions.

Tables can be *temporary* or *permanent*. Temporary tables exist only in virtual storage for the length of time during which they remain open. Temporary tables are always deleted at the end of an ISPF session. Permanent tables are stored on disk and exist across sessions. They can be accessed by more than one dialog, and the Dialog Manager ensures data integrity by its provision of concurrency control.*

The control date table used in the sample dialog is a permanent table because it saves data across sessions. Unlike the values saved in the application profile pool, the data in this table are accessible by all dialog users. The table does not consist of data saved on a per user basis.

Tables may be opened by functions for purposes of update or for read-only access. Options 1, 2, and 4 selectable from the menus of figures 9-1 and 9-2 open tables with read-only access. They are retrieval

---

*ISPF's table integrity feature assumes that all users who update a given table have the same first library definition for **ISPTLIB**. See the manual *ISPF Dialog Management Services* and the publications of the GUIDE ISPF Project for important details on ISPF's locking mechanism.

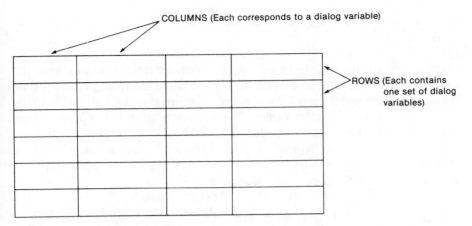

Diagram 9-1. ISPF tables.

functions. Option 3, the update function, opens the table with update access.

Dialog Manager tables are defined as *keyed* or *unkeyed*. Keyed tables can be directly processed on the basis of a key data field defined when the table is created. Key tables can also be processed sequentially by row. Like unkeyed tables, row processing is facilitated by the *Current Row Pointer* (CRP). The CRP points to the next sequentially accessed table row.

Keyed tables can be defined with more than one data field specified as *key*. Successful retrieval of rows with more than a single data element defined as key means that all key fields match their counterparts in the retrieved row.

Unkeyed tables can only be processed sequentially by Dialog Manager services that refer to the current row pointer. Dialog Manager terminology labels unkeyed fields as *name* fields.

The control date table used in this example dialog is a keyed table. The Cost Center (**COSCTR**) and Sub-cost Center (**SUBCTR**) fields are specified as *key* when the table is created, as shown in diagram 9-2. The other three fields in the table are denoted as *name* fields.

Diagram 9-2. Example dialog table layout.

COBOL FUNCTION THAT RETRIEVES
A TABLE ROW

Option 1 from the Accounting Control Administration menu allows the user to retrieve and view a specific row of the accounting control date table. The user enters the Cost Center and Sub-cost Center, which represent key values for the table. The function supporting this option displays the name fields from the retrieved row, which include the User Representative, Distribution Code, and Invoice Control Date fields, or it displays a message informing the user that no information exists in the table for the Center Codes specified.

The data entry panel definition presented by the function for the user's entry of the Cost Center and Sub-cost Center codes is shown in figure 9-3. An interesting feature of this panel definition is the manner in which input values are truncated to four characters in the processing section of the panel through use of the truncation built-in function. Because placeholder variables were not used in the body section of the panel, the user might well have entered up to six characters of data into each field. This panel definition handles center codes that are longer than four characters by truncating them without the user's knowledge, verifying the values as nonblank and numeric, and continuing dialog processing. Later panel examples show more sophisticated ways of handling this input editing task.

Figure 9-4 contains the panel definition for the output display panel. There is nothing new in this panel definition other than the display of the fields from the retrieved table row as highlighted, nonmodifiable output fields. The Dialog Manager takes care of substitution of the present values for these variables into the output panel prior to its display. If the user-specified key did not result in retrieval of a row of data from the table, a message is displayed informing the user on the panel of figure 9-3.

The COBOL program that handles these two panel definitions is called **CVIEW1**. Its listing is in figure 9-5.

The logic of this COBOL program is different from all functions described previously in that the function displays the data entry panel of this program (**WPAN4**, in figure 9-3) when the retrieval attempt is completed. At this point, the user enters another Cost Center/Sub-cost Center key for retrieval or presses the **END** program function key and returns to the menu of figure 9-1. The logic of the program thus dictates that the user remain in a loop, the first action of which is display of panel **WPAN4**, until he or she presses the **END** program function key. This is evident in lines 85 and 86 of the program, which perform the paragraph for table data retrieval until the user presses the **END** key.

This program's first action is to open the accounting control table for processing through the **TBOPEN** service. The **TBOPEN** service includes the parameter **NOWRITE**, which states that the program requests read-only access to the specified table. As shown in the call, the name of the accounting control data table in the example dialog is **CONTDATA**.

If the table exists, the **TBOPEN** service issues a return code of **0**. If the table does not exist, a return code of **8** is intercepted by the COBOL program, and the program exits after sending an appropriate message to the user. Note that if a table is locked by another user (**ENQ**'d), **TBOPEN** may send a return code of **12**.

The program paragraph entitled **RETRIEVAL-WORK** displays panel **WPAN4**, through which the user enters the Cost Center/Sub-cost Center codes. Assuming the user enters these data, the program issues a **TBGET** call to the Dialog Manager to retrieve the table row specified by these two data fields. Retrieval is assumed keyed since when the table was defined, these two fields were specified as the table's key. Both of the current key field values must match that of a row in the table in order for retrieval to succeed.

If retrieval succeeds, the ISPF service returns a code of **0** to the program, and the function displays the table information via a **DISPLAY** call to ISPF with panel **WPAN5**. If the call does not retrieve a table row, the program issues a **SETMSG** call to set up a message for the user. In either case, the user returns to the data entry display panel for further retrieval attempts.

After the user exits the retrieval loop, the program closes the ISPF table. This occurs in program lines 88 and 89. The **TBEND** call closes the table without altering its contents. Then the program exits with a condition code of **0** to the menu from which it was selected.

CLIST IMPLEMENTATION

The CLIST version of this function is contained in figure 9-6. It is selectable from the menu of figure 9–2. It uses the same data entry and display panels as does its COBOL counterpart.

In the CLIST, the accounting control date table is opened by this statement:

ISPEXEC TBOPEN CONTDATA NOWRITE

The **NOWRITE** parameter specifies that this function requests read-only access to the ISPF table to ensure that even if this CLIST errantly attempted to update the table, it could not do so.

Assuming the Dialog Manager's service return code is **0**, the CLIST knows the table open command succeeded.* In this case, the logic provides a **DO WHILE** construct based on the value of the variable **&CONTINU**. As long as the user does not press the **END** program function key, **&CONTINU** remains **YES**, and the user will return to display of the data entry panel for this function.

From the data entry panel, the user enters the two fields that represent the key of the table: the Cost Center and Sub-cost Center. With this information, the CLIST attempts a direct retrieval with the current

---

*Like the other table services examples, this CLIST function simplifies table processing logic by ignoring the possibility of **TBOPEN** service return codes other than 0 and 8.

values of these two variables in line 59. If retrieval succeeds, the return code of **0** indicates this to the CLIST, and the data display panel **WPAN5** appears on the user's screen. Otherwise a message that retrieval failed is displayed.

The display of the retrieved row could have been accomplished by using a CLIST variable for the panel name:

```
SET PANL = WPAN5
ISPEXEC DISPLAY PANEL(&PANL)
```

This technique of specifying parameter values in ISPF invocations as variables can give the CLIST developer added flexibility in the code.

The user exits from interaction with this function by pressing the **END** program function key in response to display of the data entry panel, **WPAN4**. When this occurs, the CLIST closes the accounting control data table through the **TBEND** command. This command closes the table without updating it. Then the CLIST exits to the Accounting Control Administration Subsystem menu.

Figure 9-1. WSAMENC panel definition.

```
)BODY
%-------------- WEST DEPARTMENT ACCOUNTS RECEIVABLE --------------------------
%                  ACCOUNTING CONTROL ADMINISTRATION
%
%SELECT OPTION ===>_ZCMD+
%
%
%   1   +VIEW ACCOUNTING CONTROL PARAMETERS FOR A SPECIFIED CENTER
%
%   2   +VIEW ALL ACCOUNTING CONTROL PARAMETERS
%
%   3   +ADD, UPDATE OR DELETE ACCOUNTING PARAMETERS FOR A SPECIFIED CENTER
%
%   4   +SCAN ACCOUNTING CONTROL PARAMETERS
%
%
%
%
+PRESS%END+KEY TO RETURN TO APPLICATION MASTER MENU
%
%
)INIT
    .HELP    = WH007
)PROC
    &ZSEL = TRANS( TRUNC (&ZCMD,'.')
                   1,'PGM(CVIEW1)'
                   2,'PGM(CVIEW2)'
                   3,'PGM(CUPD)'
                   4,'PGM(CSCAN)'
                 ' ',' '
                   *,'?' )

)END
```

Figure 9-2. WSAMENU panel definition.

```
)BODY
%-------------- WEST DEPARTMENT ACCOUNTS RECEIVABLE ---------------------------
%                  ACCOUNTING CONTROL ADMINISTRATION
%
%SELECT OPTION ===>_ZCMD+
%
%
%   1   +VIEW ACCOUNTING CONTROL PARAMETERS FOR A SPECIFIED CENTER
%
%   2   +VIEW ALL ACCOUNTING CONTROL PARAMETERS
%
%   3   +ADD, UPDATE OR DELETE ACCOUNTING PARAMETERS FOR A SPECIFIED CENTER
%
%   4   +SCAN ACCOUNTING CONTROL PARAMETERS
%
%
%
%
+PRESS%END+KEY TO RETURN TO APPLICATION MASTER MENU
%
%
)INIT
   .HELP    = WH007
)PROC
   &ZSEL = TRANS( TRUNC (&ZCMD,'.')
                 1,'CMD(XVIEW1)'
                 2,'CMD(XVIEW2)'
                 3,'CMD(XUPD)'
                 4,'CMD(XSCAN)'
               ' ',' '
                 *,'?' )

)END
```

Figure 9-3. WPAN4 panel definition.

```
)BODY
%-------------- WEST DEPARTMENT ACCOUNTS RECEIVABLE ----------------------------
%               ACCOUNTING CONTROL ADMINISTRATION
+
%VIEW ACCOUNTING CONTROL PARAMETERS FOR A SPECIFIED CENTER:
+
+    ENTER COST CENTER CODES:
+
+
+    COST CENTER     %===>_COSCTR+
+    SUB-COST CENTER%===>_SUBCTR+
+
+
+
+
+PRESS%END+KEY TO EXIT
)INIT
   .HELP  = WH008
)PROC
   &COSCTR = TRUNC (&COSCTR, 4)
   VER (&COSCTR, NONBLANK, NUM, MSG=WDAR004D)
   &SUBCTR = TRUNC (&SUBCTR, 4)
   VER (&SUBCTR, NONBLANK, NUM, MSG=WDAR004D)
)END
```

Figure 9-4. WPAN5 panel definition.

```
)BODY
%-------------- WEST DEPARTMENT ACCOUNTS RECEIVABLE ---------------------------
%                   ACCOUNTING CONTROL ADMINISTRATION
+
%VIEW ACCOUNTING CONTROL PARAMETERS FOR A SPECIFIED CENTER:
+
+
+    FOR COST CENTER OF%&COSCTR.-&SUBCTR.:
+
+
+    USER REPRESENTATIVE IS:%&CONTACT
+    USER DISTRIBUTION CODE:%&DISTRIB
+    INVOICE CONTROL DATE  :%&INVDATE
+
+
+
+
+
+PRESS%END+KEY TO EXIT
)INIT
   .HELP  = WH009
)END
```

Figure 9-5. CVIEW1 COBOL function.

```
       IDENTIFICATION DIVISION.                                      00010000
       PROGRAM-ID. CVIEW1.                                           00020000
      ***************************************************************00030000
      *  NAME: CVIEW1                                  BY: H. FOSDICK *00040000
      *                                                              *00050000
      *  PURPOSE: THIS ROUTINE ILLUSTRATES THE ISPF TABLE SERVICES   *00060000
      *  BY DISPLAYING ONE ROW OF TABLE INFORMATION TO THE USER.     *00070000
      *                                                              *00080000
      ***************************************************************00090000
       ENVIRONMENT DIVISION.                                         00100000
       DATA DIVISION.                                                00110000
                                                                     00120000
                                                                     00130000
       WORKING-STORAGE SECTION.                                      00140000
                                                                     00150000
                                                                     00160000
      *  SERVICE CALL TYPES:                                         00170000
                                                                     00180000
       01  TBOPEN            PIC X(8)      VALUE 'TBOPEN  '.          00190000
       01  TBEND             PIC X(8)      VALUE 'TBEND   '.          00200000
       01  TBGET             PIC X(8)      VALUE 'TBGET   '.          00210000
       01  DISPLAY-PANEL     PIC X(8)      VALUE 'DISPLAY '.          00220000
       01  SETMSG            PIC X(8)      VALUE 'SETMSG  '.          00230000
                                                                     00240000
                                                                     00250000
      *  OPTION TO SPECIFY WHEN OPENING A TABLE WITHOUT UDPATE INTENT:00260000
                                                                     00270000
       01  NOWRITE           PIC X(8)      VALUE 'NOWRITE '.          00280000
                                                                     00290000
                                                                     00300000
      *  NAMES OF THE DISPLAY PANELS:                                00310000
                                                                     00320000
       01  PANEL-NAME4       PIC X(8)      VALUE 'WPAN4   '.          00330000
       01  PANEL-NAME5       PIC X(8)      VALUE 'WPAN5   '.          00340000
                                                                     00350000
                                                                     00360000
      *  NAME OF THE ACCOUNTING CONTROL DATA TABLE:                  00370000
                                                                     00380000
       01  TABLE-NAME        PIC X(8)      VALUE 'CONTDATA'.          00390000
                                                                     00400000
                                                                     00410000
      *  MESSAGES:                                                   00420000
                                                                     00430000
       01  NO-CONTROL-DATA-MSG    PIC X(8)     VALUE 'WDAR004A'.      00440000
       01  ENTER-ACCTING-DATA-MSG PIC X(8)     VALUE 'WDAR004B'.      00450000
       01  ENTRY-NOT-FOUND-MSG    PIC X(8)     VALUE 'WDAR004C'.      00460000
                                                                     00470000
                                                                     00480000
      *  THIS VARIABLE ENSURES RETURN TO DISPLAYING ORIGINAL PANEL:  00490000
                                                                     00500000
       01  CONTINU           PIC X(3)      VALUE 'YES'.               00510000
                                                                     00520000
                                                                     00530000
                                                                     00540000
       PROCEDURE DIVISION.                                           00550000
                                                                     00560000
                                                                     00570000
      *                                                              00580000
      *  OPEN THE ISPF TABLE CONTAINING ACCOUNTING CONTROL DATA:     00590000
      *                                                              00600000
                                                                     00610000
           CALL 'ISPLINK' USING  TBOPEN                              00620000
                                 TABLE-NAME                          00630000
                                 NOWRITE.                            00640000
                                                                     00650000
                                                                     00660000
      *                                                              00670000
      *  IF TABLE DOESNOT EXIST, INFORM USER AND EXIT:               00680000
      *                                                              00690000
                                                                     00700000
           IF RETURN-CODE = 8                                        00710000
                                                                     00720000
               CALL 'ISPLINK' USING  SETMSG                          00730000
                                     NO-CONTROL-DATA-MSG             00740000
                                                                     00750000
                                                                     00760000
      *                                                              00770000
      *  DISPLAY DATA UNTIL THE USER PRESSES 'END' KEY:              00780000
      *                                                              00790000
                                                                     00800000
           ELSE                                                      00810000
                                                                     00820000
               MOVE 'YES' TO CONTINU                                 00830000
                                                                     00840000
               PERFORM RETRIEVAL-WORK THRU RETRIEVAL-WORK-EXIT       00850000
                   UNTIL CONTINU = 'NO '                             00860000
```

(continued)

Figure 9-5. (*Continued*)

```
           CALL 'ISPLINK' USING   TBEND                            00870000
                                  TABLE-NAME.                      00880000
                                                                   00890000
                                                                   00900000
                                                                   00910000
*                                                                  00920000
*   SET NORMAL RETURN CODE AND EXIT:                               00930000
*                                                                  00940000
                                                                   00950000
       MOVE 0 TO RETURN-CODE.                                      00960000
       GOBACK.                                                     00970000
                                                                   00980000
    MAIN-LINE-EXIT.                                                00990000
                                                                   01000000
                                                                   01010000
                                                                   01020000
                                                                   01030000
                                                                   01040000
    RETRIEVAL-WORK.                                                01050000
                                                                   01060000
                                                                   01070000
*                                                                  01080000
*   DISPLAY DATA ENTRY PANEL FOR USER TO ENTER THE KEYS            01090000
*   OF THE DESIRED TABLE ROW:                                      01100000
*                                                                  01110000
                                                                   01120000
       CALL 'ISPLINK' USING   DISPLAY-PANEL                        01130000
                              PANEL-NAME4                          01140000
                              ENTER-ACCTING-DATA-MSG.              01150000
                                                                   01160000
                                                                   01170000
*                                                                  01180000
*   PREPARE TO EXIT IF USER PRESSES THE 'END' KEY:                 01190000
*                                                                  01200000
                                                                   01210000
       IF RETURN-CODE = 8                                          01220000
                                                                   01230000
           MOVE 'NO ' TO CONTINU                                   01240000
                                                                   01250000
                                                                   01260000
*                                                                  01270000
*   RETRIEVE THE USER-SPECIFIED ROW FROM THE TABLE:                01280000
*                                                                  01290000
                                                                   01300000
       ELSE                                                        01310000
                                                                   01320000
           CALL 'ISPLINK'  USING  TBGET                            01330000
                                  TABLE-NAME                       01340000
                                                                   01350000
*                                                                  01360000
*   DISPLAY DATA OR 'NOT FOUND' MESSAGE TO USER:                   01370000
*                                                                  01380000
                                                                   01390000
           IF RETURN-CODE = 0                                      01400000
                                                                   01410000
               CALL 'ISPLINK' USING   DISPLAY-PANEL                01420000
                                      PANEL-NAME5                  01430000
                                                                   01440000
           ELSE                                                    01450000
                                                                   01460000
               CALL 'ISPLINK' USING   SETMSG                       01470000
                                      ENTRY-NOT-FOUND-MSG.         01480000
                                                                   01490000
                                                                   01500000
    RETRIEVAL-WORK-EXIT.                                           01510000
       EXIT.                                                       01520000
```

Figure 9-6. XVIEW1 CLIST function.

```
00010000   PROC 0
00020000   CONTROL MSG NOFLUSH
00030000   /*******************************************************************/
00040000   /* NAME: XVIEW1                        BY: H. FOSDICK        */
00050000   /*                                                          */
00060000   /* PURPOSE: THIS CLIST ILLUSTRATES ISPF TABLE SERVICES BY   */
00070000   /* DISPLAYING ONE ROW OF TABLE INFORMATION TO THE USER.     */
00080000   /*                                                          */
00090000   /*******************************************************************/
00100000
00110000   ISPEXEC  CONTROL  ERRORS  CANCEL
00120000
00130000   /*                                                          */
00140000   /*  OPEN THE ISPF TABLE CONTAINING ACCOUNTING CONTROL DATA: */
00150000   /*                                                          */
00160000
00170000   ISPEXEC  TBOPEN  CONTDATA  NOWRITE
00180000
00190000
00200000   /*                                                          */
00210000   /*  IF TABLE DOESNOT EXIST, INFORM USER AND EXIT:           */
00220000   /*                                                          */
00230000
00240000   IF &LASTCC = 8 THEN +
00250000       ISPEXEC SETMSG MSG(WDAR004A)
00260000
00270000   ELSE DO
00280000
00290000
00300000   /*                                                          */
00310000   /* OTHERWISE, DISPLAY DATA UNTIL THE USER PRESSES 'END' KEY */
00320000   /*                                                          */
00330000
00340000       SET CONTINU = YES
00350000
00360000       DO WHILE &CONTINU = YES
00370000
00380000          /*                                                          */
00390000          /*  DISPLAY DATA ENTRY PANEL FOR USER TO ENTER THE KEYS     */
00400000          /*  OF THE DESIRED TABLE ROW:                               */
00410000          /*                                                          */
00420000
00430000          ISPEXEC  DISPLAY  PANEL(WPAN4)  MSG(WDAR004B)
00440000
00450000
00460000          /*                                                          */
00470000          /*  PREPARE TO EXIT IF THE USER PRESSES THE 'END' KEY:      */
00480000          /*                                                          */
00490000
00500000          IF &LASTCC = 8 THEN +
00510000              SET CONTINU = NO
00520000
00530000             /*                                                          */
00540000             /*  RETRIEVE THE USER-SPECIFIED ROW FROM THE TABLE:         */
00550000             /*                                                          */
00560000
00570000          ELSE DO
00580000
00590000             ISPEXEC  TBGET  CONTDATA
00600000
00610000                /*                                                          */
00620000                /* DISPLAY DATA OR 'NOT FOUND' MESSAGE TO USER:             */
00630000                /*                                                          */
00640000
00650000             IF &LASTCC = 0 THEN +
00660000                 ISPEXEC  DISPLAY  PANEL(WPAN5)
00670000
00680000             ELSE +
00690000                 ISPEXEC  SETMSG  MSG(WDAR004C)
00700000          END
00710000       END
00720000
00730000
00740000       /*                                                          */
00750000       /* CLOSE THE TABLE WITHOUT ALTERING ANY DATA:               */
00760000       /*                                                          */
00770000
00780000       ISPEXEC  TBEND  CONTDATA
00790000
00800000   END
00810000
00820000
00830000   EXIT CODE(0)
```

10

Table Retrieval Functions

This chapter describes two more functions that retrieve data from an ISPF-maintained permanent table. The first of these two functions displays all the data in the table. In a manner analogous to that of the file viewing capability of option 2 of the master menu, this function allows the user to scroll the screen display up or down in order to view all the data contained in the table. The second retrieval function allows the user to search the table for one or more values. These values do *not* have to be key values. This free-form searching of a table on dynamically specified name fields is referred to as the *scanning* capability of the Dialog Manager's table services.

In terms of the Accounts Receivable system, the two functions are selectable as options 2 and 4 from the Accounting Control Administration Subsystem menu. Option 2 permits users to view all the information in the accounting control date table. Users select option 4 to search for a specific row of accounting control information, but unlike menu option 1, they do not have to know the Cost Center and Subcost Center codes for the data they wish to retrieve. Instead option 4 allows them to search the accounting control table by entering the User Representative Contact Name, the Distribution Code, or the Invoice Control Date. These data fields can be supplied in any combination to retrieve the desired row in the accounting control data table.

TABLE DISPLAY BY A COBOL PROGRAM

The COBOL version of the function that displays the entire contents of the accounting control date table is shown in figure 10-1. The program is named **CVIEW2**.

The single panel definition associated with this transaction is illustrated in figure 10-2. Figure 10-3 shows what this panel looks like when it is displayed on the terminal user's screen. There is no data entry screen definition for this function because the entire contents of the accounting control table are always displayed.

The panel definition in figure 10-2 contains two new sections: the *attribute section* and the *model section*. The attribute section defines one or more special characters for use as attribute characters in the body of the panel definition. This line:

   @ TYPE(OUTPUT) INTENS(LOW)

defines the @ (''at'') symbol as an attribute character for the body of the panel definition. This attribute character describes fields that output data at low intensity. Some of the more common keywords that may appear in the attribute section of panel definitions and their values are as follows:

TYPE		Type of field
	TEXT	Protected field
	INPUT	Input (unprotected) field
	OUTPUT	Output (protected) field
INTENS		Display intensity of a field
	HIGH	Highlighted display
	LOW	Low (normal) intensity display
	NON	Nondisplay field (used only for input fields)
CAPS		Defines upper-case translation for input and output fields
	ON	Automatic translation of the field to upper-case
	OFF	Disables automatic field translation to upper-case
JUST		Justification for input and output fields
	LEFT	Left justification for the field
	RIGHT	Right justification for the field
	ASIS	No justification
SKIP		Defines the autoskip attribute for text and output fields
	ON	The cursor skips this field
	OFF	The cursor does not skip this field

The default attribute characters (%, +, and __) can also be replaced by means of the **DEFAULT** keyword on either the)**ATTR** or)**BODY** section statement, as follows:

)**ATTR DEFAULT(!$;)**

The three characters following the **DEFAULT** keyword positionally correspond to and replace the system-defined attribute characters. Thus, ! takes the place of %, $ substitutes for +, and ; replaces __. In this way the panel designer can change the default attribute characters to any other symbols. This technique is useful if one of the default attribute characters is required in the text of the panel.

Many installations' standards require attribute sections in all panel definitions. This approach documents the panel code.

The other new section of the **WPAN6** panel definition is the model section. The purpose of this section is to define the layout of information that displays from a Dialog Manager table on this panel. The model section is used only for *table display services*.

The model section allows the panel designer to specify an appropriate format for display of the table information on the screen. Each row of the table results in an additional line of information inserted into the format described by the variable locations in the screen model section.

There are several other items of note in this panel definition. First, the system variable **ZCMD** appears in the upper left-hand corner of the body section of the definition. The Dialog Manager requires table output panel definitions to contain a command input field; the panel designer has done this by including **ZCMD** as the first variable in the panel. The control variable **.CURSOR** is set to the field **&AMT** in the initialization section of this panel definition, ensuring that the cursor rests on the scroll amount field when the user views this screen. In effect, the user is not aware of the presence of the command input field because the panel designer has disguised its presence through this technique.

The scroll amount field is also required on a panel definition for table display. It is the second input field occurring in the panel, after the command input field. The scroll amount field enables the user to specify how he or she wishes to scroll the table data on the screen if the entire table cannot be displayed on a single logical screen. When the user first views this display panel, the scroll amount is preset to the default value of **PAGE**, and the cursor appears at the beginning of the scroll amount field.

The code of the **CVIEW2** program in figure 10-1 is quite simple. The first sentence in the PROCEDURE DIVISION attempts to open the accounting control date table. The **TBOPEN** call serves this purpose, and the parameters on this service indicate the Dialog Manager table name and read-only access to the table. If the table opens successfully, the program uses the **TBDISPL** command to display the table via the panel definition. The Dialog Manager services for table display handle all interaction with the terminal user as he or she scrolls the table to view it. When the terminal user presses the **END** program function key to exit display of the table, this program invokes the **TBEND** service to close the accounting control date table. Then the program returns the user to the "Accounting Control Administration" menu by exiting with a return code of **0**.

TABLE DISPLAY BY A CLIST

The CLIST encoding of this function is even briefer than the COBOL program. The code of the **XVIEW2** CLIST is provided in figure 10-4. Similar to all the other CLISTs, this function uses the same panel definition as does its COBOL counterpart.

After initializing its ISPF environment through invocation of the **CONTROL** service, the CLIST uses **TBOPEN** to open the accounting control date table. This service specifies the **NOWRITE** parameter, which ensures that the table will not be updated (even inadvertently) by this function and allows the table to be read by other users concurrently. All retrieval-only functions should use the **NOWRITE** parameter.

If the table does not exist, the CLIST sets up a message for the terminal user that no accounting control data exist to be viewed. If the table does exist, the CLIST uses the **TBDISPL** service to display the table data to the user. At this point, the user may scroll the table information as desired. After pressing the **END** program function key, the user returns control to this function. The function closes the accounting control date table through the **TBEND** service. **TBEND** closes the table without updating any of the data within it.

Like its COBOL program equivalent, this CLIST assumes that if the table of accounting control data exists, it contains at least one row of information. Although one could have written this dialog function with logic to check for this odd condition of an empty table, this circumstance never obtains in this application because it makes no sense from the user's viewpoint. In response to any non-0 return code from its attempt to open the control date table, this function rejects the user's query with an error message.

COBOL FUNCTION TO SCAN THE TABLE

By selecting option 4 from the Accounting Control Administration Subsystem menu, the user can search the accounting control date table for particular records. This search differs from that provided by menu option 1 because the user does not specify the key fields of the table. Instead he or she enters any combination of name fields. In the terminology of the Dialog Manager, this search of a table on dynamically specified nonkey fields is called *scanning*.

Selecting option 4 presents the user with the screen generated from the panel definition of figure 10–5. From this screen, the user enters any combination of one or more of the three input fields shown. Recall that these three fields were defined as nonkey or *name* fields to the Dialog Manager when the accounting control date table was created.

Like the panel definition of figure 10–2, this screen definition includes an attribute section. The defined attribute character is used to display the field **&OUTLINE** near the bottom of the screen. This field provides an extra message line maintained by the function logic (*not* through use of the Dialog Manager's message display services.) This message line supplies the user with the Cost Center and Sub-cost Center fields for retrieved records. It demonstrates another way to display data conditionally.

The COBOL version of the table scanning function is included as figure 10–6. The program explicitly defines dialog variables through the use of the **VDEFINE** service because its code directly inspects the values of these variables. If the **VDEFINE** calls were not made, the compiled program could only work with dialog variables implicitly.

In the PROCEDURE DIVISION of the program, the program explicitly defines its variables. Then it opens the accounting control date table for processing via a **TBOPEN** call. If the table opens successfully, the program performs the table scanning paragraph continually until the user exits by pressing the **END** or **RETURN** program function keys.

In the **SCAN-WORK** paragraph, the program first issues a **TBVCLEAR** call to the Dialog Manager. This service sets all the dialog variables that correspond to columns in the accounting control date table to nulls. In effect, it clears these variables. **TBVCLEAR** is issued as part of the procedure to initialize for a table scan.

The program then displays panel **WPAN9** to the user. If the user enters one or more of the *name* search arguments provided for in that screen, the program positions the current row pointer (CRP) to the top of the table. This is accomplished through the **TBTOP** service call. The CRP now points before the first row of the accounting control date table. This permits table scanning to search the table sequentially, starting with the first row in the table. Searching continues until either a row is found matching the search criteria or the end of the table. Should a row be found that matches the search criteria, ISPF points the CRP to that row.

After initializing the CRP, the program calls the ISPF **TBSARG** service. **TBSARG** establishes the search argument for the table scan. The table variables that currently have values will be specified as the search arguments: thus the variables the user enters constitute the search criteria.

Immediately after the **TBSARG** call, the program scans the table. The **TBSCAN** call achieves this. The search arguments used in the **TBSCAN** call are those established through the prior **TBSARG** invocation.

The return code from the scan service indicates whether a row was retrieved matching the user-specified criteria. If this return code is **0**, the program displays panel **WPAN9** to the user with the retrieved data on screen. The Cost Center and Sub-cost Center fields are displayed on the extra message line, conveyed via the field **&OUTLINE**. Thus the user views all the fields of the retrieved accounting control date table row.

If the retrieval attempt does not succeed, panel **WPAN9** is redisplayed with an appropriate message. The user may continue the table search process. Should the user exit from this function, the program calls the **VDELETE** service to eliminate the effects of the earlier **VDEFINE** calls.

There are several final points to note concerning this function. First, the program always displays only the first table row that matches the user-specified variable value(s). This is because the program issues a **TBTOP** call to reset the CRP to the top of the table prior to each sequential scan. One could easily alter the program logic to retrieve the next occurrence of a row matching the search parameter(s) by not resetting the CRP.

Second, a retrieved row must match all the user-specified search arguments. The **TBSARG** call may establish multiple fields as an *argument list* for the subsequent **TBSCAN** invocation.

CLIST FUNCTION TO SCAN THE TABLE

The CLIST version appears in figure 10-7. This CLIST duplicates the function of the COBOL program and uses the same data display panel.

The CLIST opens the accounting control date table for retrieval through the **TBOPEN** service. If the table opens successfully the procedure places the user into a **DO WHILE** loop that permits him or her to search the table for as long as desired before returning to the menu panel.

As in the COBOL program, the **TBVCLEAR** service clears all variables corresponding to table columns to nulls. This service provides a clean slate for the subsequent **TBSARG** and **TBSCAN** invocations. It does not alter the position of the CRP.

The **DISPLAY** command displays the search argument entry panel to the user. If the user enters one or more values into this screen, the CLIST sets the CRP position to the top of the table through issuing the **TBTOP** command. Then the CLIST establishes the input variable value(s) as the search argument for the table scan command through invocation of the **TBSARG** service. The subsequent **TBSCAN** command attempts to retrieve a row in the table based on the user-supplied field value(s).

If the ISPF return code indicates successful retrieval, panel **WPAN9** is displayed with the retrieved row values. The variable **&OUTLINE** appears near the bottom of the screen with the Cost Center and Subcost Center fields for the table row.

If the return code indicates that the Dialog Manager could not retrieve a table row matching all the specified variable values of the search argument list, the CLIST displays a message to this effect to the user.

Prior to the user's exit from the function, the function closes the accounting control date table through the **TBEND** service. The CLIST exits by setting its return code to **0**.

Figure 10-1. CVIEW2 COBOL function.

```
IDENTIFICATION DIVISION.                                              00010000
PROGRAM-ID. CVIEW2.                                                   00020000
*********************************************************************00030000
*  NAME: CVIEW2                                    BY: H. FOSDICK  *00040000
*                                                                 *00050000
*  PURPOSE: THIS ROUTINE ILLUSTRATES THE ISPF TABLE DISPLAY       *00060000
*  PANEL SERVICE.  IT ALLOWS THE USER TO VIEW THE ACCOUNTING      *00070000
*  CONTROL DATA TABLE AS A SCROLLABLE TABLE.                      *00080000
*                                                                 *00090000
*  NOTE: IF THE TABLE EXISTS, THIS ROUTINE ASSUMES IT CONTAINS    *00100000
*  AT LEAST ONE ROW.                                              *00110000
*                                                                 *00120000
*********************************************************************00130000
ENVIRONMENT DIVISION.                                                00140000
DATA DIVISION.                                                       00150000
                                                                     00160000
                                                                     00170000
WORKING-STORAGE SECTION.                                             00180000
                                                                     00190000
                                                                     00200000
*  SERVICE CALL TYPES:                                              00210000
                                                                     00220000
01  TBOPEN            PIC X(8)      VALUE 'TBOPEN  '.               00230000
01  TBEND             PIC X(8)      VALUE 'TBEND   '.               00240000
01  TBDISPL           PIC X(8)      VALUE 'TBDISPL '.               00250000
01  SETMSG            PIC X(8)      VALUE 'SETMSG  '.               00260000
                                                                     00270000
                                                                     00280000
*  OPTION TO SPECIFY WHEN OPENING A TABLE WITHOUT UDPATE INTENT:    00290000
                                                                     00300000
01  NOWRITE           PIC X(8)      VALUE 'NOWRITE '.               00310000
                                                                     00320000
                                                                     00330000
*  NAME OF THE TABLE OUTPUT PANEL TO DISPLAY:                       00340000
                                                                     00350000
01  PANEL-NAME        PIC X(8)      VALUE 'WPAN6   '.               00360000
                                                                     00370000
                                                                     00380000
*  NAME OF THE ACCOUNTING CONTROL DATA TABLE:                       00390000
                                                                     00400000
01  TABLE-NAME        PIC X(8)      VALUE 'CONTDATA'.               00410000
                                                                     00420000
                                                                     00430000
*  MESSAGES:                                                        00440000
                                                                     00450000
01  EXIT-MESSAGE-MSG      PIC X(8)      VALUE 'WDAR004E'.           00460000
01  NO-CONTROL-DATA-MSG   PIC X(8)      VALUE 'WDAR004A'.           00470000
                                                                     00480000
                                                                     00490000
                                                                     00500000
PROCEDURE DIVISION.                                                  00510000
                                                                     00520000
                                                                     00530000
*                                                                   00540000
*  OPEN THE ISPF TABLE CONTAINING ACCOUNTING CONTROL DATA:          00550000
*                                                                   00560000
                                                                     00570000
    CALL 'ISPLINK' USING   TBOPEN                                   00580000
                           TABLE-NAME                               00590000
                           NOWRITE.                                 00600000
                                                                     00610000
                                                                     00620000
*                                                                   00630000
*  IF TABLE DOESNOT EXIST, INFORM USER AND EXIT:                    00640000
*                                                                   00650000
                                                                     00660000
    IF RETURN-CODE NOT = 0                                          00670000
                                                                     00680000
        CALL 'ISPLINK' USING   SETMSG                               00690000
                               NO-CONTROL-DATA-MSG                  00700000
                                                                     00710000
                                                                     00720000
*                                                                   00730000
*  OTHERWISE, DISPLAY ALL THE ACCOUNTING CONTROL                    00740000
*  INFORMATION FROM THE TABLE VIA 'TBDISPL':                        00750000
*                                                                   00760000
                                                                     00770000
    ELSE                                                            00780000
                                                                     00790000
        CALL 'ISPLINK' USING   TBDISPL                              00800000
                               TABLE-NAME                           00810000
                               PANEL-NAME                           00820000
                               EXIT-MESSAGE-MSG                     00830000
                                                                     00840000
        CALL 'ISPLINK' USING   TBEND                                00850000
                               TABLE-NAME.                          00860000
                                                                     00870000
                                                                     00880000
                                                                     00890000
    MOVE 0 TO RETURN-CODE.                                          00900000
    GOBACK.                                                         00910000
```

Figure 10-2. WPAN6 panel definition.

```
)ATTR
  a TYPE(OUTPUT) INTENS(LOW)
)BODY
%-------------- WEST DEPARTMENT ACCOUNTS RECEIVABLE ---------------------------
+ _ZCMD          %ACCOUNTING CONTROL ADMINISTRATION          %SCROLL ===>_AMT +
+
%VIEW ACCOUNTING CONTROL PARAMETERS FOR ALL CENTERS:
+
+
+ COST         SUBCOST        USER                                  INVOICE
+CENTER        CENTER         CONTACT        DISTRIBUTION           DATE
+
)MODEL
 aCOSCTR       aSUBCTR        aCONTACT       aDISTRIB      aINVDATE
)INIT
   .HELP   = WH010
   &AMT    = PAGE
   .CURSOR = AMT
)END
```

Figure 10-3. WPAN6 screen as displayed.

```
-------------- WEST DEPARTMENT ACCOUNTS RECEIVABLE ---- LINE 000001 COL 001 080
                ACCOUNTING CONTROL ADMINISTRATION            SCROLL ===> PAGE

VIEW ACCOUNTING CONTROL PARAMETERS FOR ALL CENTERS:


   COST        SUBCOST        USER                              INVOICE
   CENTER      CENTER         CONTACT        DISTRIBUTION         DATE

   1100        1000           FLINT          2022               03/02/85
   2260        8600           DAMIEN         3343               01/06/85
   2260        8400           BECKLEY        6140               11/04/84
   1242        2000           FREDERIK       1010               01/01/85
   1242        1010           MURRAY         3343               12/01/84
   1242        1000           PLUM           3343               11/11/84
   1242        1222           POLK           6424               11/11/84
******************************** BOTTOM OF DATA ********************************
```

Figure 10-4. XVIEW2 CLIST function.

```
00010000  PROC 0
00020000  CONTROL MSG NOFLUSH
00030000  /******************************************************************/
00040000  /* NAME: XVIEW2                          BY: H. FOSDICK      */
00050000  /* */
00060000  /* PURPOSE: THIS CLIST ILLUSTRATES THE ISPF TABLE DISPLAY   */
00070000  /* PANEL SERVICE.  IT ALLOWS THE USER TO VIEW THE ACCOUNTING*/
00080000  /* CONTROL DATA TABLE AS A SCROLLABLE TABLE.               */
00090000  /* */
00100000  /* NOTE: IF THE TABLE EXISTS, THIS CLIST ASSUMES IT        */
00110000  /* CONTAINS AT LEAST ONE ROW.                              */
00120000  /* */
00130000  /******************************************************************/
00140000
00150000  ISPEXEC  CONTROL  ERRORS  CANCEL
00160000
00170000  /* */
00180000  /*   OPEN THE ISPF TABLE CONTAINING ACCOUNTING CONTROL DATA: */
00190000  /* */
00200000
00210000  ISPEXEC  TBOPEN  CONTDATA  NOWRITE
00220000
00230000
00240000  /* */
00250000  /*   IF TABLE DOESNOT EXIST, INFORM USER AND EXIT:          */
00260000  /* */
00270000
00280000  IF &LASTCC ¬= 0 THEN +
00290000      ISPEXEC SETMSG MSG(WDAR004A)
00300000
00310000
00320000      /* */
00330000      /* OTHERWISE, DISPLAY ALL THE ACCOUNTING CONTROL       */
00340000      /* INFORMATION FROM THE TABLE VIA 'TBDISPL':           */
00350000      /* */
00360000
00370000  ELSE DO
00380000
00390000      ISPEXEC  TBDISPL  CONTDATA  PANEL(WPAN6)  MSG(WDAR004E)
00400000
00410000
00420000      /* */
00430000      /* CLOSE THE TABLE WITHOUT ALTERING ANY DATA:          */
00440000      /* */
00450000
00460000      ISPEXEC  TBEND  CONTDATA
00470000
00480000  END
00490000
00500000
00510000  EXIT CODE(0)
```

Figure 10-5. WPAN9 panel definition.

```
)ATTR
  a TYPE(OUTPUT) INTENS(HIGH)
)BODY
%-------------- WEST DEPARTMENT ACCOUNTS RECEIVABLE ---------------------------
%                   ACCOUNTING CONTROL ADMINISTRATION
+
%SCAN ACCOUNTING CONTROL PARAMETERS:
+
+ENTER PARAMETERS YOU WISH TO SEARCH FOR:
+
+
+   USER REPRESENTATIVE IS%===>_CONTACT +
+   USER DISTRIBUTION CODE%===>_DISTRIB +
+   INVOICE CONTROL DATE  %===>_INVDATE +       ('MM/DD/YY')
+
+
aOUTLINE
+
+
+
+PRESS%END+KEY TO EXIT
)INIT
  .HELP  = WH013
)PROC
   VER (&CONTACT, ALPHA)
   VER (&DISTRIB, NUM)
   VER (&INVDATE, PICT, '99/99/99', MSG=WDAR002C)
)END
```

Figure 10-6. CSCAN COBOL function.

```
       IDENTIFICATION DIVISION.                                      00010000
       PROGRAM-ID. CSCAN.                                            00020000
      ***************************************************************00030000
      *  NAME: CSCAN                                    BY: H. FOSDICK *00040000
      *                                                              *00050000
      *  PURPOSE: THIS ROUTINE ILLUSTRATES THE TABLE SCAN FACILITY   *00060000
      *  IN ALLOWING THE USER TO SEARCH FOR NON-KEY (NAME) PARAMETERS *00070000
      *  IN THE ACCOUNTING CONTROL DATA TABLE.                       *00080000
      *                                                              *00090000
      *  NOTE: THIS ROUTINE ALWAYS DISPLAYS THE FIRST TABLE ROW      *00100000
      *  TO MATCH THE USER'S SEARCH CRITERIA ONLY.                   *00110000
      *                                                              *00120000
      ***************************************************************00130000
       ENVIRONMENT DIVISION.                                         00140000
       DATA DIVISION.                                                00150000
                                                                     00160000
                                                                     00170000
       WORKING-STORAGE SECTION.                                      00180000
                                                                     00190000
                                                                     00200000
                                                                     00210000
      *  SERVICE CALL TYPES:                                         00220000
                                                                     00230000
       01  DISPLAY-PANEL     PIC X(8)      VALUE 'DISPLAY '.         00240000
       01  TBEND             PIC X(8)      VALUE 'TBEND   '.         00250000
       01  TBOPEN            PIC X(8)      VALUE 'TBOPEN  '.         00260000
       01  TBVCLEAR          PIC X(8)      VALUE 'TBVCLEAR'.         00270000
       01  TBTOP             PIC X(8)      VALUE 'TBTOP   '.         00280000
       01  TBSARG            PIC X(8)      VALUE 'TBSARG  '.         00290000
       01  TBSCAN            PIC X(8)      VALUE 'TBSCAN  '.         00300000
       01  VDEFINE           PIC X(8)      VALUE 'VDEFINE '.         00310000
       01  VDELETE           PIC X(8)      VALUE 'VDELETE '.         00320000
       01  SETMSG            PIC X(8)      VALUE 'SETMSG  '.         00330000
                                                                     00340000
                                                                     00350000
      *  NAME OF THE TABLE TO SCAN:                                  00360000
                                                                     00370000
       01  TABLE-NAME        PIC X(8)      VALUE 'CONTDATA'.         00380000
                                                                     00390000
                                                                     00400000
      *  NAME OF THE DATA ENTRY/DISPLAY PANEL:                       00410000
                                                                     00420000
       01  PANEL-NAME        PIC X(8)      VALUE 'WPAN9   '.         00430000
                                                                     00440000
                                                                     00450000
      *  OPTION FOR OPENING ISPF TABLE WITHOUT UPDATE INTENT:        00460000
                                                                     00470000
       01  NOWRITE           PIC X(8)      VALUE 'NOWRITE '.         00480000
                                                                     00490000
                                                                     00500000
      *  DATA TYPE PARAMETER FOR ALL 'VDEFINE' CALLS:                00510000
                                                                     00520000
       01  CHAR              PIC X(8)      VALUE 'CHAR    '.         00530000
                                                                     00540000
                                                                     00550000
      *  MESSAGES:                                                   00560000
                                                                     00570000
       01  NO-CONTROL-DATA-MSG       PIC X(8)     VALUE 'WDAR004A'.  00580000
       01  PROCESSING-TERMINATED-MSG PIC X(8)     VALUE 'WDAR000A'.  00590000
       01  ENTER-SCANNING-FIELDS-MSG PIC X(8)     VALUE 'WDAR006C'.  00600000
       01  DATA-FOUND-MSG            PIC X(8)     VALUE 'WDAR006A'.  00610000
       01  SCAN-FAILED-MSG           PIC X(8)     VALUE 'WDAR006B'.  00620000
                                                                     00630000
                                                                     00640000
      *  LOOP CONTROL VARIABLE FOR REDISPLAY OF ORIGINAL PANEL:      00650000
                                                                     00660000
       01  CONTINU           PIC X(3)      VALUE 'YES'.              00670000
                                                                     00680000
                                                                     00690000
      *  DEFINE STORAGE SPACE FOR DIALOG VARIABLES:                  00700000
                                                                     00710000
       01  COSCTR            PIC X(4)      VALUE SPACES.             00720000
       01  SUBCTR            PIC X(4)      VALUE SPACES.             00730000
       01  CONTACT           PIC X(8)      VALUE SPACES.             00740000
       01  DISTRIB           PIC X(8)      VALUE SPACES.             00750000
       01  INVDATE           PIC X(8)      VALUE SPACES.             00760000
       01  OUTLINE.                                                  00770000
           05  LITERAL-1        PIC X(16)   VALUE 'FOR COST CENTER '.00780000
           05  OUTLINE-COSCTR   PIC X(4)    VALUE SPACES.            00790000
           05  LITERAL-2        PIC X(3)    VALUE ' - '.             00800000
           05  OUTLINE-SUBCTR   PIC X(4)    VALUE SPACES.            00810000
                                                                     00820000
                                                                     00830000
      *  DEFINE THE LENGTH OF EACH DIALOG VARIABLE:                  00840000
                                                                     00850000
       01  COSCTR-LENGTH     PIC 9(6)      VALUE    4  COMP.         00860000
       01  SUBCTR-LENGTH     PIC 9(6)      VALUE    4  COMP.         00870000
       01  CONTACT-LENGTH    PIC 9(6)      VALUE    8  COMP.         00880000
```

```
 01   DISTRIB-LENGTH      PIC 9(6)      VALUE   8   COMP.            00890000
 01   INVDATE-LENGTH      PIC 9(6)      VALUE   8   COMP.            00900000
 01   OUTLINE-LENGTH      PIC 9(6)      VALUE  27   COMP.            00910000
                                                                    00920000
                                                                    00930000
*   DEFINE DIALOG VARIABLE NAMES FOR ISPF DIALOG MANAGER:           00940000
                                                                    00950000
 01   COSCTR-NAME         PIC X(8)      VALUE   '(COSCTR)'.         00960000
 01   SUBCTR-NAME         PIC X(8)      VALUE   '(SUBCTR)'.         00970000
 01   CONTACT-NAME        PIC X(9)      VALUE   '(CONTACT)'.        00980000
 01   DISTRIB-NAME        PIC X(9)      VALUE   '(DISTRIB)'.        00990000
 01   INVDATE-NAME        PIC X(9)      VALUE   '(INVDATE)'.        01000000
 01   OUTLINE-NAME        PIC X(9)      VALUE   '(OUTLINE)'.        01010000
                                                                    01020000
                                                                    01030000
                                                                    01040000
     PROCEDURE DIVISION.                                            01050000
                                                                    01060000
                                                                    01070000
                                                                    01080000
*                                                                   01090000
*   DEFINE ALL DIALOG FUNCTION VARIABLES TO ISPF DIALOG MANAGER:    01100000
*                                                                   01110000
         PERFORM DEFINE-VARIABLES THRU DEFINE-VARIABLES-EXIT.       01120000
                                                                    01130000
                                                                    01140000
*                                                                   01150000
*   OPEN THE ISPF TABLE CONTAINING ACCOUNTING CONTROL DATA:         01160000
*                                                                   01170000
                                                                    01180000
         CALL 'ISPLINK' USING  TBOPEN                               01190000
                               TABLE-NAME                           01200000
                               NOWRITE.                             01210000
                                                                    01220000
                                                                    01230000
*                                                                   01240000
*   IF THE TABLE DOESNOT EXIST, INFORM USER AND EXIT:               01250000
*                                                                   01260000
                                                                    01270000
         IF RETURN-CODE NOT = 0                                     01280000
                                                                    01290000
             CALL 'ISPLINK'  USING  SETMSG                          01300000
                                    NO-CONTROL-DATA-MSG             01310000
                                                                    01320000
         ELSE                                                       01330000
                                                                    01340000
                                                                    01350000
*                                                                   01360000
*   OTHERWISE, PROCESS USER SCAN REQUESTS AGAINST THE TABLE         01370000
*   UNTIL HE PRESSES THE 'END' KEY.   THEN CLOSE THE TABLE:         01380000
*                                                                   01390000
                                                                    01400000
             MOVE 'YES' TO CONTINU                                  01410000
                                                                    01420000
             PERFORM SCAN-WORK THRU SCAN-WORK-EXIT UNTIL            01430000
                  CONTINU = 'NO '                                   01440000
                                                                    01450000
             CALL 'ISPLINK'  USING  TBEND                           01460000
                                    TABLE-NAME.                     01470000
                                                                    01480000
                                                                    01490000
*                                                                   01500000
*   DELETE ALL DIALOG FUNCTION VARIABLES RE ISPF DIALOG MANAGER:    01510000
*                                                                   01520000
                                                                    01530000
         PERFORM DELETE-VARIABLES THRU DELETE-VARIABLES-EXIT.       01540000
                                                                    01550000
                                                                    01560000
                                                                    01570000
         MOVE 0 TO RETURN-CODE.                                     01580000
         GOBACK.                                                    01590000
                                                                    01600000
     MAIN-LINE-EXIT.                                                01610000
                                                                    01620000
                                                                    01630000
                                                                    01640000
                                                                    01650000
     SCAN-WORK.                                                     01660000
                                                                    01670000
*                                                                   01680000
*   CLEAR ALL VARIABLES, DISPLAY THE DATA ENTRY PANEL:              01690000
*                                                                   01700000
                                                                    01710000
         MOVE SPACES TO OUTLINE.                                    01720000
                                                                    01730000
         CALL 'ISPLINK'  USING  TBVCLEAR                            01740000
                                TABLE-NAME.                         01750000
```

(continued)

Figure 10-6. *(Continued)*

```
                                                              01760000
      CALL 'ISPLINK'  USING  DISPLAY-PANEL                    01770000
                             PANEL-NAME                       01780000
                             ENTER-SCANNING-FIELDS-MSG.       01790000
                                                              01800000
                                                              01810000
*                                                             01820000
*  IF USER PRESSES 'END' KEY, SET UP MESSAGE AND EXIT:        01830000
*                                                             01840000
                                                              01850000
      IF RETURN-CODE NOT = 0                                  01860000
                                                              01870000
          CALL 'ISPLINK'  USING  SETMSG                       01880000
                                 PROCESSING-TERMINATED-MSG    01890000
                                                              01900000
          MOVE 'NO ' TO CONTINU                               01910000
                                                              01920000
                                                              01930000
      ELSE                                                    01940000
                                                              01950000
                                                              01960000
*                                                             01970000
*  SCAN ONLY IF USER ENTERED AT LEAST ONE PARAMETER:          01980000
*                                                             01990000
                                                              02000000
          IF (CONTACT NOT = SPACES OR                         02010000
              DISTRIB NOT = SPACES OR                         02020000
              INVDATE NOT = SPACES)                           02030000
                                                              02040000
                                                              02050000
                                                              02060000
*                                                             02070000
*  INITIALIZE CURRENT ROW POINTER (CRP) TO TOP.  ESTABLISH    02080000
*  SEARCH ARGUMENT(S), THEN SCAN TABLE:                       02090000
*                                                             02100000
                                                              02110000
              CALL 'ISPLINK'  USING  TBTOP                    02120000
                                     TABLE-NAME               02130000
                                                              02140000
              CALL 'ISPLINK'  USING  TBSARG                   02150000
                                     TABLE-NAME               02160000
                                                              02170000
              CALL 'ISPLINK'  USING  TBSCAN                   02180000
                                     TABLE-NAME               02190000
                                                              02200000
                                                              02210000
*                                                             02220000
*  OUTPUT THE RETRIEVED DATA OR A 'NOT FOUND' MESSAGE:        02230000
*                                                             02240000
                                                              02250000
              IF RETURN-CODE = 0                              02260000
                                                              02270000
                  MOVE COSCTR TO OUTLINE-COSCTR OF OUTLINE    02280000
                  MOVE SUBCTR TO OUTLINE-SUBCTR OF OUTLINE    02290000
                  MOVE 'FOR COST CENTER ' TO LITERAL-1 OF OUTLINE02300000
                  MOVE ' - ' TO LITERAL-2 OF OUTLINE          02310000
                                                              02320000
                  CALL 'ISPLINK'  USING  DISPLAY-PANEL        02330000
                                         PANEL-NAME           02340000
                                         DATA-FOUND-MSG       02350000
                                                              02360000
              ELSE                                            02370000
                                                              02380000
                  CALL 'ISPLINK'  USING  DISPLAY-PANEL        02390000
                                         PANEL-NAME           02400000
                                         SCAN-FAILED-MSG.     02410000
                                                              02420000
  SCAN-WORK-EXIT.                                             02430000
      EXIT.                                                   02440000
                                                              02450000
                                                              02460000
                                                              02470000
                                                              02480000
                                                              02490000
  DEFINE-VARIABLES.                                           02500000
                                                              02510000
                                                              02520000
                                                              02530000
*                                                             02540000
*  DEFINE ALL DIALOG FUNCTION VARIABLES TO ISPF DIALOG MANAGER:02550000
*                                                             02560000
      CALL 'ISPLINK'  USING  VDEFINE                          02570000
                             COSCTR-NAME                      02580000
                             COSCTR                           02590000
                             CHAR                             02600000
                             COSCTR-LENGTH.                   02610000
      CALL 'ISPLINK'  USING  VDEFINE                          02620000
                             SUBCTR-NAME                      02630000
```

```
                                SUBCTR                                  02640000
                                CHAR                                    02650000
                                SUBCTR-LENGTH.                          02660000
     CALL 'ISPLINK'  USING      VDEFINE                                 02670000
                                CONTACT-NAME                            02680000
                                CONTACT                                 02690000
                                CHAR                                    02700000
                                CONTACT-LENGTH.                         02710000
     CALL 'ISPLINK'  USING      VDEFINE                                 02720000
                                DISTRIB-NAME                            02730000
                                DISTRIB                                 02740000
                                CHAR                                    02750000
                                DISTRIB-LENGTH.                         02760000
     CALL 'ISPLINK'  USING      VDEFINE                                 02770000
                                INVDATE-NAME                            02780000
                                INVDATE                                 02790000
                                CHAR                                    02800000
                                INVDATE-LENGTH.                         02810000
     CALL 'ISPLINK'  USING      VDEFINE                                 02820000
                                OUTLINE-NAME                            02830000
                                OUTLINE                                 02840000
                                CHAR                                    02850000
                                OUTLINE-LENGTH.                         02860000
                                                                        02870000
 DEFINE-VARIABLES-EXIT.                                                 02880000
     EXIT.                                                              02890000
                                                                        02900000
                                                                        02910000
                                                                        02920000
                                                                        02930000
 DELETE-VARIABLES.                                                      02940000
                                                                        02950000
*                                                                       02960000
**   DELETE ALL DIALOG FUNCTION VARIABLES RE ISPF DIALOG MANAGER:       02970000
*                                                                       02980000
                                                                        02990000
     CALL 'ISPLINK'  USING      VDELETE                                 03000000
                                COSCTR-NAME.                            03010000
     CALL 'ISPLINK'  USING      VDELETE                                 03020000
                                SUBCTR-NAME.                            03030000
     CALL 'ISPLINK'  USING      VDELETE                                 03040000
                                CONTACT-NAME.                           03050000
     CALL 'ISPLINK'  USING      VDELETE                                 03060000
                                DISTRIB-NAME.                           03070000
     CALL 'ISPLINK'  USING      VDELETE                                 03080000
                                INVDATE-NAME.                           03090000
     CALL 'ISPLINK'  USING      VDELETE                                 03100000
                                OUTLINE-NAME.                           03110000
                                                                        03120000
 DELETE-VARIABLES-EXIT.                                                 03130000
     EXIT.                                                              03140000
```

Figure 10-7. XSCAN CLIST function.

```
00010000 PROC 0
00020000 CONTROL MSG NOFLUSH
00030000 /*******************************************************************/
00040000 /* NAME: XSCAN                             BY: H. FOSDICK   */
00050000 /*                                                         */
00060000 /* PURPOSE: THIS CLIST ILLUSTRATES THE TABLE SCAN FACILITY */
00070000 /* IN ALLOWING THE USER TO SEARCH FOR NON-KEY (NAME)       */
00080000 /* PARAMETERS IN THE ACCOUNTING CONTROL DATA TABLE.        */
00090000 /*                                                         */
00100000 /* NOTE: THIS ROUTINE ALWAYS DISPLAYS THE FIRST TABLE ROW  */
00110000 /* TO MATCH THE USER'S SEARCH CRITERIA ONLY.               */
00120000 /*                                                         */
00130000 /*******************************************************************/
00140000
00150000 ISPEXEC  CONTROL   ERRORS   CANCEL
00160000
00170000 /*                                                         */
00180000 /*   OPEN THE ISPF TABLE CONTAINING ACCOUNTING CONTROL DATA: */
00190000 /*                                                         */
00200000
00210000 ISPEXEC   TBOPEN  CONTDATA  NOWRITE
00220000
00230000
00240000 /*                                                         */
00250000 /*   IF TABLE DOESNOT EXIST, INFORM USER AND EXIT:          */
00260000 /*                                                         */
00270000
00280000 IF &LASTCC ¬= 0 THEN +
00290000     ISPEXEC SETMSG MSG(WDAR004A)
00300000
00310000
00320000 ELSE DO
00330000
00340000     SET CONTINU = YES
00350000
00360000     DO WHILE &CONTINU = YES
00370000
00380000
00390000         /*                                                 */
00400000         /* CLEAR ALL VARIABLES, DISPLAY THE DATA ENTRY PANEL: */
00410000         /*                                                 */
00420000
00430000         SET OUTLINE =
00440000
00450000         ISPEXEC  TBVCLEAR  CONTDATA
00460000
00470000         ISPEXEC  DISPLAY   PANEL(WPAN9)  MSG(WDAR006C)
00480000
00490000
00500000         /*                                                 */
00510000         /* IF USER PRESSES 'END' KEY, SET UP MESSAGE AND EXIT: */
00520000         /*                                                 */
00530000
00540000         IF &LASTCC ¬= 0 THEN DO
00550000
00560000             ISPEXEC SETMSG MSG(WDAR000A)
00570000             SET CONTINU = NO
00580000             END
00590000
00600000         ELSE DO
00610000
00620000             /*                                             */
00630000             /* ONLY SCAN IF USER ENTERED AT LEAST ONE PARAMETER:*/
00640000             /*                                             */
00650000
00660000             IF &CONTACT ¬= &STR() OR &DISTRIB ¬= &STR() OR +
00670000                &STR(&INVDATE)  ¬= &STR()  THEN DO
00680000
00690000
00700000                 /*                                         */
00710000                 /* INITIALIZE CURRENT ROW POINTER (CRP) TO TOP, */
00720000                 /* ESTABLISH SEARCH ARGUMENT(S), SCAN TABLE: */
00730000                 /*                                         */
00740000
00750000                 ISPEXEC TBTOP   CONTDATA
00760000                 ISPEXEC TBSARG CONTDATA
00770000                 ISPEXEC TBSCAN CONTDATA
00780000
00790000
00800000                 /*                                         */
00810000                 /* OUTPUT DATA OR 'NOT FOUND' MESSAGE:      */
00820000                 /*                                         */
00830000
00840000                 IF &LASTCC = 0 THEN DO
00850000
00860000                     SET OUTLINE = +
00870000                         &STR(FOR COST CENTER &COSCTR - &SUBCTR)
00880000                     ISPEXEC  DISPLAY   PANEL(WPAN9)  MSG(WDAR006A)
00890000                     END
```

```
00900000
00910000                        ELSE +
00920000                            ISPEXEC  DISPLAY   PANEL(WPAN9)  MSG(WDAR006B)
00930000
00940000               END
00950000            END
00960000
00970000       END
00980000
00990000       /*                                                    */
01000000       /* CLOSE THE TABLE WITHOUT ALTERING ANY DATA:          */
01010000       /*                                                    */
01020000
01030000       ISPEXEC  TBEND  CONTDATA
01040000
01050000    END
01060000
01070000
01080000  EXIT CODE(0)
```

11

Table Creation and Maintenance

This chapter concludes the discussion of the example dialog by presenting the function that provides for creation and maintenance of the accounting control date table. From the viewpoint of the terminal user, this menu selection allows deletion, addition, and alteration of the accounting control data associated with any particular Cost Center/Sub-cost Center. This information is used, through a different master menu selection, to print the Distribution Report of accounts receivable invoices and to distribute that report within the company. From the standpoint of the Dialog Manager's table services, this is the function that initially creates the permanent table used by the other functions in this dialog. Users add, delete, and update rows of table information through this function. Since the table is keyed, all services depend on user specification of an appropriate key. Addition of new data to the table requires use of a unique and previously unused key; updating or deleting a row mandates specification of a key already in the table.

PANEL DEFINITIONS

The panels defined for use by this function are presented in figures 11-1 and 11-2. The former defines the screen the user views when selecting this option from the selection menu. This screen requires three basic pieces of input data: the Cost Center code, the Sub-cost Center code, and the transaction type. Recall that the two center codes together compose the key of the accounting control date table. The transaction type is specified as **A**, **U**, or **D**, for adding a new row of data to the table, updating data within an existing row, or deleting a row of data from the table, respectively. The first operation requires a new (unused) key to be entered, and the latter two transactions mean that an existing key must be supplied. When two or more fields are named as *key fields* during the creation of the table, from then on they may be considered as a single logical key.

149

There are a few points of interest in the panel definitions. Figure 11-1 again illustrates the use of the system variable **Z** in its role as a *placeholder* variable. This technique allows the designer to limit the length of input data for fields to fewer characters than exist in the variable names. The name-list to which the control variable **.ZVARS** is set in the initialization section of this panel definition indicates that the placeholder variable represents the variable **&COSCTR** in its first appearance in the body section of the panel definition and the variable **&SUBCTR** in its second occurrence. A placeholder variable was not used for the transaction type because its variable name consists of a single letter (**&T**).

Assuming the user inputs a correct key combination for an add transaction or an existing key for update and delete transactions, he or she views the screen generated by the panel definition of figure 11-2 next. This panel definition illustrates use of the panel **IF** statement. In the panel's initialization section, the value of the dialog variable **&T** is tested. This variable should contain a transaction code of **A**, **U**, or **D**. If the transaction code value is **A**, the three variables displayed to the user are set to blanks. Thus when the user asks to enter new data, he or she views a screen with blank fields in which to enter the new data. Should the transaction code indicate an update or delete transaction, the values in the appropriate row are displayed on this screen. In the case of an update transaction, the user types over and modifies one or more of these variables. After he or she presses the **ENTER** key, these values are updated in the table. In the case of a delete transaction, the current values of the table row to delete are shown. If the user wishes to confirm deletion of this data, he or she presses the **ENTER** key. And to abort the delete, he or she can press the **END** program function key to back him or her out of the delete request.

IF statements may be used to test the current values of variables and conditionally take some action based on those values. In the example, the **IF** statement enables the panel designer to specify initialization processing that occurs only in the case that the terminal user requests addition of data to the table. In this case, three variables display upon the transaction screen as blanks, allowing the user to enter data for the new table row.

The most important thing to remember about the **IF** statement is this: *the IF statement is indentation sensitive.* In other words, **IF** logic is dependent on the proper vertical alignment of the source code. This principle is quite different from the implementation of **IF** logic with compiled programming languages like COBOL or PL/I. Depending on the degree of nesting embodied in the **IF** statements of a panel definition, it can lead to some frustrating errors.

Here are some example **IF** statements:

```
1.  IF (&DISTRIB = &A)
2.  IF (&DISTRIB = ' ')
3.  IF (&DISTRIB = A,B)
```

```
4.   IF (&DISTRIB = A)
         IF    (&DISTRIB   =   &B)
            &CONTACT   =   QUAIFE
         &INVDATE   =   &DATE
      &DONE   =   YES
```

In the first example, if the value of variable **&DISTRIB** is equal to that of variable **&A**, then action(s) following the **IF** test are executed. Otherwise execution resumes with the next statement vertically aligned with (or starting to the left of) the **IF** statement. In the second example, the **IF** test is true if the value of variable **&DISTRIB** is null or contains blanks. Should the test prove false, processing continues with the next statement whose vertical alignment is in the same (or a lesser) column as that of the **IF** statement.

In the third example, the statement is true if the value of variable **&DISTRIB** is the literal value **A** or the value **B**.

In the final example, if the value of variable **&DISTRIB** is equal to the literal string **A**, execution proceeds with the statement that tests **&DISTRIB** with the value in variable **&B**. If this second **IF** test evaluates as true, then **&CONTACT** is set to **QUAIFE**. Whether this occurs or not, **&INVDATE** is set to **&DATE**. Then the statement **&DONE = YES** is executed.

If the original **IF** test of **(&DISTRIB = A)** was false, then the only statement executed is the one that sets the value of **&DONE** to **YES**.

COBOL UPDATE PROGRAM

Figure 11–3 shows the code of the COBOL update program. The member name of this function in the program library is **CUPD**.

The storage declarations for the Dialog Manager service calls in the program include these services: **TBCREATE, TBOPEN, TBGET, TBADD, TBPUT, TBDELETE,** and **TBCLOSE**. Notice that the program **VDEFINE**s all the dialog variables with which it works.

In the PROCEDURE DIVISION of the program, the table **CONTDATA** is opened with update intent via a **TBOPEN** call. The update access right is specified by the parameter **WRITE**.

If the **TBOPEN** call returns a nonzero return code, the program assumes that the table **CONTDATA** does not yet exist.* It creates the table through issuing a **TBCREATE** command call naming the table **CONTDATA**. This call specifies all the fields contained in each table row. Two name-lists accomplish this. The first states that program variables **COSCTR** and **SUBCTR** are table keys. The second specifies the nonkey variables stored in the table: **CONTACT, DISTRIB,** and **INVDATE**.

Following the table creation logic, the program performs the para-

---

*In a multiuser environment, **TBOPEN** may issue a return code of **12** if another user has locked (**ENQ**'d) the table. The program logic is also simplified with respect to the possibility of a non-0 return code from the **TBCREATE** service.

graph **UPDATE-WORK** until the user presses the **END** program function key. This paragraph presents the screen of the panel definition in figure 11-1 to the user. Recall that through this screen, the user specifies a Cost Center/Sub-cost Center key and the transaction type. Assuming the user enters this information, the program performs paragraph **INVALID-TRANSACTION-CHECK** in order to verify that the combination of key and transaction code is acceptable. This paragraph attempts to read a row in the table based on the user-provided key, accomplished through the **TBGET** service call of program lines 270 and 271. A user-specified transaction code of **A** should result in a failed direct retrieval; transaction codes of **U** and **D** must result in successful retrieval of a table row. If these conditions are not met, this paragraph sets up an appropriate error message in the program variable **MSG**.

Assuming that **INVALID-TRANSACTION-CHECK** routine did not find an error, **UPDATE-WORK** routine displays the panel of figure 11-2. The user enters new data for an add transaction or updates the data displayed for an update transaction. For a delete transaction, the user presses the **ENTER** key to confirm the deletion.

If the user presses the **ENTER** key to continue the transaction, the COBOL program executes the paragraph **ACTUAL-TABLE-UPDATE**. This code calls an ISPF service to effect the appropriate action against the table. Thus, it executes a **TBADD**, **TBPUT**, or **TBDELETE** call and then sets up a suitable message through the **SETMSG** call.

Whichever update call is issued against the table, that call operates on the basis of the row identified by the unique key of the Cost Center/Sub-cost Center fields. The action on the **TBADD**, **TBPUT**, and **TBDELETE** calls is affected by the Dialog Manager's knowledge that this is a keyed table. Update of a table without keys differs in that call actions depend solely on the position of the current row pointer within the table.

When the user presses the **END** program function key to exit this function, the program issues a **TBCLOSE** service call. The **TBCLOSE** service is distinguished from the **TBEND** invocations demonstrated earlier in that **TBCLOSE** both closes and saves a table. For permanent tables, this means that **TBCLOSE** writes the table to disk. Use **TBCLOSE** when updating permanent tables.

CLIST UPDATE FUNCTION

The CLIST version of the table create and update function is presented in figure 11-4. As one would expect, this CLIST involves considerably less code than its COBOL counterpart, in part, because **VDEFINE** and **VDELETE** services are not used in command procedures.

The first ISPF table service invocation in the CLIST attempts to open the accounting date table through the **TBOPEN** command. If a non-zero return code is encountered, the CLIST creates the table. This is achieved through the **TBCREATE** command. In this command, the **KEYS** keyword specifies a name-list containing fields that will be the key of this table, and the **NAMES** keyword indicates the other fields each table row contains.

The function next displays the screen of the panel definition in figure 11-1. Here, the user enters the key fields and a transaction code of **A** (for add), **U** (for update), or **D** (for delete). Assuming the user presses the **ENTER** key, the CLIST verifies that a row with the key of an add transaction does not yet exist in the table or that the key entered for update or delete transactions already exists in the table. This validation procedure is contained in lines 64 through 90.

Assuming a valid transaction, the CLIST displays the data entry/ update/delete screen of figure 11-2. On this screen, the user enters the data to add for an add transaction or changes data as desired for an update transaction. For a delete transaction, he or she views the data displayed on this screen and presses the **ENTER** key to confirm the deletion.

Lines 121 through 158 test the transaction code entered by the user. This code issues a call to Dialog Manager services to effect the user's processing choice against the table. A **TBADD**, **TBPUT**, or **TBDE-LETE** command is issued. In all cases, an appropriate action message is set up for the user through a **SETMSG** invocation.

As in the COBOL program, the row manipulation commands **TBADD**, **TBPUT**, and **TBDELETE** operate on the table row specified by the two key fields because the table was originally established as keyed via the **TBCREATE** command of lines 23 through 29. Where tables are defined via **TBCREATE** without key(s), these row manipulation commands operate on the basis of the current row pointer position within the table.

When the user finishes maintaining the table, the following line is executed:

ISPEXEC TBCLOSE CONTDATA

This command closes the table, writing it to the disk, and updating it in the process. Recall that the **TBEND** command was used where the table was opened for read-only access.

Figure 11-1. WPAN7 panel definition.

```
)BODY
%-------------- WEST DEPARTMENT ACCOUNTS RECEIVABLE --------------------------
%                    ACCOUNTING CONTROL ADMINISTRATION
+
%ADD, UPDATE OR DELETE ACCOUNTING PARAMETERS FOR A SPECIFIED CENTER:
+
+
+
+    ENTER COST CENTER CODES:
+
+    COST CENTER      %===>_Z   +
+    SUB-COST CENTER%===>_Z   +
+
+
+    TRANSACTION TYPE DESIRED%===>_T+        (ADD, UPDATE OR DELETE)
+
+
+
+PRESS%END+KEY TO EXIT
)INIT
    .HELP  = WH011
    .ZVARS = '(COSCTR SUBCTR)'
)PROC
    VER (&COSCTR, NONBLANK, NUM, MSG=WDAR004D)
    VER (&SUBCTR, NONBLANK, NUM, MSG=WDAR004D)
    VER (&T, NB, LIST, A, U, D,  MSG=WDAR005A)
)END
```

Figure 11-2. WPAN8 panel definition.

```
)BODY
%-------------- WEST DEPARTMENT ACCOUNTS RECEIVABLE ---------------------------
%                   ACCOUNTING CONTROL ADMINISTRATION
+
%ADD, UPDATE OR DELETE ACCOUNTING PARAMETERS FOR A SPECIFIED CENTER:
+
+
+    FOR COST CENTER OF%&COSCTR.-&SUBCTR.:
+
+
+    USER REPRESENTATIVE IS %===>_CONTACT +
+    USER DISTRIBUTION CODE %===>_DISTRIB +
+    INVOICE CONTROL DATE   %===>_INVDATE +    ('MM/DD/YY')
+
+
)INIT
    .HELP  = WH012
    IF (&T = A)
        &CONTACT = ' '
        &DISTRIB = ' '
        &INVDATE = ' '
)PROC
    VER (&CONTACT, NONBLANK, ALPHA)
    VER (&DISTRIB, NONBLANK, NUM)
    VER (&INVDATE, NONBLANK, PICT, '99/99/99', MSG=WDAR002C)
)END
```

Figure 11-3. CUPD COBOL function.

```
        IDENTIFICATION DIVISION.                                            00010000
        PROGRAM-ID. CUPD.                                                   00020000
******************************************************************************00030000
*    NAME: CUPD                                           BY: H. FOSDICK   *00040000
*                                                                          *00050000
*    PURPOSE: THIS ROUTINE ILLUSTRATES ISPF TABLE SERVICES IN             *00060000
*    ALLOWING THE USER TO ADD, UPDATE OR DELETE A ROW OF COST             *00070000
*    CENTER DATA IN THE ACCOUNTING CONTROL DATA TABLE.   IF THE           *00080000
*    TABLE OF ACCOUNTING CONTROL DATA DOES NOT EXIST, THIS ROUTINE        *00090000
*    CREATES IT.                                                          *00100000
*                                                                          *00110000
******************************************************************************00120000
        ENVIRONMENT DIVISION.                                               00130000
        DATA DIVISION.                                                      00140000
                                                                            00150000
                                                                            00160000
        WORKING-STORAGE SECTION.                                            00170000
                                                                            00180000
                                                                            00190000
                                                                            00200000
*    SERVICE CALL TYPES:                                                    00210000
                                                                            00220000
        01  DISPLAY-PANEL      PIC X(8)      VALUE 'DISPLAY '.              00230000
        01  TBCREATE           PIC X(8)      VALUE 'TBCREATE'.              00240000
        01  TBOPEN             PIC X(8)      VALUE 'TBOPEN  '.              00250000
        01  TBGET              PIC X(8)      VALUE 'TBGET   '.              00260000
        01  TBADD              PIC X(8)      VALUE 'TBADD   '.              00270000
        01  TBPUT              PIC X(8)      VALUE 'TBPUT   '.              00280000
        01  TBDELETE           PIC X(8)      VALUE 'TBDELETE'.              00290000
        01  TBCLOSE            PIC X(8)      VALUE 'TBCLOSE '.              00300000
        01  VDEFINE            PIC X(8)      VALUE 'VDEFINE '.              00310000
        01  VDELETE            PIC X(8)      VALUE 'VDELETE '.              00320000
        01  SETMSG             PIC X(8)      VALUE 'SETMSG  '.              00330000
                                                                            00340000
                                                                            00350000
*    NAME OF THE TABLE TO WORK WITH:                                        00360000
                                                                            00370000
        01  TABLE-NAME         PIC X(8)      VALUE 'CONTDATA'.              00380000
                                                                            00390000
                                                                            00400000
*    NAMES OF THE DATA ENTRY/DISPLAY PANELS:                                00410000
                                                                            00420000
        01  PANEL-NAME-7       PIC X(8)      VALUE 'WPAN7   '.              00430000
        01  PANEL-NAME-8       PIC X(8)      VALUE 'WPAN8   '.              00440000
                                                                            00450000
                                                                            00460000
*    OPTION FOR OPENING ISPF TABLE WITH UPDATE INTENT:                      00470000
                                                                            00480000
        01  WWRITE             PIC X(8)      VALUE 'WRITE   '.              00490000
                                                                            00500000
                                                                            00510000
*    DATA TYPE PARAMETER FOR ALL 'VDEFINE' CALLS:                           00520000
                                                                            00530000
        01  CHAR               PIC X(8)      VALUE 'CHAR    '.              00540000
                                                                            00550000
                                                                            00560000
*    MESSAGES:                                                              00570000
                                                                            00580000
        01  MSG                        PIC X(8)      VALUE SPACES.         00590000
        01  PROCESSING-TERMINATED-MSG  PIC X(8)      VALUE 'WDAR000A'.     00600000
        01  ENTER-CENTER-CODES-MSG     PIC X(8)      VALUE 'WDAR005B'.     00610000
        01  NO-SUCH-COST-CENTER-MSG    PIC X(8)      VALUE 'WDAR005G'.     00620000
        01  INVALID-ADD-ATTEMPT-MSG    PIC X(8)      VALUE 'WDAR005H'.     00630000
        01  PRESS-ENTER-MSG            PIC X(8)      VALUE 'WDAR005C'.     00640000
        01  DATA-ADDED-MSG             PIC X(8)      VALUE 'WDAR005D'.     00650000
        01  DATA-UPDATED-MSG           PIC X(8)      VALUE 'WDAR005E'.     00660000
        01  DATA-DELETED-MSG           PIC X(8)      VALUE 'WDAR005F'.     00670000
                                                                            00680000
                                                                            00690000
*    LIST OF TABLE KEY FIELDS AND NAME FIELDS FOR CREATION OF TABLE:00700000
                                                                            00710000
        01  KEY-LIST     PIC X(15)   VALUE '(COSCTR SUBCTR)'.              00720000
        01  NAME-LIST    PIC X(25)   VALUE '(CONTACT DISTRIB INVDATE)'.    00730000
                                                                            00740000
                                                                            00750000
*    LOOP CONTROL VARIABLES FOR INDICATING END OF TRANSACTIONS              00760000
                                                                            00770000
        01  CONTINU            PIC X(3)      VALUE 'YES'.                  00780000
        01  STOP-FLAG          PIC X(3)      VALUE 'NO '.                  00790000
                                                                            00800000
                                                                            00810000
*    DEFINE STORAGE SPACE FOR DIALOG VARIABLES:                            00820000
                                                                            00830000
        01  COSCTR             PIC X(4)      VALUE SPACES.                 00840000
        01  SUBCTR             PIC X(4)      VALUE SPACES.                 00850000
        01  TRANS-TYPE         PIC X(1)      VALUE SPACES.                 00860000
        01  CONTACT            PIC X(8)      VALUE SPACES.                 00870000
        01  DISTRIB            PIC X(8)      VALUE SPACES.                 00880000
        01  INVDATE            PIC X(8)      VALUE SPACES.                 00890000
```

```
                                                                    00900000
                                                                    00910000
*   DEFINE THE LENGTH OF EACH DIALOG VARIABLE:                      00920000
                                                                    00930000
01   COSCTR-LENGTH        PIC 9(6)      VALUE    4   COMP.          00940000
01   SUBCTR-LENGTH        PIC 9(6)      VALUE    4   COMP.          00950000
01   TRANS-TYPE-LENGTH    PIC 9(6)      VALUE    1   COMP.          00960000
01   CONTACT-LENGTH       PIC 9(6)      VALUE    8   COMP.          00970000
01   DISTRIB-LENGTH       PIC 9(6)      VALUE    8   COMP.          00980000
01   INVDATE-LENGTH       PIC 9(6)      VALUE    8   COMP.          00990000
                                                                    01000000
                                                                    01010000
*   DEFINE DIALOG VARIABLE NAMES FOR ISPF DIALOG MANAGER:           01020000
                                                                    01030000
01   COSCTR-NAME          PIC X(8)      VALUE   '(COSCTR)'.         01040000
01   SUBCTR-NAME          PIC X(8)      VALUE   '(SUBCTR)'.         01050000
01   CONTACT-NAME         PIC X(9)      VALUE   '(CONTACT)'.        01060000
01   DISTRIB-NAME         PIC X(9)      VALUE   '(DISTRIB)'.        01070000
01   INVDATE-NAME         PIC X(9)      VALUE   '(INVDATE)'.        01080000
01   TRANS-TYPE-NAME      PIC X(3)      VALUE   '(T)'.              01090000
                                                                    01100000
                                                                    01110000
                                                                    01120000
PROCEDURE DIVISION.                                                 01130000
                                                                    01140000
                                                                    01150000
*                                                                   01160000
*   DEFINE ALL DIALOG FUNCTION VARIABLES TO ISPF DIALOG MANAGER:    01170000
*                                                                   01180000
                                                                    01190000
    PERFORM DEFINE-VARIABLES THRU DEFINE-VARIABLES-EXIT.            01200000
                                                                    01210000
                                                                    01220000
*                                                                   01230000
*   OPEN THE ISPF TABLE CONTAINING ACCOUNTING CONTROL DATA:         01240000
*                                                                   01250000
                                                                    01260000
    CALL 'ISPLINK' USING  TBOPEN                                    01270000
                          TABLE-NAME                                01280000
                          WWRITE.                                   01290000
                                                                    01300000
*                                                                   01310000
                                                                    01320000
*   IF THE TABLE DOESNOT EXIST, CREATE IT:                          01330000
*                                                                   01340000
                                                                    01350000
    IF RETURN-CODE NOT = 0                                          01360000
                                                                    01370000
        CALL 'ISPLINK'  USING   TBCREATE                            01380000
                                TABLE-NAME                          01390000
                                KEY-LIST                            01400000
                                NAME-LIST.                          01410000
                                                                    01420000
                                                                    01430000
*                                                                   01440000
*   DISPLAY DATA ENTRY PANEL FOR UPDATES UNTIL USER HITS 'END' KEY: 01450000
*                                                                   01460000
                                                                    01470000
    MOVE ENTER-CENTER-CODES-MSG TO MSG.                             01480000
                                                                    01490000
    MOVE 'YES' TO CONTINU.                                          01500000
                                                                    01510000
                                                                    01520000
    PERFORM UPDATE-WORK THRU UPDATE-WORK-EXIT UNTIL                 01530000
        CONTINU = 'NO '.                                            01540000
                                                                    01550000
                                                                    01560000
*                                                                   01570000
*   CLOSE THE TABLE AND UPDATE ANY ALTERED DATA ON DISK:            01580000
*                                                                   01590000
                                                                    01600000
                                                                    01610000
    CALL 'ISPLINK'  USING  TBCLOSE                                  01620000
                           TABLE-NAME.                              01630000
                                                                    01640000
                                                                    01650000
*                                                                   01660000
*   DELETE ALL DIALOG FUNCTION VARIABLES RE ISPF DIALOG MANAGER:    01670000
*                                                                   01680000
                                                                    01690000
    PERFORM DELETE-VARIABLES THRU DELETE-VARIABLES-EXIT.            01700000
                                                                    01710000
                                                                    01720000
                                                                    01730000
    MOVE 0 TO RETURN-CODE.                                          01740000
    GOBACK.                                                         01750000
                                                                    01760000
```

(continued)

Figure 11-3. (*Continued*)

```
    MAIN-LINE-EXIT.                                             01770000
                                                                01780000
                                                                01790000
                                                                01800000
                                                                01810000
    UPDATE-WORK.                                                01820000
                                                                01830000
*                                                               01840000
*   DISPLAY DATA ENTRY PANEL FOR USER TO ENTER THE KEYS OF THE  01850000
*   DESIRED TABLE ROW:                                          01860000
*                                                               01870000
                                                                01880000
        CALL 'ISPLINK'  USING   DISPLAY-PANEL                   01890000
                                PANEL-NAME-7                    01900000
                                MSG.                            01910000
                                                                01920000
*                                                               01930000
*   PREPARE TO EXIT IF USER PRESSES 'END' KEY:                  01940000
*                                                               01950000
                                                                01960000
        IF RETURN-CODE NOT = 0                                  01970000
                                                                01980000
            MOVE 'NO ' TO CONTINU                               01990000
                                                                02000000
            CALL 'ISPLINK'  USING  SETMSG                       02010000
                                PROCESSING-TERMINATED-MSG       02020000
                                                                02030000
        ELSE                                                    02040000
                                                                02050000
*                                                               02060000
*   SEND MESSAGE TO USER ON INVALID ADD, UPDATE OR DELETE ATTEMPT: 02070000
*                                                               02080000
                                                                02090000
            MOVE 'NO ' TO STOP-FLAG                             02100000
                                                                02110000
            PERFORM INVALID-TRANSACTION-CHECK THRU              02120000
                INVALID-TRANSACTION-CHECK-EXIT                  02130000
                                                                02140000
*                                                               02150000
*   PROCESS A VALID UPDATE ATTEMPT:                             02160000
*                                                               02170000
                                                                02180000
            IF  STOP-FLAG  = 'NO '                              02190000
                                                                02200000
                                                                02210000
*                                                               02220000
*   DISPLAY THE DATA ADD, UPDATE, OR DELETE PANEL:              02230000
*                                                               02240000
                                                                02250000
                                                                02260000
                CALL 'ISPLINK'  USING  DISPLAY-PANEL            02270000
                                PANEL-NAME-8                    02280000
                                PRESS-ENTER-MSG                 02290000
                                                                02300000
                                                                02310000
*                                                               02320000
*   IF THE 'END' KEY WAS PRESSED, SET UP EXIT MESSAGE:          02330000
*                                                               02340000
                                                                02350000
                IF RETURN-CODE = 8                              02360000
                                                                02370000
                    CALL 'ISPLINK'  USING SETMSG                02380000
                                PROCESSING-TERMINATED-MSG       02390000
                                                                02400000
                                                                02410000
*                                                               02420000
*   IF THE 'END' KEY WAS NOT PRESSED, PERFORM THE ACTUAL TABLE  02430000
*   UPDATE AND SEND THE USER AN APPROPRIATE MESSAGE:            02440000
*                                                               02450000
                                                                02460000
                ELSE                                            02470000
                                                                02480000
                    PERFORM ACTUAL-TABLE-UPDATE THRU            02490000
                        ACTUAL-TABLE-UPDATE-EXIT.               02500000
                                                                02510000
                                                                02520000
    UPDATE-WORK-EXIT.                                           02530000
        EXIT.                                                   02540000
                                                                02550000
                                                                02560000
                                                                02570000
                                                                02580000
                                                                02590000
    INVALID-TRANSACTION-CHECK.                                  02600000
                                                                02610000
                                                                02620000
*                                                               02630000
*   THIS CODE DETECTS IF THE USER IS ATTEMPTING TO ADD A DUPLICATE 02640000
```

```
*   RECORD, OR UPDATE OR DELETE A NON-EXISTING RECORD.   IF SO, IT      02650000
*   SETS UP AN APPROPRIATE ERROR MESSAGE AND FLIPS 'STOP-FLAG' ON       02660000
*                                                                       02670000
                                                                        02680000
                                                                        02690000
        CALL 'ISPLINK'  USING  TBGET                                    02700000
                               TABLE-NAME.                              02710000
                                                                        02720000
        IF RETURN-CODE  =  8                                            02730000
                                                                        02740000
            IF  (TRANS-TYPE = 'U' OR TRANS-TYPE = 'D')                  02750000
                                                                        02760000
                MOVE NO-SUCH-COST-CENTER-MSG TO MSG                     02770000
                MOVE 'YES' TO STOP-FLAG                                 02780000
                                                                        02790000
            ELSE                                                        02800000
                                                                        02810000
                NEXT SENTENCE                                           02820000
                                                                        02830000
        ELSE                                                            02840000
                                                                        02850000
            IF  (TRANS-TYPE = 'A')                                      02860000
                                                                        02870000
                MOVE INVALID-ADD-ATTEMPT-MSG TO MSG                     02880000
                MOVE 'YES' TO STOP-FLAG.                                02890000
                                                                        02900000
                                                                        02910000
INVALID-TRANSACTION-CHECK-EXIT.                                         02920000
    EXIT.                                                               02930000
                                                                        02940000
                                                                        02950000
                                                                        02960000
                                                                        02970000
                                                                        02980000
ACTUAL-TABLE-UPDATE.                                                    02990000
                                                                        03000000
                                                                        03010000
*                                                                       03020000
*   THIS PARAGRAPH PERFORMS THE ACTUAL UPDATE OF THE ACCOUNTING         03030000
*   CONTROL DATA TABLE.  IT ADDS, UPDATES OR DELETES A ROW:             03040000
*                                                                       03050000
                                                                        03060000
                                                                        03070000
        IF TRANS-TYPE = 'A'                                             03080000
                                                                        03090000
                                                                        03100000
            CALL 'ISPLINK'  USING  TBADD                                03110000
                                   TABLE-NAME                           03120000
                                                                        03130000
            CALL 'ISPLINK'  USING  SETMSG                               03140000
                                   DATA-ADDED-MSG                       03150000
                                                                        03160000
        ELSE                                                            03170000
                                                                        03180000
            IF TRANS-TYPE = 'U'                                         03190000
                                                                        03200000
                                                                        03210000
                CALL 'ISPLINK'  USING  TBPUT                            03220000
                                       TABLE-NAME                       03230000
                                                                        03240000
                CALL 'ISPLINK'  USING  SETMSG                           03250000
                                       DATA-UPDATED-MSG                 03260000
                                                                        03270000
            ELSE                                                        03280000
                                                                        03290000
                CALL 'ISPLINK'  USING  TBDELETE                         03300000
                                       TABLE-NAME                       03310000
                                                                        03320000
                CALL 'ISPLINK'  USING  SETMSG                           03330000
                                       DATA-DELETED-MSG.                03340000
                                                                        03350000
                                                                        03360000
ACTUAL-TABLE-UPDATE-EXIT.                                               03370000
    EXIT.                                                               03380000
                                                                        03390000
                                                                        03400000
                                                                        03410000
                                                                        03420000
                                                                        03430000
DEFINE-VARIABLES.                                                       03440000
                                                                        03450000
                                                                        03460000
                                                                        03470000
*                                                                       03480000
*   DEFINE ALL DIALOG FUNCTION VARIABLES TO ISPF DIALOG MANAGER:        03490000
*                                                                       03500000
```

(continued)

Figure 11-3. (*Continued*)

```
          CALL 'ISPLINK'  USING  VDEFINE                              03510000
                                 COSCTR-NAME                          03520000
                                 COSCTR                               03530000
                                 CHAR                                 03540000
                                 COSCTR-LENGTH.                       03550000
          CALL 'ISPLINK'  USING  VDEFINE                              03560000
                                 SUBCTR-NAME                          03570000
                                 SUBCTR                               03580000
                                 CHAR                                 03590000
                                 SUBCTR-LENGTH.                       03600000
          CALL 'ISPLINK'  USING  VDEFINE                              03610000
                                 TRANS-TYPE-NAME                      03620000
                                 TRANS-TYPE                           03630000
                                 CHAR                                 03640000
                                 TRANS-TYPE-LENGTH.                   03650000
          CALL 'ISPLINK'  USING  VDEFINE                              03660000
                                 CONTACT-NAME                         03670000
                                 CONTACT                              03680000
                                 CHAR                                 03690000
                                 CONTACT-LENGTH.                      03700000
          CALL 'ISPLINK'  USING  VDEFINE                              03710000
                                 DISTRIB-NAME                         03720000
                                 DISTRIB                              03730000
                                 CHAR                                 03740000
                                 DISTRIB-LENGTH.                      03750000
          CALL 'ISPLINK'  USING  VDEFINE                              03760000
                                 INVDATE-NAME                         03770000
                                 INVDATE                              03780000
                                 CHAR                                 03790000
                                 INVDATE-LENGTH.                      03800000
                                                                      03810000
      DEFINE-VARIABLES-EXIT.                                          03820000
          EXIT.                                                       03830000
                                                                      03840000
                                                                      03850000
                                                                      03860000
                                                                      03870000
                                                                      03880000
      DELETE-VARIABLES.                                               03890000
                                                                      03900000
                                                                      03910000
      *                                                               03920000
      **                                                              03930000
      **  DELETE ALL DIALOG FUNCTION VARIABLES RE ISPF DIALOG MANAGER: 03930000
      **                                                              03940000
                                                                      03950000
          CALL 'ISPLINK'  USING  VDELETE                              03960000
                                 COSCTR-NAME.                         03970000
          CALL 'ISPLINK'  USING  VDELETE                              03980000
                                 SUBCTR-NAME.                         03990000
          CALL 'ISPLINK'  USING  VDELETE                              04000000
                                 CONTACT-NAME.                        04010000
          CALL 'ISPLINK'  USING  VDELETE                              04020000
                                 DISTRIB-NAME.                        04030000
          CALL 'ISPLINK'  USING  VDELETE                              04040000
                                 INVDATE-NAME.                        04050000
          CALL 'ISPLINK'  USING  VDELETE                              04060000
                                 TRANS-TYPE-NAME.                     04070000
                                                                      04080000
      DELETE-VARIABLES-EXIT.                                          04090000
          EXIT.                                                       04100000
```

Figure 11-4. XUPD CLIST function.

```
00010000    PROC 0
00020000    CONTROL MSG NOFLUSH
00030000    /*****************************************************************/
00040000    /* NAME: XUPD                              BY: H. FOSDICK       */
00050000    /*                                                              */
00060000    /* PURPOSE: THIS CLIST ILLUSTRATES ISPF TABLE SERVICES IN       */
00070000    /* ALLOWING THE USER TO ADD, UPDATE OR DELETE A ROW OF          */
00080000    /* COST CENTER DATA IN THE ACCOUNTING CONTROL DATA TABLE.       */
00090000    /* IF THE TABLE OF ACCOUNTING CONTROL DATA DOES NOT EXIST,      */
00100000    /* THIS ROUTINE CREATES IT.                                     */
00110000    /*                                                              */
00120000    /*****************************************************************/
00130000
00140000    ISPEXEC  CONTROL  ERRORS  CANCEL
00150000
00160000    /*                                                              */
00170000    /*   OPEN THE ISPF TABLE CONTAINING ACCOUNTING CONTROL DATA:    */
00180000    /*                                                              */
00190000
00200000    ISPEXEC  TBOPEN  CONTDATA  WRITE
00210000
00220000
00230000    /*                                                              */
00240000    /*   IF TABLE DOESNOT EXIST, CREATE IT:                         */
00250000    /*                                                              */
00260000
00270000    IF &LASTCC ¬= 0 THEN +
00280000        ISPEXEC  TBCREATE  CONTDATA  KEYS  (COSCTR SUBCTR) +
00290000                                    NAMES (CONTACT DISTRIB INVDATE)
00300000
00310000
00320000    /*                                                              */
00330000    /* DISPLAY DATA ENTRY PANEL UNTIL USER PRESSES 'END' KEY:       */
00340000    /*                                                              */
00350000
00360000    SET MSG = WDAR005B
00370000    SET CONTINU = YES
00380000
00390000
00400000    DO WHILE &CONTINU = YES
00410000
00420000        /*                                                          */
00430000        /*   DISPLAY DATA ENTRY PANEL FOR USER TO ENTER THE KEYS */
00440000        /*   OF THE DESIRED TABLE ROW:                              */
00450000        /*                                                          */
00460000
00470000        ISPEXEC  DISPLAY  PANEL(WPAN7)  MSG(&MSG)
00480000
00490000
00500000        /*                                                          */
00510000        /*   PREPARE TO EXIT IF THE USER PRESSES THE 'END' KEY:     */
00520000        /*                                                          */
00530000
00540000        IF &LASTCC ¬= 0 THEN DO
00550000
00560000            SET CONTINU = NO
00570000            ISPEXEC  SETMSG  MSG(WDAR000A)
00580000
00590000            END
00600000
00610000
00620000        ELSE DO
00630000
00640000            /*                                                      */
00650000            /* SEND MESSAGE TO USER ON INVALID ADD, UPDATE OR       */
00660000            /* DELETE ATTEMPT:                                      */
00670000            /*                                                      */
00680000
00690000            SET STOP = NO
00700000
00710000            ISPEXEC  TBGET  CONTDATA
00720000
00730000            IF &LASTCC = 8 THEN DO
00740000
00750000                IF &T = U OR &T = D THEN DO
00760000
00770000                    SET MSG = WDAR005G
00780000                    SET STOP = YES
00790000                    END
00800000
00810000                END
00820000
00830000            ELSE DO
00840000
00850000                IF &T = A THEN DO
00860000
```

(continued)

Figure 11-4. *(Continued)*

```
00870000                     SET MSG = WDAR005H
00880000                     SET STOP = YES
00890000                     END
00900000          END
00910000
00920000
00930000          /*                                                    */
00940000          /* PROCESS A VALID UPDATE ATTEMPT:                     */
00950000          /*                                                    */
00960000
00970000          IF &STOP = NO THEN DO
00980000
00990000
01000000              /*                                                */
01010000              /* DISPLAY THE DATA ADD, UPDATE, OR DELETE PANEL:  */
01020000              /*                                                */
01030000
01040000              ISPEXEC  DISPLAY  PANEL(WPAN8)  MSG(WDAR005C)
01050000
01060000
01070000              /*                                                */
01080000              /* IF THE 'END' KEY WAS PRESSED, SET UP EXIT MSG:  */
01090000              /*                                                */
01100000
01110000              IF &LASTCC = 8 THEN +
01120000                  ISPEXEC  SETMSG  MSG(WDAR000A)
01130000
01140000
01150000              /*                                                */
01160000              /* IF THE 'END' KEY WAS NOT PRESSED:               */
01170000              /*                                                */
01180000
01190000              ELSE DO
01200000
01210000                  /*                                            */
01220000                  /*  PROCESS AN 'ADD':                         */
01230000                  /*                                            */
01240000
01250000                  IF &T = A  THEN DO
01260000                      ISPEXEC  TBADD   CONTDATA
01270000                      ISPEXEC  SETMSG  MSG(WDAR005D)
01280000
01290000                      END
01300000
01310000                  ELSE DO
01320000
01330000
01340000                      /*                                        */
01350000                      /*  PROCESS AN 'UPDATE':                   */
01360001                      /*                                        */
01370000
01380000                      IF &T = U  THEN DO
01390000
01400000                          ISPEXEC  TBPUT   CONTDATA
01410000                          ISPEXEC  SETMSG  MSG(WDAR005E)
01420000
01430000                          END
01440000
01450000
01460000                      /*                                        */
01470000                      /*  PROCESS A 'DELETE':                    */
01480000                      /*                                        */
01490000
01500000                      ELSE DO
01510000
01520000                          ISPEXEC  TBDELETE  CONTDATA
01530000                          ISPEXEC  SETMSG  MSG(WDAR005F)
01540000
01550000                          END
01560000
01570000                          END
01580000                      END
01590000                  END
01600000              END
01610000          END
01620000      END
01630000
01640000
01650000      /*                                                        */
01660000      /* CLOSE THE TABLE AND UPDATE ANY ALTERED DATA ON DISK:    */
01670000      /*                                                        */
01680000
01690000      ISPEXEC  TBCLOSE  CONTDATA
01700000
01710000
01720000      EXIT CODE(0)
```

12

Additional Features

During 1984 and 1985, a new version of the ISPF Dialog Manager became available. Called *Version 2*, this program product adds 25 new dialog services and enhances 14 of the existing ones. This chapter describes the more important of these extensions to the Dialog Manager, as well as reviewing some features of the older Version 1 product not covered previously. Remember that this book is introductory; it does not provide exhaustive coverage of Dialog Manager features. See the vendor's reference manuals listed in appendix B for information concerning advanced ISPF services.

ENHANCED TERMINAL SUPPORT

The new version of the Dialog Manager permits dialog functions to specify color and extended highlighting attributes for terminals having those features. Thus dialog functions can take full advantage of the capabilities of 3279 terminals, for example.

Version 2 supports the Graphical Data Display Manager (GDDM) for format and display of screens. New Dialog Manager services **GRINIT**, **GRTERM**, and **GRERROR** permit functions to display graphics via panel definitions.

Version 2 introduces dynamic panel definitions. This feature allows dialog developers to declare all or part of a panel definition as dynamically generated. Dialog functions dynamically fill in this portion of the panel definition with data they deem appropriate.

Finally, the new ISPF extends support to the new 3290 series of terminals. This includes the ability to split the terminal screen vertically as well as horizontally. As with the horizontal split-screen feature, the vertical split-screen facility occurs in a manner transparent to user-developed functions.

TABLE SERVICES

The sample dialog of the previous chapters illustrated the following Dialog Manager table services:

TBADD	Add a row to a table
TBCLOSE	Close and save a table
TBCREATE	Create a new table and open it for processing
TBDELETE	Delete a row from a table
TBDISPL	Display all or selected rows of a table
TBEND	Close a table without saving
TBGET	Retrieve a row from a table
TBOPEN	Open a permanent table for processing
TBPUT	Update a row within a table
TBSARG	Establish a search argument
TBSCAN	Search a table for a specified row
TBTOP	Set the current row pointer ahead of the first table row
TBVCLEAR	Set dialog variables that correspond to table columns to nulls

In addition, the Dialog Manager provides several services for table handling that were not illustrated in the sample dialog. These Version 1 services and their uses are listed below:

TBBOTTOM	Set the row pointer to the last row of the table and retrieve that row
TBERASE	Delete a table from the table output library
TBEXIST	Check for the existence of a keyed row within a table
TBMOD	Update a row in a table
TBQUERY	Retrieve information about a table
TBSAVE	Save a table
TBSKIP	Manipulate the current row pointer forward or backward n rows then retrieve the row to which it points

Version 2 of the Dialog Manager enhances several of the above services. For example, the new **NOREAD** parameter available with the **TBBOTTOM, TBGET, TBSCAN,** and **TBSKIP** services allows functions to position the current row pointer to the specified row without altering dialog variables in the function pool. The new **POSITION** parameter available on these same services returns the current row pointer to the function.

Two new table services have been added with Version 2. The **TBSORT** service permits functions to sort the rows of a table. The new **ORDER** parameter available on the **TBADD, TBMOD,** and **TBPUT** services maintains the sorted table in order.

The second new Version 2 table service is **TBSTATS**. It retains status information on the contents and usage of tables.

You may wish to examine the vendor's reference manual *Interactive System Productivity Facility: Version 2, What's New in ISPF?* for a detailed listing of new and enhanced table services.

LIBRARY ACCESS SERVICES

Version 2 of the Dialog Manager introduces a major new class of services, *Library Access Services*. This group of 16 commands offers a comprehensive facility to manipulate members within ISPF libraries. The services provide this feature in a manner that is largely independent of the operating system under which the dialog is developed. However, since data set naming conventions are a significant aspect of system dependency, there are some differences in these commands between operating environments.

The following library access services provide for record-oriented processing of library members:

LMCLOSE	Close a data set
LMGET	Read a record from the data set
LMOPEN	Open a data set for processing
LMPUT	Write a record to a data set

The following new services permit higher-level member manipulation for controlled libraries:

LMERASE	Erase a ISPF library or data set
LMFREE	Release the data set of a specified data set ID.
LMINIT	Establish a relationship between one or more ISPF libraries or a data set and a *data set ID*— other library access services then refer to these files by the data set ID.
LMMADD	Add a member to an ISPF library
LMMDEL	Delete a member from an ISPF library
LMMFIND	Find a member of an ISPF library and optionally lock the member
LMMLIST	Create a member list for an ISPF library
LMMREN	Rename a member of an ISPF library
LMMREP	Replace a member of an ISPF library
LMPROM	Promote a member or data set to a controlled ISPF library
LMQUERY	Retrieve information concerning a data set with a specified data set ID.
LMRENAME	Rename an ISPF library.

Functions written in compiled programming languages access the library services like they do other ISPF services: through calls to the **ISPLINK** (or **ISPLNK**) interface routine. This is significant because it extends library management facilities to programmers who work with compiled programming languages. Previously programmers could only conveniently encode certain of these functions in command procedures.

Version 2 ISPF services for library access are further described in the manual *ISPF/Program Development Facility Services*. The next two chapters include several example programs that demonstrate the library management commands.

SUPPORT FOR RELATIONAL DATABASE MANAGEMENT SYSTEMS

Version 2 of the Dialog Manager supports the relational database management systems (DBMS) introduced by IBM during the 1980s. In the MVS/TSO environment, the relational DBMS is called Database 2 and is most often known by its acronym, **DB2**. In the VM and VSE environments, the relational DBMS product is called Structured Query Language/Data System (SQL/DS).

From the standpoint of the applications programmer, DB2 and SQL/DS may be considered as essentially the same product adapted to their respective operating systems. Both products support the Structured Query Language (SQL) as their code-oriented interface to the relational database manager. SQL may be used to write either stand-alone queries and updates against the databases or as a language to embed in programs written in high-level procedural languages such as COBOL or PL/I.

ISPF Dialog Manager support for DB2 and SQL/DS means that compiled programs that make calls to the ISPF Dialog Manager may also make calls to DB2 and SQL/DS. Thus COBOL and PL/I programs can use the Dialog Manager for screen management and DB2 or SQL/DS for data management. The full capabilities of both the Dialog Manager and relational data management products are available to programmers within their programs. Of course, use of the ISPF Dialog Manager is exactly as shown in this book; no special program changes are required to use the Dialog Manager in conjunction with these database products.

Chapter 15 provides an example COBOL program that uses both the ISPF Dialog Manager and DB2. The purpose of this program is to show how a program dialog function can make use of the Dialog Manager services and also the capabilities of database management systems like DB2. Because this book cannot cover the extensive topic of programming with Database 2, it is assumed you have some familiarity in coding with that product. Further information on the DB2 and SQL/DS database management systems may be found through the bibliography of reference manuals in appendix B.

SUPPORT FOR ADDITIONAL LANGUAGES AND SYSTEMS

Version 2 of the Dialog Manager supports several additional programming languages. Under MVS and VM these include VS FORTRAN,

Pascal, and APL2. VM also extends support to the REXX interpretive command language.

A version of the ISPF Dialog Manager and ISPF/PDF was introduced in 1985 for the SSX/VSE (Small Systems Executive/Virtual Storage Extended) operating system, a form of the VSE operating system run on entry-level mainframes. Thus, the ISPF Dialog Manager now supports both the SSX and DOS versions of the VSE operating system.

IMPLICATIONS OF ISPF DIALOG MANAGER ENHANCEMENTS

The introduction of Dialog Manager improvements to support IBM's relational database management systems, new programming languages, and new operating systems confirm ISPF's strategic role in the marketplace. The vendor continues to improve the product, broaden its relationships to other software products, and render it available under all its mainframe operating systems.

13

Library Access Services

The previous chapter briefly described the Dialog Manager services for manipulation of data sets that are members of libraries or are sequential data sets. These library access services are newly offered in Version 2 of the ISPF Dialog Manager; you must have this version of the product or a later one in order to use them.

This chapter describes the functions and use of these library management services in detail. It and the next chapter provide three sample programs to illustrate use of the services. As before, these three programs are implemented in both the COBOL and CLIST languages.

These programs are not part of the West Department Accounts Receivable system that has served as the example previously in this book. Instead, these three programs provide utility functions for programmers through the use of library access services.

All three programs were written for the MVS operating system. As will become evident during the discussion, there are some operating-system dependencies involved in the ISPF library management services because file naming conventions and file organizations are defined differently by the MVS, VM, and VSE operating systems. *Subsequent discussion of library access services in this chapter assumes the use of the MVS operating system in order to simplify explanation.* Use of the library access services under the VM and VSE operating systems is highly similar other than differences in file naming conventions and file organization.

SCOPE OF LIBRARY ACCESS SERVICES

Under the MVS operating system, the library access services provide capabilities to manipulate three kinds of data sets:

ISPF-controlled libraries and their members
MVS Partitioned Data Sets (PDS) and their members
Standard sequential files

ISPF-controlled libraries refer to MVS cataloged partitioned data sets with three-level names in this form:

'project-name.group-name.type'

where **project-name** is the common name for all libraries in the same project, **group-name** identifies a particular set of libraries, and **type** indicates the nature of the information kept in the individual members within the library. For example, **type** might denote that all the members in the library contain COBOL programs.

A specific member within an ISPF-controlled library is referred to in the same manner as a member within a MVS partitioned data set:

'project-name.group-name.type(member)'

ISPF's facilities for controlled libraries allow installations to manage their many files as members of a hierarchy of partitioned data sets. For example, a COBOL program that is only in the design or testing phase might be included in an ISPF-controlled source code test library. After it has been thoroughly tested, that program might be moved into a source code production library at a higher level within the ISPF-controlled library hierarchy.

ISPF/PDF provides its *Library Management Facility* to enforce appropriate administration of these controlled libraries. The library access services illustrated in this chapter provide programmers capabilities to administer ISPF-controlled libraries through their programs via invocation of Dialog Manager services. These Dialog Manager services for ISPF-controlled libraries also operate on MVS partitioned data sets (PDSs). These partitioned data sets must have three-level names of the form described already for ISPF-controlled libraries. The Dialog Manager's library access services additionally can be used to manipulate standard MVS sequential files.

The Dialog Manager's library access services do not operate on any other kinds of data sets. For example, VSAM files and various forms of database organization (DL/1, IMS, DB2, and SQL/DS) are not supported by ISPF's library access services.

PROGRAM EXAMPLES

Three MVS program examples illustrate library access services in this chapter and the next. The first program provides a simple **OSCOPY** utility: it copies an existing MVS sequential file into a newly created MVS sequential file. After the file has been copied, this program deletes the original file. Thus the original sequential file is effectively moved to a new sequential file.

This first program illustrates the basic library access services that initialize and open files for use (**LMINIT** and **LMOPEN**), read records from an input data set and write them to an output data set (**LMGET** and **LMPUT**), close and free files after use (**LMCLOSE** and **LMFREE**), and delete files with three-level names (**LMERASE**).

The second program example provides a utility analogous to that of the first program except that it operates on members within partitioned data sets. In other words, it copies a member from one partitioned data set to another. As in the first program, the data set to copy is assumed to exist. The target member, however, may either exist or be newly created in this second program.

The second program example illustrates many of the same library access services as the first. These services, however, are applied to partitioned data sets. Additionally the second example shows how to use the **LMMFIND** service to locate a member within a PDS, and the **LMMREP** function, to replace (or add) the copied member to the target PDS.

The third program example is named **PDSLISTC**. It uses library access services to retrieve the names of all members of a specified partitioned data set in alphabetical order. It also retrieves some the system-maintained statistics for each member. These statistics include the TSO userid of the last person to update (or create) the library member, the last modification date for the member, and the current number of records in the member. The program writes a record for each member and its statistics to a newly created MVS sequential file. After a record has been written for each member of the PDS, the program allows the terminal user to inspect the member list.

This program demonstrates many of the same library access service routines illustrated by the first two utilities. Several new services are included as well. Among them are **LMMLIST**, which retrieves a member name and its statistics via the Dialog Manager; an invocation of **LMMLIST**, which frees the virtual storage acquired by the first call of **LMMLIST**; and a new format for the ISPF **BROWSE** service. (The **BROWSE** service was introduced in chapter 4.)

For clarity of illustration, all three of these utility programs were written with a minimalist philosophy; that is, in a production environment, these programs would be front-ended by Dialog Manager panels for data entry, validation, and display. Since previous chapters covered the techniques required for panel design and data input to programs, these utilities exclude that code in order to present the library access services more simply and clearly.

OSCOPYC: A COBOL UTILITY TO COPY AN MVS SEQUENTIAL FILE

This program example copies all records from an MVS sequential file to a newly created MVS sequential file. After the copy is completed, the program deletes the original data set. Figure 13-1 contains the source code for the COBOL version of this program. Program messages issued by this program (and the other utilities of this chapter) are contained in figure 13-2.

In the code of figure 13-1, this program first invokes the **VDEFINE** service with the program variables referenced in subsequent program calls to ISPF. Recall that the **VDEFINE** service renders variables within a compiled program accessible to the Dialog Manager.

Following definition of program variables to ISPF, this program uses the **LMINIT** service to initialize the input file for the copy operation. The **LMINIT** function performs an important service prerequisite to the use of all other library management services: it associates a data set specified in the program with a system-generated *dataid*. This unique dataid is used to refer to the file in all subsequent calls to the Dialog Manager.

Thus, the **LMINIT** service and the concept of the dataid together limit the operating system dependency of ISPF programs. Operating system dependent file references are restricted in the program to **LMINIT** calls. Subsequent invocations of library access services do not refer to operating-system dependent file names but to the dataids associated with files through the **LMINIT** calls.

The general format of the **LMINIT** service is:

```
CALL 'ISPLINK' USING LMINIT
                     data-var-id
                     project-name
                     group1-name
                     group2-name
                     group3-name
                     group4-name
                     type
                     dsname
                     ddname
                     serial
                     password
                     access-mode
                     org-var
```

The **LMINIT** service is used in the **OSCOPYC** program in two different ways. In the first invocation, the program associates a three-level file name with a dataid. This represents the program's input file. In the second invocation of **LMINIT**, the program associates its output file **DDNAME** with a dataid.

Here is the first call to **LMINIT**:

```
CALL 'ISPLINK' USING LMINIT
                     DSIDINA
                     B B B B B B
                     INPUT-SEQ-FILE-NAME
                     B B B
                     ENQ-SHR.
```

The parameter **DSIDINA** is a program variable that contains the name of the variable into which the Dialog Manager will place the dataid associated with the file. Notice that variable **DSIDINA** is not itself where ISPF places the dataid; it is, rather, a variable that contains the name of the variable (**DSIDIN**) where ISPF is to place the input file's dataid. The variable into which the dataid is returned should be defined as an alphanumeric field of eight characters:

01 DSIDIN   PIC X(8)   VALUE SPACES.

This is important because the dataid will not likely consist solely of digits. Declaring this storage as **PICTURE 9(8)** can cause errors.

The next nonblank call parameter is **INPUT-SEQ-FILE-NAME**. This program variable specifies the three-level qualified data set name that will be associated with the dataid returned by the call. A look at the WORKING STORAGE section of the program shows that the input file name is hard-coded as **'ZHMF01.INFILE.DATA'**.

The final parameter in this call, **ENQ-SHR**, specifies a disposition of **SHR** for this file. That is, this file is used only for input so its use can be concurrently shared with other programs that read it. Data sets can also be initialized with the options **EXCLU** (exclusive data set use) or **MOD** (for adding records at the end of an existing data set).

Many of the unused parameters of this **LMINIT** invocation allow for specification of a three-level qualified data set name through indicating the data set's **project-name, group-name**, and **type**. This is as explained already concerning file-naming conventions for ISPF-controlled libraries and MVS partitioned data sets. There are several **group-name**s in the call format because up to four libraries can be concatenated for one **LMINIT** reference. Although these parameters are not used in the particular call shown here, they still must be specified (as blank) because the parameters in this call are all positional. Omitted parameters are thus specified as blank fields in COBOL programs. Here is how the omitted parameters are defined in this program:

```
01 B        PIC X(8)        VALUE SPACES.
```

The last parameter in the formal service call format, **org-var**, can be omitted from this program call because it occurs after the last specified variable in the parameter list. If present, **org-var** provides the name of the variable into which ISPF returns the data set organization of the file. ISPF returns **PO** for partitioned data sets or **PS** for sequential data sets.

In summary, the **LMINIT** service invocation allows the program to retrieve a dataid with which the specified input data set name is thereafter associated. This dataid is used in subsequent ISPF service invocations in order to refer to the input file.

After a file is initialized for use through **LMINIT**, it is opened via the **LMOPEN** function. This call appears:

```
CALL 'ISPLINK' USING LMOPEN
               DSIDIN
               OPTION-INPUT
```

The second parameter specifies the dataid of the input file. The variable named **DSIDIN** is where this dataid is stored. This is unlike the **LMINIT** service, which instead specifies the *name of the variable* (through **DSIDINA**) that will hold the file's dataid. The variable **OPTION-INPUT** means that this file is opened for data **INPUT**. **OUTPUT** is the alternative specification.

In addition to these parameters, the **LMOPEN** function does offer optionally encoded parameters for the return of the file's logical record length (**LRECL**), its record format (**RECFM**), and its data set organization (**DSORG**). Thus, **LMOPEN** optionally returns data set information to the invoking program.

After the input sequential file is initialized and opened, these same services are executed for the output file. Recall that this output file will be a new MVS sequential data set. It is allocated for the use of this program before the program is executed.

Whereas the **LMINIT** call for the input file specified the data set name (**DSNAME**) for that file, in the case of the output file, the function's **LMINIT** call specifies a **DDNAME**. Looking at the program's storage area shows that the **DDNAME** referred to by this program is **NEWFILE**. Since **NEWFILE** is the **DDNAME** of a new file to be used by this program, this file must have been allocated prior to program execution. This is accomplished through the TSO **ALLOCATE** command in the online environment.

Thus an **LMINIT** call can refer to either a **DSNAME** or a **DDNAME** to initialize a file. In the case of the **DSNAME** parameter, the referenced data set must already exist. In the case of the **DDNAME** parameter, the referenced file must have been previously allocated for the program's use. In the instance of a new data set, this allocation must specify the data set's record format, organization, logical record length, and block size.

The **OSCOPYC** program, then, was called by a CLIST that allocated the **DDNAME NEWFILE** to a new data set. Here are the lines from this calling CLIST that allocated the new data set:

```
ATTR ATTR1 BLKSIZE(6080) LRECL(80) RECFM(F B) DSORG(PS)
ALLOCATE FILE(NEWFILE) DA('ZHMF01.NEWFILE.DATA') +
     NEW SPACE(3) TRACKS USING(ATTR1)
```

This calling CLIST did not allocate or reference the input data set for the COBOL program **OSCOPYC**. Instead the **OSCOPYC** program used the **DSNAME** form of the **LMINIT** call to directly specify the input data set name of **'ZHMF01.INFILE.DATA'**.

The third way a data set can be specified via **LMINIT** is through the parameters to name the **project-name**, **group-name**, and **type** of an ISPF-controlled library or MVS partitioned data set. Since this approach was not adopted in this program, these positional parameters have been indicated as omitted in the **LMINIT** calls through the blank variable named **B**.

After input and output files have been initialized and opened, the program performs the paragraph **COPY-PARAGRAPH**. This code copies the records from the input file to the output file. The first ISPF call in this paragraph invokes the **LMGET** service. **LMGET** retrieves a record from the input file:

```
CALL 'ISPLINK' USING LMGET
                DSIDIN
                MODE-INVAR
                DATALOCA
```

DATALENA
MAXLEN.

As in the **LMOPEN** service, the second parameter in the call supplies the dataid of the affected file. **MODE-INVAR** specifies **INVAR,** which means that the retrieved record will be moved into the data location variable in the program. The next parameter indicates the name of the variable into which the record will be placed. The last two variables denote the name of the variable into which **LMGET** stores the actual length of the record read and the maximum length of the record to read.

There are several points you must be aware of when using **LMGET.** First, the parameters concerned with the data location and data length provide the *variable names* of where the record and its length are to be placed. Do not become confused and place the names of those variables themselves in the **LMGET** call. The following is incorrect:

```
CALL 'ISPLINK' USING LMGET
               DSIDIN
               MODE-INVAR
               DATALOC
               DATALEN
               MAXLEN.
```

Second, the parameter for specifying the maximum length of the record to read should refer to a *nonzero positive numeric value.* In COBOL, **MAXLEN** can be declared as a signed binary data item:

```
01 MAXLEN        PIC S9(8)       VALUE +80 COMP.
```

The return code from the **LMGET** service tells whether a record was retrieved: **0** means a record was read, and **8** represents an end-of-file condition.

If a record was read, the program writes it to the output file through the use of the **LMPUT** function. This function's format is similar to that of the **LMGET** call:

```
CALL 'ISPLINK' USING LMPUT
               DSIDOUT
               MODE-INVAR
               DATALOCA
               MAXLEN
```

Notice the specification of a variable name in the data location parameter **(DATALOCA)** and the reference to a positive nonzero numeric value as the length of the logical record to write **(MAXLEN).** Like **LMGET, LMPUT** can only be issued on a file that has been both initialized (via **LMINIT**) and opened (via **LMOPEN**). Attempts to use **LMGET** or **LMPUT** on files that have not been both initialized and opened result in error return codes.

After the input file has been copied, the **OSCOPYC** program must close and free the two files. The **LMCLOSE** and **LMFREE** services accomplish these tasks. **LMCLOSE** and **LMFREE** are the inverses of **LMOPEN** and **LMINIT**, respectively. Thus a program that performs an **LMINIT** should later **LMFREE** that file; a program that performs an **LMOPEN** should later **LMCLOSE** that file.

Both **LMCLOSE** and **LMFREE** calls contain only two parameters: the service name and the dataid of the file to close or free. Both input and output files must be closed and freed.

The logic of this program is designed such that whenever an **LMINIT** or **LMOPEN** function succeeds, a flag is set to indicate the successful operation. These flags are later individually tested to see which files have been initialized and/or opened. This ensures that although other calls to the Dialog Manager may have failed, any initialized or opened file will be freed or closed.

Finally, if calls to ISPF have succeeded in the program, the program deletes the input file through the **LMERASE** service. This invocation lists the three level qualifiers in the name of the file to delete:

```
CALL 'ISPLINK' USING LMERASE
               HIGH-LEVEL
               NEXT-LEVEL
               LOW-LEVEL
```

Although the three level qualifiers specify an MVS sequential file, they could have as well referred to the **project-name**, **group-name**, and **type** of an ISPF library.

Following the completion of the **LMERASE** function, the program removes variable names associated with this program function via the **VDELETE** service. Then the program exits.

OSCOPY: A CLIST UTILITY TO COPY A SEQUENTIAL FILE

Figure 13-3 contains the CLIST version of this dialog function to copy an MVS sequential file. As in the COBOL version, the routine is written for clarity of illustration. It could easily be generalized by adding panels for user input of data set names rather than hard-coding these names. Instead a minimalist design was pursued to render the program code as brief and as comprehensible as possible.

This CLIST first allocates the new output file for the copy. Then it initializes the flags that signal whether its files have been initialized and opened. The procedure next initializes the input file through the **LMINIT** service:

```
ISPEXEC LMINIT DATAID(DSIDIN) +
        DATASET('&HIGHLVL..&NEXTLVL..&LOWLVL') ENQ(SHR)
```

As in the COBOL program, this **LMINIT** service refers to a data set name. The CLIST keyword **DATASET** denotes this choice. Since this is an input file, the file locking mechanism is specified as **SHR**, in contrast with output files, normally specified as **EXCLU** or **MOD**.

Recall that the **LMINIT** call in the COBOL program required the presence of positional parameters in the call format even though they were not used. Since CLIST invocations of Dialog Manager services use keyword parameters, there is no need to "dummy out" unused parameters.

If the attempt to initialize the input data set succeeds, the flag named **ININIT** is set to **YES**. Before the function ends, it tests this flag to ensure that a corresponding **LMFREE** service frees the initialized file.

The initialized data set is next opened for input:

```
ISPEXEC LMOPEN DATAID(&DSIDIN) OPTION(INPUT)
```

A tricky aspect of the encoding is ensuring that the dataid is properly substituted into the code. The symbolic variable **&DSIDIN** accomplishes this.

The output file, newly allocated at the start of this CLIST, is now initialized. As in the COBOL program, the CLIST uses the **DDNAME** format of the **LMINIT** service. Since the file is written to, the **LMINIT** command specifies exclusive use of the output file through the **EXCLU** keyword.

After the initialized output data set is opened, the CLIST's **DO WHILE** loop copies records from the input file to the output data set. The **LMGET** service retrieves records from the input file:

```
ISPEXEC LMGET DATAID(&DSIDIN) MODE(INVAR) +
    DATALOC(RECORD) DATALEN(RECLEN) MAXLEN(80)
```

Again, **DATALOC** refers to where the Dialog Manager moves the retrieved record. **INVAR** denotes that ISPF move the input record to this variable, and **DATALEN** tells ISPF where to indicate how many bytes were read. **MAXLEN** states the maximum number of bytes to store in the data location variable. The **LMPUT** invocation that writes the record references these same variables:

```
ISPEXEC LMPUT DATAID(&DSIDOUT) MODE(INVAR) +
    DATALOC(RECORD) DATALEN(&RECLEN)
```

After all records have been read from the input file, the **LMGET** service produces a return code of **8**, indicating end-of-file on the input file. The CLIST exits the loop, which copies records from input to output files.

Now the flag indicating successful opening of the input file is tested. If it is on, the **LMCLOSE** command closes the input file. Similarly the flag denoting the initialization of that file is tested. An initialized file is freed through the **LMFREE** service. Then the output file is closed if it is open and freed if it was initialized.

Finally, the CLIST deletes the input file through the **LMERASE** service. **LMERASE** can be used only on data sets having three-level qualified names. The CLIST exits by returning its last error code from the Dialog Manager services.

Figure 13-1. OSCOPYC COBOL function.

```
      IDENTIFICATION DIVISION.                                     00010000
      PROGRAM-ID. OSCOPYC.                                         00020000
     *************************************************************00030000
     *  NAME: OSCOPYC                                BY: H. FOSDICK *00040000
     *                                                            *00050000
     *  PURPOSE: THIS PROGRAM COPIES AN MVS SEQUENTIAL FILE TO A  *00060000
     *  NEW MVS SEQUENTIAL FILE.  AFTER THE COMPLETION OF THE COPY,*00070000
     *  THE PROGRAM 'LMERASES' THE ORIGINAL FILE.  IT IS ASSUMED THAT *00080000
     *  THE FILE TO COPY EXISTS, AND THAT BOTH FILES HAVE 3-LEVEL *00090000
     *  QUALIFIED DATA SET NAMES.                                 *00100000
     *                                                            *00110000
     *************************************************************00120000
      ENVIRONMENT DIVISION.                                        00130000
      DATA DIVISION.                                               00140000
                                                                   00150000
                                                                   00160000
      WORKING-STORAGE SECTION.                                     00170000
                                                                   00180000
                                                                   00190000
                                                                   00200000
     *  SERVICE CALL TYPES:                                        00210000
                                                                   00220000
      01  LMINIT           PIC X(8)    VALUE 'LMINIT  '.           00230000
      01  LMOPEN           PIC X(8)    VALUE 'LMOPEN  '.           00240000
      01  LMGET            PIC X(8)    VALUE 'LMGET   '.           00250000
      01  LMPUT            PIC X(8)    VALUE 'LMPUT   '.           00260000
      01  LMCLOSE          PIC X(8)    VALUE 'LMCLOSE '.           00270000
      01  LMFREE           PIC X(8)    VALUE 'LMFREE  '.           00280000
      01  LMERASE          PIC X(8)    VALUE 'LMERASE '.           00290000
      01  VDEFINE          PIC X(8)    VALUE 'VDEFINE '.           00300035
      01  VDELETE          PIC X(8)    VALUE 'VDELETE '.           00310035
      01  SETMSG           PIC X(8)    VALUE 'SETMSG  '.           00320043
                                                                   00330000
                                                                   00340000
     *  FLAG INDICATES ERROR HAS OCCURRED IF NOT 0:                00350000
                                                                   00360000
      01  ERROR-FLAG       PIC S9(8)   VALUE +0  COMP.             00370044
                                                                   00380000
                                                                   00390000
     *  THESE FOUR FLAGS INDICATE THE STATUS OF THE INPUT AND OUTPUT 00400000
     *  FILES AND WHETHER THEY HAVE BEEN INITIALIZED AND/OR OPENED: 00410000
                                                                   00420000
      01  ININIT           PIC X(3)    VALUE 'NO '.                00430000
      01  INOPEN           PIC X(3)    VALUE 'NO '.                00440000
      01  OUTINIT          PIC X(3)    VALUE 'NO '.                00450000
      01  OUTOPEN          PIC X(3)    VALUE 'NO '.                00460000
                                                                   00470000
                                                                   00480000
     *  HERE IS THE SEQUENTIAL INPUT FILE NAME, BOTH IN FULL FORM  00490000
     *  AND AS SPLIT BETWEEN ITS THREE LEVEL QUALIFIERS.  THE      00500000
     *  LEVELS ARE USED AS INDIVIDUAL PARAMETERS DURING THE        00510042
     *  'LMERASE' SERVICE CALL:                                    00520042
                                                                   00530000
      01  INPUT-SEQ-FILE-NAME PIC X(46)                            00540002
                            VALUE '''ZHMF01.INFILE.DATA'''.        00550001
      01  HIGH-LEVEL       PIC X(8)    VALUE 'ZHMF01  '.           00560042
      01  NEXT-LEVEL       PIC X(8)    VALUE 'INFILE  '.           00570042
      01  LOW-LEVEL        PIC X(8)    VALUE 'DATA    '.           00580042
                                                                   00590042
                                                                   00600042
     *  THE OUTPUT FILE IS SPECIFIED VIA A 'DDNAME' IN THE         00610042
     *  'LMINIT' INITIALIZATION SERVICE CALL:                      00620042
                                                                   00630042
      01  DDNAME           PIC X(8)    VALUE  'NEWFILE '.          00640042
                                                                   00650000
                                                                   00660000
     *  THE VARIOUS LEVELS OF LOCKS ON DATASETS INITIALIZED        00670042
     *  VIA 'LMINIT' SERVICE CALLS:                                00680042
                                                                   00690042
      01  ENQ-SHR          PIC X(8)    VALUE 'SHR     '.           00700042
      01  ENQ-EXCLU        PIC X(8)    VALUE 'EXCLU   '.           00710042
                                                                   00720000
                                                                   00730000
     *  FOR DATA SET ID'S RETURNED VIA 'LMINIT' INITIALIZATION SERVICE.00740042
     *  NOTE THAT THE 'LMINIT' CALL REFERS TO A VARIABLE THAT ITSELF 00750042
     *  CONTAINS THE NAME OF THE VARIABLE WHERE ISPF RETURNS A DATAID: 00760042
                                                                   00770002
      01  DSIDINA          PIC X(8)    VALUE  'DSIDIN  '.          00780042
      01  DSIDIN           PIC X(8)    VALUE  SPACES.              00790042
      01  DSIDOUTA         PIC X(8)    VALUE  'DSIDOUT '.          00800042
      01  DSIDOUT          PIC X(8)    VALUE  SPACES.              00810042
                                                                   00820002
                                                                   00830002
     *  OPTION PARAMETER FOR OPENING DATA SETS AS 'INPUT' OR 'OUTPUT': 00840003
                                                                   00850002
      01  OPTION-INPUT     PIC X(8)    VALUE  'INPUT   '.          00860042
      01  OPTION-OUTPUT    PIC X(8)    VALUE  'OUTPUT  '.          00870042
                                                                   00880013
```

```
*  BLANK PARAMETER FOR 'LMINIT' SERVICE CALLS.  THIS IS REQUIRED   00890013
*  BECAUSE THE CALL PARAMETERS ARE POSITIONAL:                     00900042
                                                                   00910042
                                                                   00920013
   01  B                    PIC X(8)      VALUE SPACES.            00930042
                                                                   00940005
                                                                   00950005
*  FLAG INDICATES END-OF-FILE CONDITION ON INPUT FILE DURING       00960005
*  THE COPY TO THE NEW FILE:                                       00970005
                                                                   00980005
   01  LEAVE-FLAG           PIC X(3)      VALUE 'NO '.             00990042
                                                                   01000005
                                                                   01010005
*  PARAMETERS FOR 'LMGET' AND 'LMPUT' REPRESENTING WHERE THE       01020042
*  DATA IS MOVED TO/FROM AND THE LENGTH OF THE MOVE:               01030042
                                                                   01040005
   01  DATALOCA             PIC X(8)      VALUE 'DATALOC '.        01050042
   01  DATALOC              PIC X(80)     VALUE SPACES.            01060042
   01  DATALENA             PIC X(8)      VALUE 'DATALEN '.        01070042
   01  DATALEN              PIC X(8)      VALUE SPACES.            01080042
                                                                   01090005
                                                                   01100005
*  MODE OF 'LMGET' AND 'LMPUT' IS 'INVAR':                         01110005
                                                                   01120005
   01  MODE-INVAR   PIC X(8)      VALUE 'INVAR   '.                01130005
                                                                   01140006
                                                                   01150006
*  LENGTH OF DATA RECORD FOR 'LMGET' & 'LMPUT' CALLS:              01160042
                                                                   01170006
   01  MAXLEN       PIC S9(8)      VALUE +80 COMP.                 01180040
                                                                   01190035
                                                                   01200035
*  PARAMETERS USED IN 'VDEFINE' OF VARIABLES TO ISPF:              01210035
                                                                   01220035
   01  DSIDIN-LENGTH   PIC 9(6)    VALUE  8  COMP.                 01230035
   01  DSIDOUT-LENGTH  PIC 9(6)    VALUE  8  COMP.                 01240035
   01  DATALOC-LENGTH  PIC 9(6)    VALUE 80 COMP.                  01250041
   01  DATALEN-LENGTH  PIC 9(6)    VALUE  8  COMP.                 01260041
                                                                   01270035
   01  DSIDIN-NAME     PIC X(8)    VALUE  '(DSIDIN)'.              01280035
   01  DSIDOUT-NAME    PIC X(9)    VALUE  '(DSIDOUT)'.             01290036
   01  DATALOC-NAME    PIC X(9)    VALUE  '(DATALOC)'.             01300040
   01  DATALEN-NAME    PIC X(9)    VALUE  '(DATALEN)'.             01310040
                                                                   01320035
   01  CHAR            PIC X(8)    VALUE  'CHAR    '.              01330035
                                                                   01340000
                                                                   01350000
*  MESSAGES:                                                       01360000
                                                                   01370000
   01  LMINIT-FAILED-INP-MSG    PIC X(8)    VALUE 'WDAR001A'.      01380000
   01  LMOPEN-FAILED-INP-MSG    PIC X(8)    VALUE 'WDAR001B'.      01390000
   01  LMINIT-FAILED-OUT-MSG    PIC X(8)    VALUE 'WDAR001C'.      01400000
   01  LMOPEN-FAILED-OUT-MSG    PIC X(8)    VALUE 'WDAR001D'.      01410000
   01  LMGET-FAILED-MSG         PIC X(8)    VALUE 'WDAR001E'.      01420000
   01  LMPUT-FAILED-MSG         PIC X(8)    VALUE 'WDAR001F'.      01430000
   01  LMCLOSE-FAILED-INP-MSG   PIC X(8)    VALUE 'WDAR001G'.      01440000
   01  LMFREE-FAILED-INP-MSG    PIC X(8)    VALUE 'WDAR001H'.      01450000
   01  LMCLOSE-FAILED-OUT-MSG   PIC X(8)    VALUE 'WDAR001I'.      01460000
   01  LMFREE-FAILED-OUT-MSG    PIC X(8)    VALUE 'WDAR001J'.      01470000
   01  LMERASE-FAILED-MSG       PIC X(8)    VALUE 'WDAR001K'.      01480000
   01  OSCOPY-COMPLETED-OK-MSG  PIC X(8)    VALUE 'WDAR001L'.      01490000
                                                                   01500000
                                                                   01510042
                                                                   01520042
                                                                   01530000
PROCEDURE DIVISION.                                                01540000
                                                                   01550000
                                                                   01560042
                                                                   01570042
*                                                                  01580042
*  DEFINE NECESSARY VARIABLES TO ISPF:                             01590042
*                                                                  01600042
                                                                   01610000
      PERFORM DEFINE-VARIABLES THROUGH DEFINE-VARIABLES-EXIT.      01620035
                                                                   01630042
                                                                   01640042
                                                                   01650000
*  INITIALIZE THE INPUT FILE FOR THE COPY THROUGH 'LMINIT'.        01660015
*  PARAMETERS ARE POSITIONAL: 'B' INDICATES AN OMITTED PARAMETER:  01670042
*                                                                  01680000
                                                                   01690036
      CALL  'ISPLINK'  USING  LMINIT                               01700036
                              DSIDINA                              01710038
                              B  B  B  B  B  B                     01720036
                              INPUT-SEQ-FILE-NAME                  01730036
                              B  B  B                              01740036
                              ENQ-SHR.                             01750036
```

(continued)

Figure 13-1. (*Continued*)

```
        MOVE  RETURN-CODE  TO  ERROR-FLAG.                      01760002
                                                               01770002
        IF  ERROR-FLAG  >  0                                    01780002
                                                               01790002
            CALL  'ISPLINK'  USING  SETMSG                      01800002
                                    LMINIT-FAILED-INP-MSG       01810002
                                                               01820002
                                                               01830002
        ELSE                                                    01840002
                                                               01850002
            MOVE  'YES'  TO  ININIT.                            01860002
                                                               01870002
                                                               01880002
*                                                               01890000
*   OPEN THE INPUT FILE FOR THE COPY:                           01900002
*                                                               01910000
                                                               01920000
        IF  ERROR-FLAG  =  0                                    01930027
                                                               01940002
            CALL  'ISPLINK'  USING  LMOPEN                      01950002
                                    DSIDIN                      01960031
                                    OPTION-INPUT                01970002
                                                               01980000
            MOVE  RETURN-CODE  TO  ERROR-FLAG                   01990002
                                                               02000002
            IF  ERROR-FLAG  >  0                                02010002
                                                               02020002
                CALL  'ISPLINK'  USING  SETMSG                  02030002
                                        LMOPEN-FAILED-INP-MSG   02040002
                                                               02050002
            ELSE                                                02060002
                                                               02070002
                MOVE  'YES'  TO  INOPEN.                        02080002
                                                               02090000
                                                               02100000
*                                                               02110000
*   INITIALIZE THE OUTPUT FILE FOR THE COPY, BY THE 'LMINIT'    02120003
*   SERVICE SPECIFYING A DDNAME:                                02130003
*                                                               02140000
                                                               02150003
        IF  ERROR-FLAG  =  0                                    02160027
                                                               02170003
            CALL  'ISPLINK'  USING  LMINIT                      02180003
                                    DSIDOUTA                    02190038
                                    B   B   B   B   B   B       02200003
                                    DDNAME                      02210003
                                    B   B                       02220003
                                    ENQ-EXCLU                   02230003
                                                               02240003
            MOVE  RETURN-CODE  TO  ERROR-FLAG                   02250003
                                                               02260003
            IF  ERROR-FLAG  >  0                                02270003
                                                               02280003
                CALL  'ISPLINK'  USING  SETMSG                  02290003
                                        LMINIT-FAILED-OUT-MSG   02300003
                                                               02310003
            ELSE                                                02320003
                                                               02330003
                MOVE  'YES'  TO  OUTINIT.                       02340003
                                                               02350003
                                                               02360003
*                                                               02370003
*   OPEN THE OUTPUT FILE FOR THE COPY:                          02380003
*                                                               02390003
                                                               02400003
        IF  ERROR-FLAG  =  0                                    02410027
                                                               02420003
            CALL  'ISPLINK'  USING  LMOPEN                      02430003
                                    DSIDOUT                     02440003
                                    OPTION-OUTPUT               02450003
                                                               02460003
            MOVE  RETURN-CODE  TO  ERROR-FLAG                   02470003
                                                               02480003
            IF  ERROR-FLAG  >  0                                02490003
                                                               02500003
                CALL  'ISPLINK'  USING  SETMSG                  02510003
                                        LMOPEN-FAILED-OUT-MSG   02520003
                                                               02530003
            ELSE                                                02540003
                                                               02550003
                MOVE  'YES'  TO  OUTOPEN.                       02560003
                                                               02570003
                                                               02580003
*                                                               02590003
*   COPY THE RECORDS FROM THE SEQUENTIAL INPUT FILE TO THE      02600003
*   SEQUENTIAL OUTPUT FILE:                                     02610003
*                                                               02620003
                                                               02630003
```

```
       PERFORM  COPY-PARAGRAPH  THRU  COPY-PARAGRAPH-EXIT         02640003
            UNTIL  ERROR-FLAG  NOT =  0                           02650003
            OR     LEAVE-FLAG  NOT =  'NO '.                      02660003
                                                                 02670000
                                                                 02680003
                                                                 02690000
*                                                                02700003
*  IF THE INPUT FILE WAS OPENED, CLOSE IT:                       02710000
*                                                                02720000
                                                                 02730003
       IF  INOPEN = 'YES'                                        02740004
                                                                 02750004
            CALL  'ISPLINK'  USING    LMCLOSE                    02760004
                                      DSIDIN                     02770004
                                                                 02780004
            IF  RETURN-CODE  >  0                                02790004
                                                                 02800004
                 MOVE  RETURN-CODE  TO  ERROR-FLAG               02810004
                                                                 02820004
                 CALL  'ISPLINK'  USING  SETMSG                  02830004
                                  LMCLOSE-FAILED-INP-MSG.        02840004
                                                                 02850004
*                                                                02860004
*  IF THE INPUT FILE WAS INITIALIZED, FREE IT:                   02870004
*                                                                02880004
                                                                 02890004
       IF  ININIT = 'YES'                                        02900004
                                                                 02910004
            CALL  'ISPLINK'  USING    LMFREE                     02920004
                                      DSIDIN                     02930004
                                                                 02940004
            IF  RETURN-CODE  >  0                                02950004
                                                                 02960004
                 MOVE  RETURN-CODE  TO  ERROR-FLAG               02970004
                                                                 02980004
                 CALL  'ISPLINK'  USING  SETMSG                  02990004
                                  LMFREE-FAILED-INP-MSG.         03000004
                                                                 03010004
                                                                 03020004
                                                                 03030004
                                                                 03040004
*                                                                03050004
*  IF THE OUTPUT FILE WAS OPENED, CLOSE IT:                      03060004
*                                                                03070004
                                                                 03080004
       IF  OUTOPEN = 'YES'                                       03090004
                                                                 03100004
            CALL  'ISPLINK'  USING    LMCLOSE                    03110004
                                      DSIDOUT                    03120004
            IF  RETURN-CODE  >  0                                03130004
                                                                 03140004
                 MOVE  RETURN-CODE  TO  ERROR-FLAG               03150004
                                                                 03160004
                 CALL  'ISPLINK'  USING  SETMSG                  03170004
                                  LMCLOSE-FAILED-OUT-MSG.        03180004
                                                                 03190004
                                                                 03200004
*                                                                03210004
*  IF THE OUTPUT FILE WAS INITIALIZED, FREE IT:                  03220004
*                                                                03230004
                                                                 03240004
       IF  OUTINIT = 'YES'                                       03250004
                                                                 03260004
            CALL  'ISPLINK'  USING    LMFREE                     03270004
                                      DSIDOUT                    03280004
                                                                 03290004
            IF  RETURN-CODE  >  0                                03300004
                                                                 03310004
                 MOVE  RETURN-CODE  TO  ERROR-FLAG               03320004
                                                                 03330004
                 CALL  'ISPLINK'  USING  SETMSG                  03340004
                                  LMFREE-FAILED-OUT-MSG.         03350004
                                                                 03360004
                                                                 03370004
                                                                 03380004
*                                                                03390004
*  IF NO ERROR HAS OCCURRED, 'LMERASE' THE INPUT FILE:           03400004
*                                                                03410004
       IF  ERROR-FLAG  =  0                                      03420004
                                                                 03430004
            CALL  'ISPLINK'  USING    LMERASE                    03440004
                                      HIGH-LEVEL                 03450004
                                      NEXT-LEVEL                 03460004
                                      LOW-LEVEL                  03470004
                                                                 03480004
            MOVE  RETURN-CODE  TO  ERROR-FLAG                    03490004
                                                                 03500004
```

(continued)

Figure 13-1. (*Continued*)

```
          IF   ERROR-FLAG  >  0                                03510004
                                                               03520004
                 CALL  'ISPLINK'  USING  SETMSG                03530004
                                         LMERASE-FAILED-MSG.   03540004
                                                               03550004
                                                               03560042
*                                                              03570000
*  IF ALL WENT WELL, WRITE A MESSAGE.  'VDELETE' ALL VARIABLES 03580042
*  KNOWN TO ISPF AND EXIT:                                     03590042
*                                                              03600000
                                                               03610000
     IF   ERROR-FLAG  =  0                                     03620004
                                                               03630004
                 CALL  'ISPLINK'  USING  SETMSG                03640004
                                         OSCOPY-COMPLETED-OK-MSG. 03650004
                                                               03660000
                                                               03670000
     PERFORM DELETE-VARIABLES THROUGH DELETE-VARIABLES-EXIT.   03680035
                                                               03690000
                                                               03700042
     MOVE  ERROR-FLAG  TO  RETURN-CODE.                        03710004
     GOBACK.                                                   03720000
                                                               03730000
 MAIN-LINE-EXIT.                                               03740000
                                                               03750034
                                                               03760034
                                                               03770034
                                                               03780034
 COPY-PARAGRAPH.                                               03790034
                                                               03800034
                                                               03810042
*                                                              03820034
*   RETRIEVE A RECORD FROM THE INPUT FILE:                     03830034
*                                                              03840034
                                                               03850042
     CALL 'ISPLINK'  USING   LMGET                             03860034
                             DSIDIN                            03870034
                             MODE-INVAR                        03880034
                             DATALOCA                          03890040
                             DATALENA                          03900040
                             MAXLEN.                           03910034
                                                               03920034
     MOVE  RETURN-CODE  TO  ERROR-FLAG.                        03930034
                                                               03940034
     IF   ERROR-FLAG  >  8                                     03950034
                                                               03960034
          CALL  'ISPLINK'  USING  SETMSG                       03970034
                                  LMGET-FAILED-MSG.            03980034
                                                               03990034
*                                                              04000042
*  RETURN CODE OF 8 SIGNIFIES END-OF-FILE ON INPUT FILE:       04010034
*                                                              04020034
                                                               04030034
     IF   ERROR-FLAG  =  8                                     04040034
                                                               04050034
          MOVE  'YES'  TO  LEAVE-FLAG                          04060034
                                                               04070034
          MOVE  0  TO  ERROR-FLAG.                             04080034
                                                               04090034
                                                               04100034
*                                                              04110034
*  IF A RECORD WAS READ, WRITE IT TO OUTPUT FILE:              04120034
*                                                              04130034
                                                               04140034
     IF   ERROR-FLAG  =  0  AND  LEAVE-FLAG  =  'NO '          04150034
                                                               04160034
          CALL 'ISPLINK'  USING   LMPUT                        04170034
                                  DSIDOUT                      04180034
                                  MODE-INVAR                   04190034
                                  DATALOCA                     04200034
                                  MAXLEN                       04210040
                                                               04220040
          MOVE  RETURN-CODE  TO  ERROR-FLAG                    04230034
                                                               04240034
          IF   ERROR-FLAG  >  0                                04250034
                                                               04260034
                 CALL  'ISPLINK'  USING  SETMSG                04270034
                                         LMPUT-FAILED-MSG.     04280034
                                                               04290034
                                                               04300034
 COPY-PARAGRAPH-EXIT.                                          04310034
     EXIT.                                                     04320034
                                                               04330034
                                                               04340040
                                                               04350040
                                                               04360040
                                                               04370040
 DEFINE-VARIABLES.                                             04380040
```

```
                                                                04390040
                                                                04400042
                                                                04410040
*                                                               04420040
**  DEFINE NECESSARY VARIABLES TO ISPF DIALOG MANAGER:          04430040
*                                                               04440040
    CALL 'ISPLINK'  USING  VDEFINE                              04450040
                           DSIDIN-NAME                          04460040
                           DSIDIN                               04470040
                           CHAR                                 04480040
                           DSIDIN-LENGTH.                       04490040
    CALL 'ISPLINK'  USING  VDEFINE                              04500040
                           DSIDOUT-NAME                         04510040
                           DSIDOUT                              04520040
                           CHAR                                 04530040
                           DSIDOUT-LENGTH.                      04540040
    CALL 'ISPLINK'  USING  VDEFINE                              04550040
                           DATALOC-NAME                         04560040
                           DATALOC                              04570040
                           CHAR                                 04580040
                           DATALOC-LENGTH.                      04590040
    CALL 'ISPLINK'  USING  VDEFINE                              04600040
                           DATALEN-NAME                         04610040
                           DATALEN                              04620040
                           CHAR                                 04630040
                           DATALEN-LENGTH.                      04640040
                                                                04650040
                                                                04660040
DEFINE-VARIABLES-EXIT.                                          04670040
    EXIT.                                                       04680040
                                                                04690040
                                                                04700040
                                                                04710040
                                                                04720040
DELETE-VARIABLES.                                               04730040
                                                                04740040
                                                                04750042
*                                                               04760040
**  DELETE ALL DIALOG MANAGER VARIABLES RE ISPF DIALOG MANAGER: 04770042
*                                                               04780040
                                                                04790040
    CALL 'ISPLINK'  USING  VDELETE                              04800040
                           DSIDIN-NAME.                         04810040
    CALL 'ISPLINK'  USING  VDELETE                              04820040
                           DSIDOUT-NAME.                        04830040
    CALL 'ISPLINK'  USING  VDELETE                              04840040
                           DATALOC-NAME.                        04850040
    CALL 'ISPLINK'  USING  VDELETE                              04860040
                           DATALEN-NAME.                        04870040
                                                                04880040
                                                                04890040
DELETE-VARIABLES-EXIT.                                          04900040
    EXIT.                                                       04910040
```

Figure 13-2. Utility functions messages.

```
WDAR001A 'LMINIT FAILED            '           .ALARM = NO
'WDAR001A- LMINIT FAILED ON INPUT FILE                          '

WDAR001B 'LMOPEN FAILED            '           .ALARM = NO
'WDAR001B- LMOPEN FAILED ON INPUT FILE                          '

WDAR001C 'LMINIT FAILED            '           .ALARM = NO
'WDAR001C- LMINIT FAILED ON OUTPUT FILE                         '

WDAR001D 'LMOPEN FAILED            '           .ALARM = NO
'WDAR001D- LMOPEN FAILED ON OUTPUT FILE                         '

WDAR001E 'LMGET FAILED             '           .ALARM = NO
'WDAR001E- LMGET FAILED WITH RETURN CODE > 8                    '

WDAR001F 'LMPUT FAILED             '           .ALARM = NO
'WDAR001F- LMPUT FAILED WHEN WRITING TO OUTPUT FILE             '

WDAR001G 'LMCLOSE FAILED           '           .ALARM = NO
'WDAR001G- LMCLOSE FAILED ON INPUT FILE                         '

WDAR001H 'LMFREE FAILED            '           .ALARM = NO
'WDAR001H- LMFREE FAILED ON INPUT FILE                          '

WDAR001I 'LMCLOSE FAILED           '           .ALARM = NO
'WDAR001I- LMCLOSE FAILED ON OUTPUT FILE                        '

WDAR001J 'LMFREE FAILED            '           .ALARM = NO
'WDAR001J- LMFREE FAILED ON OUTPUT FILE                         '

WDAR001K 'LMERASE FAILED           '           .ALARM = NO
'WDAR001K- LMERASE FAILED ON INPUT FILE                         '

WDAR001L 'OSCOPY COMPLETED OK      '           .ALARM = NO
'WDAR001L- OSCOPY COMPLETED WITH FINAL RETURN CODE OF 0         '

WDAR002A 'LMMFIND FAILED           '           .ALARM = NO
'WDAR002A- LMMFIND FAILED ON INPUT LIBRARY MEMBER               '

WDAR002B 'LMMREP FAILED            '           .ALARM = NO
'WDAR002B- LMMREP FAILED ON OUTPUT LIBRARY MEMBER               '

WDAR002C 'PDSCOPY COMPLETED OK     '           .ALARM = NO
'WDAR002C- PDSCOPY COMPLETED WITH FINAL RETURN CODE OF 0        '

WDAR003A 'LMMLIST FAILED           '           .ALARM = NO
'WDAR003A- LMMLIST FAILED DURING MEMBERNAME RETRIEVAL ATTEMPT   '

WDAR003B 'LMMLIST FAILED ON FREE'              .ALARM = NO
'WDAR003B- LMMLIST FAILED DURING FREE OF MEMBER LIST STORAGE    '

WDAR003C 'ISPF BROWSE FAILED       '           .ALARM = NO
'WDAR003C- ISPF BROWSE SERVICE FAILED ON MEMBER LIST FILE       '

WDAR003D 'PDSLIST COMPLETED OK     '           .ALARM = NO
'WDAR003D- PDSLIST COMPLETED OK WITH FINAL RETURN CODE OF 0     '
```

Figure 13-3. OSCOPY CLIST function.

```
00010000   PROC 0
00020017   CONTROL LIST
00030000   /******************************************************************/
00040000   /* NAME: OSCOPY                              BY: H. FOSDICK      */
00050000   /*                                                               */
00060018   /* PURPOSE: THIS CLIST COPIES AN MVS SEQUENTIAL FILE TO          */
00070018   /* A NEW MVS SEQUENTIAL FILE.  AFTER THE COMPLETION OF THE       */
00080018   /* COPY, THIS CLIST 'LMERASES' THE ORIGINAL FILE.  IT IS         */
00090017   /* ASSUMED THAT THE FILE TO COPY EXISTS, AND THAT BOTH           */
00100017   /* FILES HAVE 3-LEVEL QUALIFIED DATA SET NAMES.                  */
00110000   /*                                                               */
00120000   /******************************************************************/
00130000
00140000   /*                                                               */
00150022   /*    FREE PREVIOUS FILE ALLOCATION AND ALLOCATE THE OUTPUT      */
00160018   /*    DATA SET FOR THE COPY:                                     */
00170000   /*                                                               */
00180000
00190011   DELETE   'ZHMF01.NEWFILE.DATA'
00200021   FREE  FILE(NEWFILE)
00210019   FREE  ATTRLIST(ATTR1)
00220000
00230009   ATTR  ATTR1  BLKSIZE(6080)  LRECL(80)  RECFM(F B)  DSORG(PS)
00240019   ALLOCATE  FILE(NEWFILE)  DA('ZHMF01.NEWFILE.DATA')  +
00250010        NEW  SPACE(3)  TRACKS  USING(ATTR1)
00260002
00270018
00280018   /*                                                               */
00290018   /*   INITIALIZE FLAGS:                                           */
00300018   /*                                                               */
00310018
00320018   SET  ERROR   =  0        /* 0 MEANS AN ERROR HAS NOT OCCURRED. */
00330018   SET  ININIT  =  NO       /* THESE FOUR FLAGS INDICATE THE      */
00340018   SET  INOPEN  =  NO       /* STATUS OF THE INPUT AND OUTPUT     */
00350018   SET  OUTINIT =  NO       /* FILES AND WHETHER THEY HAVE BEEN   */
00360018   SET  OUTOPEN =  NO       /* INITIALIZED AND/OR OPENED.         */
00370024
00380024
00390024   /*                                                               */
00400024   /*   INITIALIZE VARIABLES FOR THE INPUT SEQUENTIAL FILE NAME:*/
00410024   /*                                                               */
00420024
00430024   SET  HIGHLVL =  ZHMF01     /* HIGH-LEVEL PART OF FILE NAME    */
00440024   SET  NEXTLVL =  INFILE     /* 2ND-LEVEL PART OF FILE NAME     */
00450025   SET  LOWLVL  =  DATA       /* 3RD-LEVEL PART OF FILE NAME     */
00460018
00470018
00480018   /*                                                               */
00490018   /*   INITIALIZE THE INPUT FILE FOR THE COPY:                     */
00500018   /*                                                               */
00510018
00520001   ISPEXEC  LMINIT  DATAID(DSIDIN)  +
00530024        DATASET('&HIGHLVL..&NEXTLVL..&LOWLVL')  ENQ(SHR)
00540018
00550000   SET  ERROR  =  &LASTCC
00560018
00570001   IF  &ERROR  >  0  THEN +
00580000        ISPEXEC  SETMSG  MSG(WDAR001A)
00590002   ELSE  +
00600002        SET  ININIT  =  YES
00610018
00620018
00630018   /*                                                               */
00640018   /*   OPEN THE INPUT FILE FOR THE COPY:                           */
00650018   /*                                                               */
00660018
00670001   IF  &ERROR  =  0  THEN  DO
00680018
0C690001        ISPEXEC  LMOPEN  DATAID(&DSIDIN)  OPTION(INPUT)
00700018
00710001        SET  ERROR  =  &LASTCC
00720018
00730001        IF  &ERROR  >  0  THEN +
00740001             ISPEXEC  SETMSG  MSG(WDAR001B)
00750002        ELSE  +
00760002             SET  INOPEN  =  YES
00770019
00780001        END
00790018
00800018
00810018   /*                                                               */
00820018   /*   INITIALIZE THE OUTPUT FILE FOR THE COPY:                    */
00830018   /*                                                               */
00840018
00850001   IF  &ERROR  =  0  THEN  DO
00860018
```

(continued)

Figure 13-3. (*Continued*)

```
00870007        ISPEXEC  LMINIT  DATAID(DSIDOUT)  DDNAME(NEWFILE)  ENQ(EXCLU)
00880018
00890001        SET  ERROR  =  &LASTCC
00900018
00910001        IF  &ERROR  >  0  THEN  +
00920004            ISPEXEC  SETMSG  MSG(WDAR001C)
00930002        ELSE  +
00940002            SET  OUTINIT  =  YES
00950019
00960001        END
00970018
00980018
00990018  /*                                                          */
01000018  /*  OPEN THE OUTPUT FILE FOR THE COPY:                      */
01010018  /*                                                          */
01020018
01030001  IF  &ERROR  =  0  THEN  DO
01040018
01050001        ISPEXEC  LMOPEN  DATAID(&DSIDOUT)  OPTION(OUTPUT)
01060018
01070001        SET  ERROR  =  &LASTCC
01080018
01090001        IF  &ERROR  >  0  THEN  +
01100001            ISPEXEC  SETMSG  MSG(WDAR001D)
01110002        ELSE  +
01120002            SET  OUTOPEN  =  YES
01130019
01140001        END
01150018
01160019
01170018
01180018  /*                                                          */
01190019  /*  THE CODE IN THIS 'DO WHILE' LOOP COPIES THE RECORDS     */
01200019  /*  FROM THE SEQUENTIAL INPUT FILE TO THE SEQUENTIAL OUTPUT */
01210019  /*  FILE.   THE VARIABLE 'LEAVE' INDICATES END-OF-FILE ON   */
01220019  /*  THE INPUT FILE AND SIGNIFIES EXIT FROM THE LOOP:        */
01230018  /*                                                          */
01240018
01250001  SET  LEAVE  =  NO
01260018
01270001  DO  WHILE  &ERROR  =  0   AND  &LEAVE  =  NO
01280019
01290019
01300019        /*                                                    */
01310019        /*  RETRIEVE A RECORD FROM THE INPUT FILE:            */
01320019        /*                                                    */
01330019
01340001        ISPEXEC  LMGET  DATAID(&DSIDIN)  MODE(INVAR)  +
01350001            DATALOC(RECORD)  DATALEN(RECLEN)  MAXLEN(80)
01360019
01370004        SET  ERROR  =  &LASTCC
01380019
01390004        IF  &ERROR  >  8  THEN  +
01400004            ISPEXEC  SETMSG  MSG(WDAR001E)
01410019
01420019        /*                                                    */
01430019        /*  RETURN CODE OF 8 SIGNIFIES END-OF-FILE ON INPUT FILE: */
01440019        /*                                                    */
01450019
01460004        IF  &ERROR  =  8  THEN  DO
01470004            SET  LEAVE  =  YES
01480004            SET  ERROR  =  0
01490004            END
01500019
01510019
01520019        /*                                                    */
01530019        /*  IF A RECORD WAS READ, WRITE IT TO OUTPUT FILE:    */
01540019        /*                                                    */
01550019
01560004        IF  &ERROR  =  0   AND  &LEAVE  =  NO  THEN  DO
01570019
01580004            ISPEXEC  LMPUT  DATAID(&DSIDOUT)  MODE(INVAR)  +
01590010                DATALOC(RECORD)  DATALEN(&RECLEN)
01600019
01610004            SET  ERROR  =  &LASTCC
01620019
01630004            IF  &ERROR  >  0  THEN  +
01640004                ISPEXEC  SETMSG  MSG(WDAR001F)
01650019
01660004            END
01670019
01680001  END
01690019
01700019
01710019
01720019  /*                                                          */
01730019  /*  IF THE INPUT FILE WAS OPENED, CLOSE IT:                 */
01740019  /*                                                          */
```

```
01750001
01760002     IF  &INOPEN  =  YES   THEN   DO
01770019
01780002          ISPEXEC  LMCLOSE  DATAID(&DSIDIN)
01790019
01800004          IF  &LASTCC  >  0  THEN  DO
01810004               SET  ERROR  =  &LASTCC
01820002               ISPEXEC  SETMSG  MSG(WDAR001G)
01830004               END
01840019
01850004          END
01860019
01870019
01880019     /*                                                        */
01890019     /*  IF THE INPUT FILE WAS INITIALIZED, FREE IT:           */
01900019     /*                                                        */
01910019
01920004     IF  &ININIT  =  YES   THEN   DO
01930019
01940004          ISPEXEC  LMFREE  DATAID(&DSIDIN)
01950019
01960004          IF  &LASTCC  >  0  THEN  DO
01970004               SET  ERROR  =  &LASTCC
01980004               ISPEXEC  SETMSG  MSG(WDAR001H)
01990004               END
02000019
02010004          END
02020019
02030019
02040019     /*                                                        */
02050019     /*  IF THE OUTPUT FILE WAS OPENED, CLOSE IT:              */
02060019     /*                                                        */
02070019
02080004     IF  &OUTOPEN  =  YES   THEN   DO
02090019
02100004          ISPEXEC  LMCLOSE  DATAID(&DSIDOUT)
02110019
02120004          IF  &LASTCC  >  0  THEN  DO
02130004               SET  ERROR  =  &LASTCC
02140004               ISPEXEC  SETMSG  MSG(WDAR001I)
02150004               END
02160019
02170004          END
02180019
02190019
02200019     /*                                                        */
02210019     /*  IF THE OUTPUT FILE WAS INITIALIZED, FREE IT:          */
02220019     /*                                                        */
02230019
02240004     IF  &OUTINIT  =  YES   THEN   DO
02250019
02260004          ISPEXEC  LMFREE  DATAID(&DSIDOUT)
02270019
02280004          IF  &LASTCC  >  0  THEN  DO
02290004               SET  ERROR  =  &LASTCC
02300004               ISPEXEC  SETMSG  MSG(WDAR001J)
02310004               END
02320019
02330004          END
02340019
02350019
02360019     /*                                                        */
02370019     /*  IF NO ERROR HAS OCCURRED, 'LMERASE' THE INPUT FILE:   */
02380019     /*                                                        */
02390019
02400002     IF  &ERROR  =  0  THEN  DO
02410019
02420024          ISPEXEC  LMERASE  PROJECT(&HIGHLVL) GROUP(&NEXTLVL) TYPE(&LOWLVL)
02430019
02440002          SET  ERROR  =  &LASTCC
02450019
02460002          IF  &ERROR  >  0  THEN  +
02470002               ISPEXEC  SETMSG  MSG(WDAR001K)
02480019
02490019          END
02500019
02510019
02520019     /*                                                        */
02530019     /*  IF ALL WENT WELL, WRITE A MESSAGE.  THEN EXIT CLIST:  */
02540019     /*                                                        */
02550019
02560016     IF  &ERROR  =  0  THEN  +
02570016          ISPEXEC  SETMSG  MSG(WDAR001L)
02580019
02590019
02600002     EXIT  CODE(&ERROR)
```

14

More on Library Access Services

The previous chapter described the Dialog Manager's library access services. An example dialog utility function illustrated use of several of the basic library access services. This chapter continues that discussion by presenting two additional program examples.

A UTILITY TO COPY A MEMBER OF A PARTITIONED DATA SET

This dialog utility copies a member from one partitioned data set to another. The input data set is assumed to exist. The output member will replace an existing member in the target partitioned data set (PDS) or add the member if it is new to that PDS.

Since the COBOL and CLIST versions of this dialog function parallel each other very closely, the discussion pertains to both versions. Figure 14-1 presents the COBOL-language version of this utility, named **PDSCOPYC**, and figure 14-2 contains its CLIST-language equivalent, named **PDSCOPY**.

The logic of this dialog function is similar to that of the **OSCOPYC/ OSCOPY** utility. The input and output partitioned data sets are initialized and opened through the **LMINIT** and **LMOPEN** dialog services. Records are read from the input file and written to output through the **LMGET** and **LMPUT** services. And the input and output partitioned data sets are closed and freed via the **LMCLOSE** and **LMFREE** calls.

But there are several important differences in this function. For example, since the **LMINIT** service invocations do not name the members involved in the **LMGET** and **LMPUT** operations, where are the members specified? For the input data set, this requires an **LMMFIND** service, which occurs immediately after the input partitioned data set is initialized and opened. A return code of **0** indicates that ISPF was able to locate the desired member within the input partitioned data set.

For the output data set member name, the **LMMREP** service is invoked after the **LMGET**s and **LMPUT**s have copied the input file. **LMMREP** updates the directory of the target PDS to replace a member. If that member does not exist, **LMMREP** will add it. A return code of **0** indicates that the directory was updated to replace a member, and a return code of **8** means that the member was added because it did not previously exist. Thus **LMMREP** either adds a new member or replaces an existing member of the output partitioned data set.

Like **LMMFIND**, the **LMMREP** service requires that both the **LMINIT** and **LMOPEN** services have been accomplished on the dataid to which it refers. Of course, the **LMMREP** service assumes that the **LMOPEN** invocation opened the dataid with the **OUTPUT** option. This makes sense because **LMMREP** would be called only as a result of output operations. **LMMREP** also requires that the **LMPUT** commands have been completed.

A difference between the COBOL version of this function and the **OSCOPYC** utility described in chapter 13 is that the service invocations for **LMINIT**, **LMOPEN**, **LMCLOSE**, and **LMFREE** refer to partitioned rather than sequential data sets. Both the input and output files are initialized through specification of **DDNAME**s in the **PDSCOPYC** COBOL program. Thus, appropriate allocation of files must have occurred through TSO **ALLOCATE** commands (as through a CLIST, for example) prior to execution of this program.

The CLIST version of this function refers directly to existing data sets in its **LMINIT** commands. Members are not specified on these commands since **LMMFIND** and **LMMREP** handle the member names.

In looking at the **LMINIT** invocations, you will recognize that the COBOL-language version of this function requests this service through an entirely new command format. The ISPF Dialog Manager services interface routine is called **ISPEXEC** rather than **ISPLINK**. Here is how the call invocation appears when using the **ISPEXEC** interface for compiled COBOL programs:

```
01 BUFFER            PIC X(120)       VALUE SPACES.
01 BUFFER-LENGTH     PIC 9(8)         VALUE 120 COMP.
                        .
                        .
                        .
MOVE 'LMINIT DATAID(DSIDIN) DDNAME(INFILE) ENQ(SHR)'
    TO BUFFER.
CALL 'ISPEXEC' USING BUFFER-LENGTH BUFFER.
```

The **ISPEXEC** interface routine provides an alternative call format for compiled programs to that required by **ISPLINK**. The call statement itself contains only two parameters, a buffer, which contains the Dialog Manager service name and its parameters, and a parameter which specifies the length of this buffer. Prior to the call to **ISPEXEC**, the program moves information into the buffer that names the ISPF service and its parameters in the same format as they would appear in an **ISPEXEC** invocation for a command procedure. In other words, the

**Table 14-1. Use of ISPLINK Versus ISPEXEC Interfaces
in Compiled Programs**

ISPLINK (ISPLNK)	ISPEXEC (ISPEX)
More commonly used from compiled programs	Supports symbolic variables
Usually more readable	Keyword parameters instead of positional parameters
Supports services that would not be valid from **ISPEXEC** (e.g., **VDEFINE** and **VDELETE**)	

contents of the buffer should appear as if this information were encoded in a CLIST.

The **ISPEXEC** form of ISPF service calls can be used for any Dialog Manager service whose use is valid from within a command procedure. Thus any valid CLIST or EXEC2 service invocation can be sent via a compiled program function through the **ISPEXEC** interface. The **ISPEXEC** interface is called **ISPEX** in FORTRAN and Pascal programs.

This book follows predominant coding practice in using the **ISPLINK** routine interface for compiled programs rather than the **ISPEXEC** interface. Why would one call the **ISPEXEC** service routine? First, it can be more convenient in certain situations. For example, in the **PDSCOPYC** program **LMINIT** calls, the **ISPEXEC** interface avoids specification of numerous positional parameters that are not relevant to the call. Use of the **ISPEXEC** interface allows omission of dummy parameters because its contents are keyword oriented.

Second, **ISPEXEC** allows symbolic variables in the buffer string. In a manner similar to their use in CLISTs and EXECs, variable names preceded by ampersands are dynamically replaced by the values of the corresponding variables. This feature is illustrated in the last example COBOL program in this chapter.

Table 14-1 summarizes the relative advantages of the two call formats available for dialog functions written in compiled programming languages. **ISPLINK** is the more commonly used.

A UTILITY TO CREATE A SORTED LIST OF MEMBER NAMES

The previous program examples provided opportunities for you to become familiar with the Dialog Manager services for library access; however, these utilities may not seem realistic from the functional standpoint. Why, for example, would you write a dialog function to perform simple copies of files when operating systems offer copy commands and utilities to perform these functions? The answer, of course, is that you would not program such a function but that the kinds of tasks library access services offer can be combined at will in dialogs to provide new functionality. For example, this last example utility program creates a new sequential file containing a sorted list of the member names of a specified MVS partitioned data set or library. For each member of the PDS, the user who last updated (or created) the file, the date of last update, and the number of records in the file are reported. This dialog function displays this file under the control of ISPF **BROWSE**. Then the function terminates when the user exits the **BROWSE** panel.

Figure 14-3 shows the COBOL-language version of this utility. As in the previous COBOL program examples, this program first defines important program variables to ISPF through the paragraph **DEFINE-VARIABLES**. Afterward, the input partitioned data set is initialized and opened using the **LMINIT** and **LMOPEN** services. The input PDS is that library whose members will constitute the output member list from this program. As with the other utility programs in this chapter, it is assumed that a valid input data set exists. The data sets to initialize are referred to through the **DDNAME** parameter in both calls to **LMINIT**.

All Dialog Manager services in this COBOL program were invoked via the **ISPEXEC** interface. Thus the encoding of the calls is nearly the same as those found in the CLIST version of this function. This CLIST is listed in figure 14-4. The COBOL **ISPEXEC** interface was illustrated so that you can compare use of this interface with the **ISPLINK** routine shown throughout this book. The only **ISPLINK** calls in this program are to the **VDEFINE** and **VDELETE** services. **ISPLINK** is employed in these cases because these services are not allowed in command languages. **ISPEXEC** does not support their use as valid **ISPEXEC** commands.

Take several minutes to inspect the calls to the Dialog Manager through the COBOL program's use of the **ISPEXEC** interface. Compare these calls to the similar invocations of ISPF services using the **ISPLINK** routine in the **PDSCOPYC** program. You may also wish to compare these program statements to the corresponding CLIST version of this dialog function provided in figure 14-4. The contents of the **BUFFER** for COBOL calls to **ISPEXEC** are the same as the parameters that follow the corresponding **ISPEXEC** command in the CLIST. The only exception to this statement is that the COBOL **LMINIT** invocations reference **DDNAME**s while one of the CLIST commands specifies a data set name via the **DATASET** keyword.

After initializing and opening the input PDS, the function does the same for the newly created output file, an OS sequential file. In the case of the COBOL version of this dialog function, the **DDNAME** form of **LMINIT** initializes the files. Thus, both input and output files must be allocated to the program prior to its execution by TSO commands or an appropriate CLIST.

Next, the dialog function executes a "read loop" (in the COBOL program's paragraph named **LIST-PARAGRAPH**) that retrieves the sorted member list. This is accomplished by repeated invocations of the **LMMLIST** (Member List) service. Here is the call in COBOL:

Table 14-2. Library Access System Variables

System Variable	Meaning	Format
ZLVERS	Version number	Between 0 and 99
ZLMOD	Modification level	Between 0 and 99
ZLCDATE	Creation date	In form **YY/MM/DD**
ZLMDATE	Date of last modification	In form **YY/MM/DD**
ZLMTIME	Time of last modification	In form **HH:MM**
ZLCNORC	Current number of records	Between 0 and 65535
ZLINORC	Initial number of records	Between 0 and 65535
ZLMNORC	Number of modified records	Between 0 and 65535
ZLUSER	User id of last user to modify the file	8-character string

```
        MOVE 'LMMLIST DATAID(&DSIDIN) OPTION(LIST)
    —    'MEMBER(MEMVAR) STATS(YES)' TO BUFFER

        CALL 'ISPEXEC' USING BUFFER-LENGTH BUFFER
```

The first time the **LMMLIST** service is invoked with the **LIST** option, it creates an alphabetically ordered member list for the indicated data set in virtual storage. The first member from this list is returned in the variable **MEMVAR**.

The **STATS** option on the **LMMLIST** service requests return of various data set statistics through predefined system variables. The available system variables are shown in table 14-2.

In this dialog function, the requirements were to list the last user to modify the file (**ZLUSER**), the date of last modification (**ZLMDATE**), and the current number of records (**ZLCNORC**). Thus these are the variables of interest returned through the **LMMLIST STATS** option. In the COBOL version of this function, ISPF was given access to appropriate program variables through use of the **VDEFINE** calls in the program paragraph **DEFINE-VARIABLES**. Since the system variables reside in the shared variable pool, the ISPF **VCOPY** service could also have been used to return their values to the program.

Subsequent invocations of the **LMMLIST** service with the **LIST** and **STATS** options continue to return the next member name (with relevant statistics) in the alphabetically ordered list. The return code of **8** from **LMMLIST** indicates that end-of-file has occurred on the input member list. After the file of members and statistics has been written, the function exits the member list retrieval loop. **LMMLIST** is then invoked one last time, this time using the **FREE** option. This frees the virtual storage member list created by the first invocation of **LMMLIST**. It is important to free the member list once its use is completed.

At this point, the function closes and frees the input PDS. It closes (but does not yet free) the output file. ISPF **BROWSE** is now invoked with the output dataid specified, permitting the user to browse the file of member names and statistics. Figure 14-5 shows how this output appears.

Table 14-3. Use of Command Procedure Dialog Functions versus Compiled COBOL Functions

Command Procedures	*Compiled COBOL*
Shorter programs, less code	Code is much more portable across operating systems
Quicker and easier to test	Faster execution of compiled dialog function
Function pool variables are automatically accessible to the command procedure, and command procedure variables are automatically accessible to ISPF	Programmer must assume responsibility for references to function pool and program variables through VDEFINEs
	Programmer skills applicable across operating systems
	Perhaps more maintainable and self-documenting code
	May have access to program or function libraries unavailable to command procedures

The **BROWSE** command with a dataid is a new form of that service available only with ISPF Version 2. The dataid must have been established via **LMINIT** (and not yet freed) in order to use this form of **BROWSE**. This format of the service is valid only through the **ISPEXEC** interface.

Following the browsing of the output file, the function frees the output data set and exits.

ISPF WITH COMPILED VERSUS COMMAND PROCEDURE FUNCTIONS

The program example presented in the previous section showed that the invocation of Dialog Manager services can appear very similar between COBOL programs and command procedures when compiled programs use the **ISPEXEC** module interface. Because of this, you might wonder when it is appropriate to use compiled language rather than command procedures in dialog functions.

Table 14-3 lists the relative advantages of program versus command functions. In general, command procedures are quicker to write. As opposed to COBOL, command procedures result in shorter routines. Command procedures do not require programmers to **VDEFINE** program variables to ISPF, nor do they contain lengthy data definition sections. Furthermore, command procedures are easier to test and debug because they are interpreted. As one example of the ease of testing, the CLIST command functions in this chapter specified **CONTROL LIST**. Combined with the Dialog Test facilities for tracing service invocations and variable changes, this renders these routines extremely easy to test.

Compiled program functions execute faster than interpreted command procedures. Compiled languages also offer greater transportability of code across operating systems. Programmer language skills, too, are applicable to various operating systems.

To some extent, the relative advantages of program versus command functions depend on the languages used in the comparison. For example, comparison of the two kinds of dialog functions is affected by whether one contrasts CLISTs with COBOL, EXEC2 versus PL/I, and so forth. In the final analysis, the chart in table 14-3 provides only general guidelines. The decision on which language(s) to use with the Dialog Manager must be made based on those factors most important to the particular installation.

Figure 14-1. PDSCOPYC COBOL function.

```
IDENTIFICATION DIVISION.                                            00010000
PROGRAM-ID. PDSCOPYC.                                               000200u0
*****************************************************************00030000
*  NAME: PDSCOPYC                                     BY: H. FOSDICK *00040000
*                                                                   *00050000
*  PURPOSE: THIS PROGRAM COPIES A MEMBER FROM ONE ISPF LIBRARY      *00060000
*  TO ANOTHER.  IT IS ASSUMED THAT THE MEMBER TO COPY EXISTS AND    *00070000
*  THAT IT CONTAINS AT LEAST ONE RECORD.                            *00080000
*                                                                   *00090000
*****************************************************************00100000
ENVIRONMENT DIVISION.                                              00110000
DATA DIVISION.                                                     00120000
                                                                   00130000
                                                                   00140000
WORKING-STORAGE SECTION.                                           00150000
                                                                   00160000
                                                                   00170000
                                                                   00180000
*  SERVICE CALL TYPES:                                             00190000
                                                                   00200000
01   LMOPEN            PIC X(8)      VALUE 'LMOPEN  '.             00210000
01   LMGET             PIC X(8)      VALUE 'LMGET   '.             00220000
01   LMPUT             PIC X(8)      VALUE 'LMPUT   '.             00230000
01   LMCLOSE           PIC X(8)      VALUE 'LMCLOSE '.             00240000
01   LMFREE            PIC X(8)      VALUE 'LMFREE  '.             00250000
01   LMMFIND           PIC X(8)      VALUE 'LMMFIND '.             00260000
01   LMMREP            PIC X(8)      VALUE 'LMMREP  '.             00270001
01   VDEFINE           PIC X(8)      VALUE 'VDEFINE '.             00280000
01   VDELETE           PIC X(8)      VALUE 'VDELETE '.             00290000
01   SETMSG            PIC X(8)      VALUE 'SETMSG  '.             00300000
                                                                   00310000
                                                                   00320000
*  FLAG INDICATES ERROR HAS OCCURRED IF NOT 0:                     00330000
                                                                   00340000
01   ERROR-FLAG        PIC S9(8)     VALUE +0   COMP.              00350002
                                                                   00360000
                                                                   00370000
*  THESE FOUR FLAGS INDICATE THE STATUS OF THE INPUT AND OUTPUT    00380000
*  FILES AND WHETHER THEY HAVE BEEN INITIALIZED AND/OR OPENED:     00390000
                                                                   00400000
01   ININIT            PIC X(3)      VALUE 'NO '.                  00410000
01   INOPEN            PIC X(3)      VALUE 'NO '.                  00420000
01   OUTINIT           PIC X(3)      VALUE 'NO '.                  00430000
01   OUTOPEN           PIC X(3)      VALUE 'NO '.                  00440000
```
(continued)

Figure 14-1. (*Continued*)

```
                                                                     00450000
                                                                     00460000
*  THE BUFFER AND BUFFER LENGTH FOR THE 'LMINIT' CALLS:              00470000
                                                                     00480000
01  BUFFER            PIC X(120)   VALUE SPACES.                     00490000
01  BUFFER-LENGTH     PIC 9(8)     VALUE 120 COMP.                   00500002
                                                                     00510000
*  FOR DATA SET ID'S RETURNED VIA 'LMINIT' INITIALIZATION SERVICE:   00520000
                                                                     00530000
                                                                     00540000
01  DSIDIN            PIC X(8)     VALUE SPACES.                     00550000
01  DSIDOUT           PIC X(8)     VALUE SPACES.                     00560000
                                                                     00570000
                                                                     00580000
*  OPTION PARAMETER FOR OPENING DATA SETS AS 'INPUT' OR 'OUTPUT':    00590000
                                                                     00600000
01  OPTION-INPUT      PIC X(8)     VALUE 'INPUT   '.                 00610000
01  OPTION-OUTPUT     PIC X(8)     VALUE 'OUTPUT  '.                 00620000
                                                                     00630000
                                                                     00640000
*  FLAG INDICATES END-OF-FILE CONDITION ON INPUT FILE DURING         00650000
*  THE COPY TO THE NEW FILE:                                         00660000
                                                                     00670000
01  LEAVE-FLAG        PIC X(3)     VALUE 'NO '.                      00680000
                                                                     03690000
                                                                     00700000
*  FLAG INDICATES WHETHER ANY RECORD(S) HAVE BEEN WRITTEN TO         00710000
*  THE OUTPUT MEMBER:                                                00720000
                                                                     00730000
01  PUT-FLAG          PIC X(3)     VALUE 'NO '.                      00740000
                                                                     00750000
                                                                     00760000
*  PARAMETERS FOR 'LMGET' AND 'LMPUT' REPRESENTING WHERE THE         00770000
*  DATA IS MOVED TO/FROM AND THE LENGTH OF THE MOVE:                 00780000
                                                                     00790000
01  DATALOCA          PIC X(8)     VALUE 'DATALOC '.                 00800000
01  DATALOC           PIC X(80)    VALUE SPACES.                     00810000
01  DATALENA          PIC X(8)     VALUE 'DATALEN '.                 00820000
01  DATALEN           PIC X(8)     VALUE SPACES.                     00830000
                                                                     00840000
                                                                     00850000
*  THE MEMBER NAMES OF THE INPUT AND OUTPUT MEMBERS:                 00860000
                                                                     00870000
01  INPUT-MEMBER-NAME  PIC X(8)    VALUE 'OLDMEMBR'.                 00880000
01  OUTPUT-MEMBER-NAME PIC X(8)    VALUE 'NEWMEMBR'.                 00890000
                                                                     00900000
                                                                     00910000
*  MODE OF 'LMGET' AND 'LMPUT' IS 'INVAR':                           00920000
                                                                     00930000
01  MODE-INVAR        PIC X(8)     VALUE 'INVAR   '.                 00940000
                                                                     00950000
                                                                     00960000
*  LENGTH OF DATA RECORD FOR 'LMGET' & 'LMPUT' CALLS:                00970000
                                                                     00980000
01  MAXLEN            PIC S9(8)    VALUE +80 COMP.                   00990000
                                                                     01000000
                                                                     01010000
*  PARAMETERS USED IN 'VDEFINE' OF VARIABLES TO ISPF:               01020000
                                                                     01030000
01  DSIDIN-LENGTH   PIC 9(6)    VALUE 8  COMP.                       01040000
01  DSIDOUT-LENGTH  PIC 9(6)    VALUE 8  COMP.                       01050000
01  DATALOC-LENGTH  PIC 9(6)    VALUE 80 COMP.                       01060000
01  DATALEN-LENGTH  PIC 9(6)    VALUE 8  COMP.                       01070000
                                                                     01080000
01  DSIDIN-NAME     PIC X(8)    VALUE '(DSIDIN)'.                    01090000
01  DSIDOUT-NAME    PIC X(9)    VALUE '(DSIDOUT)'.                   01100000
01  DATALOC-NAME    PIC X(9)    VALUE '(DATALOC)'.                   01110000
01  DATALEN-NAME    PIC X(9)    VALUE '(DATALEN)'.                   01120000
                                                                     01130000
01  CHAR            PIC X(8)    VALUE 'CHAR    '.                    01140000
                                                                     01150000
                                                                     01160000
*  MESSAGES:                                                         01170000
                                                                     01180000
01  LMINIT-FAILED-INP-MSG    PIC X(8)    VALUE 'WDAR001A'.           01190000
01  LMOPEN-FAILED-INP-MSG    PIC X(8)    VALUE 'WDAR001B'.           01200000
01  LMINIT-FAILED-OUT-MSG    PIC X(8)    VALUE 'WDAR001C'.           01210000
01  LMOPEN-FAILED-OUT-MSG    PIC X(8)    VALUE 'WDAR001D'.           01220000
01  LMGET-FAILED-MSG         PIC X(8)    VALUE 'WDAR001E'.           01230000
01  LMPUT-FAILED-MSG         PIC X(8)    VALUE 'WDAR001F'.           01240000
01  LMCLOSE-FAILED-INP-MSG   PIC X(8)    VALUE 'WDAR001G'.           01250000
01  LMFREE-FAILED-INP-MSG    PIC X(8)    VALUE 'WDAR001H'.           01260000
01  LMCLOSE-FAILED-OUT-MSG   PIC X(8)    VALUE 'WDAR001I'.           01270000
01  LMFREE-FAILED-OUT-MSG    PIC X(8)    VALUE 'WDAR001J'.           01280000
01  LMMFIND-FAILED-MSG       PIC X(8)    VALUE 'WDAR002A'.           01300000
01  LMMREP-FAILED-MSG        PIC X(8)    VALUE 'WDAR002B'.           01310000
01  PDSCOPY-COMPLETED-OK-MSG PIC X(8)    VALUE 'WDAR002C'.           01320000
                                                                     01330000
```

```
                                                       01340000
                                                       01350000
                                                       01360000
    PROCEDURE DIVISION.                                 01370000
                                                       01380000
                                                       01390000
                                                       01400000
                                                       01410000
 *                                                      01420000
 *  DEFINE NECESSARY VARIABLES TO ISPF:                 01430000
 *                                                      01440000
        PERFORM DEFINE-VARIABLES THROUGH DEFINE-VARIABLES-EXIT.   01450004
                                                       01460000
                                                       01470000
 *                                                      01480000
 *  INITIALIZE THE INPUT FILE FOR THE COPY THROUGH 'LMINIT'.   01490000
 *  NOTE USE OF THE 'ISPEXEC' CALL FORMAT TO ELMINATE CONCERN   01500000
 *  OVER POSITIONAL PARAMETERS, AS IN 'ISPLINK' CALL FORMAT:   01510000
 *                                                      01520000
                                                       01530000
                                                       01540000
        MOVE  'LMINIT DATAID(DSIDIN) DDNAME(INFILE) ENQ(SHR)'   01550000
            TO  BUFFER.                                 01560000
                                                       01570000
        CALL  'ISPEXEC'  USING  BUFFER-LENGTH  BUFFER.   01580000
                                                       01590000
                                                       01600000
        MOVE  RETURN-CODE  TO  ERROR-FLAG.             01610000
                                                       01620000
        IF  ERROR-FLAG  >  0                            01630000
                                                       01640000
            CALL 'ISPLINK'  USING  SETMSG              01650000
                                   LMINIT-FAILED-INP-MSG   01660000
                                                       01670000
        ELSE                                            01680000
                                                       01690000
            MOVE  'YES'  TO  ININIT.                    01700000
                                                       01710000
                                                       01720000
 *                                                      01730000
 *  OPEN THE INPUT FILE FOR THE COPY:                   01740000
 *                                                      01750000
                                                       01760000
        IF  ERROR-FLAG  =  0                            01770000
                                                       01780000
            CALL  'ISPLINK'  USING  LMOPEN             01790000
                                    DSIDIN              01800000
                                    OPTION-INPUT        01810000
                                                       01820000
            MOVE  RETURN-CODE  TO  ERROR-FLAG          01830000
                                                       01840000
            IF  ERROR-FLAG  >  0                        01850000
                                                       01860000
                CALL  'ISPLINK'  USING  SETMSG         01870000
                                       LMOPEN-FAILED-INP-MSG   01880000
                                                       01890000
            ELSE                                        01900000
                                                       01910000
                MOVE  'YES'  TO  INOPEN.               01920000
                                                       01930000
                                                       01940000
 *                                                      01950000
 *  CALL 'LMMFIND' TO FIND THE MEMBER TO COPY:          01960000
 *                                                      01970000
                                                       01980000
        IF  ERROR-FLAG  =  0                            01990000
                                                       02000000
            CALL  'ISPLINK'  USING  LMMFIND            02010000
                                    DSIDIN              02020000
                                    INPUT-MEMBER-NAME   02030000
                                                       02040000
            MOVE  RETURN-CODE  TO  ERROR-FLAG          02050000
                                                       02060000
            IF  ERROR-FLAG  >  0                        02070000
                                                       02080000
                CALL  'ISPLINK'  USING  SETMSG         02090000
                                       LMMFIND-FAILED-MSG.   02100000
                                                       02110000
                                                       02120000
 *                                                      02130000
 *  INITIALIZE THE OUTPUT FILE FOR THE COPY, BY THE 'LMINIT'   02140000
 *  SERVICE SPECIFYING A DDNAME:                        02150000
 *                                                      02160000
                                                       02170000
        IF  ERROR-FLAG  =  0                            02180000
                                                       02190000
```

(continued)

Figure 14-1. (Continued)

```
            MOVE                                                      02200000
            'LMINIT DATAID(DSIDOUT) DDNAME(OUTFILE) ENQ(EXCLU)'       02210000
                 TO   BUFFER                                          02220000
                                                                      02230000
            CALL  'ISPEXEC' USING  BUFFER-LENGTH  BUFFER              02240000
                                                                      02250000
            MOVE  RETURN-CODE  TO  ERROR-FLAG                         02260000
                                                                      02270000
            IF  ERROR-FLAG  >  0                                      02280000
                                                                      02290000
                CALL  'ISPLINK'  USING  SETMSG                        02300000
                                        LMINIT-FAILED-OUT-MSG         02310000
                                                                      02320000
            ELSE                                                      02330000
                                                                      02340000
                MOVE 'YES'  TO  OUTINIT.                              02350000
                                                                      02360000
                                                                      02370000
*                                                                     02380000
*   OPEN THE OUTPUT FILE FOR THE COPY:                                02390000
*                                                                     02400000
                                                                      02410000
        IF  ERROR-FLAG  =  0                                          02420000
                                                                      02430000
            CALL  'ISPLINK'  USING    LMOPEN                          02440000
                                      DSIDOUT                         02450000
                                      OPTION-OUTPUT                   02460000
                                                                      02470000
            MOVE  RETURN-CODE  TO  ERROR-FLAG                         02480000
                                                                      02490000
            IF  ERROR-FLAG  >  0                                      02500000
                                                                      02510000
                CALL  'ISPLINK'  USING  SETMSG                        02520000
                                        LMOPEN-FAILED-OUT-MSG         02530000
                                                                      02540000
            ELSE                                                      02550000
                                                                      02560000
                MOVE 'YES'  TO  OUTOPEN.                              02570000
                                                                      02580000
                                                                      02590000
*                                                                     02600000
*   COPY THE RECORDS FROM THE LIBRARY MEMBER INPUT FILE TO THE        02610000
*   OUTPUT MEMBER IN THE OTHER LIBRARY:                               02620000
*                                                                     02630000
                                                                      02640000
        PERFORM  COPY-PARAGRAPH  THRU   COPY-PARAGRAPH-EXIT           02650000
            UNTIL   ERROR-FLAG  NOT =   0                             02660000
            OR      LEAVE-FLAG  NOT =   'NO '.                        02670000
                                                                      02680000
                                                                      02690000
*                                                                     02700000
*   IF 'LMPUT' WAS PROPERLY EXECUTED FOR OUTPUT, CALL 'LMMREP'        02710000
*   TO REPLACE OUTPUT MEMBER.  RETURN CODE OF 8 WILL BE OK -          02720000
*   IT MEANS THE MEMBER IS ADDED, BECAUSE IT DID NOT PREVIOUSLY       02730000
*   EXIST:                                                            02740000
*                                                                     02750000
                                                                      02760000
        IF  ERROR-FLAG  =  0  AND  PUT-FLAG  =  'YES'                 02770001
                                                                      02780000
            CALL  'ISPLINK'  USING    LMMREP                          02790000
                                      DSIDOUT                         02800000
                                      OUTPUT-MEMBER-NAME              02810000
                                                                      02820000
            IF  RETURN-CODE  >  8                                     02830000
                                                                      02840000
                MOVE  RETURN-CODE  TO  ERROR-FLAG                     02850000
                                                                      02860000
                CALL  'ISPLINK'  USING  SETMSG                        02870000
                                        LMMREP-FAILED-MSG.            02880000
                                                                      02890000
                                                                      02900000
*                                                                     02910000
*   IF THE INPUT FILE WAS OPENED, CLOSE IT:                           02920000
*                                                                     02930000
                                                                      02940000
        IF  INOPEN  =  'YES'                                          02950000
                                                                      02960000
            CALL  'ISPLINK'  USING    LMCLOSE                         02970000
                                      DSIDIN                          02980000
                                                                      02990000
            IF  RETURN-CODE  >  0                                     03000000
                                                                      03010000
                MOVE  RETURN-CODE  TO  ERROR-FLAG                     03020000
                                                                      03030000
                CALL  'ISPLINK'  USING  SETMSG                        03040000
                                        LMCLOSE-FAILED-INP-MSG.       03050000
                                                                      03060000
                                                                      03070000
```

```
*                                                              03080000
*   IF THE INPUT FILE WAS INITIALIZED, FREE IT:                03090000
*                                                              03100000
                                                               03110000
    IF  ININIT  =  'YES'                                       03120000
                                                               03130000
        CALL  'ISPLINK'  USING   LMFREE                        03140000
                                 DSIDIN                        03150000
                                                               03160000
        IF  RETURN-CODE  >  0                                  03170000
                                                               03180000
            MOVE  RETURN-CODE  TO  ERROR-FLAG                  03190000
                                                               03200000
            CALL  'ISPLINK'  USING  SETMSG                     03210000
                                LMFREE-FAILED-INP-MSG.         03220000
                                                               03230000
                                                               03240000
                                                               03250000
*                                                              03260000
*   IF THE OUTPUT FILE WAS OPENED, CLOSE IT:                   03270000
*                                                              03280000
                                                               03290000
    IF  OUTOPEN  =  'YES'                                      03300000
                                                               03310000
        CALL  'ISPLINK'  USING   LMCLOSE                       03320000
                                 DSIDOUT                       03330000
                                                               03340000
        IF  RETURN-CODE  >  0                                  03350000
                                                               03360000
            MOVE  RETURN-CODE  TO  ERROR-FLAG                  03370000
                                                               03380000
            CALL  'ISPLINK'  USING  SETMSG                     03390000
                                LMCLOSE-FAILED-OUT-MSG.        03400000
                                                               03410000
                                                               03420000
*                                                              03430000
*   IF THE OUTPUT FILE WAS INITIALIZED, FREE IT:               03440000
*                                                              03450000
                                                               03460000
    IF  OUTINIT  =  'YES'                                      03470000
                                                               03480000
        CALL  'ISPLINK'  USING   LMFREE                        03490000
                                 DSIDOUT                       03500000
                                                               03510000
        IF  RETURN-CODE  >  0                                  03520000
                                                               03530000
            MOVE  RETURN-CODE  TO  ERROR-FLAG                  03540000
                                                               03550000
            CALL  'ISPLINK'  USING  SETMSG                     03560000
                                LMFREE-FAILED-OUT-MSG.         03570000
                                                               03580000
                                                               03590000
*                                                              03600000
*   IF ALL WENT WELL, WRITE A MESSAGE.  'VDELETE' ALL VARIABLES 03610000
*   KNOWN TO ISPF AND EXIT:                                    03620000
*                                                              03630000
                                                               03640000
    IF  ERROR-FLAG  =  0                                       03650000
                                                               03660000
            CALL  'ISPLINK'  USING  SETMSG                     03670000
                                PDSCOPY-COMPLETED-OK-MSG.      03680000
                                                               03690000
                                                               03700000
    PERFORM DELETE-VARIABLES THROUGH DELETE-VARIABLES-EXIT.    03710000
                                                               03720000
                                                               03730000
    MOVE  ERROR-FLAG  TO  RETURN-CODE.                         03740000
    GOBACK.                                                    03750000
                                                               03760000
MAIN-LINE-EXIT.                                                03770000
                                                               03780000
                                                               03790000
                                                               03800000
                                                               03810000
COPY-PARAGRAPH.                                                03820000
                                                               03830000
                                                               03840000
*                                                              03850000
*   RETRIEVE A RECORD FROM THE INPUT FILE:                     03860000
*                                                              03870000
                                                               03880000
    CALL  'ISPLINK'  USING  LMGET                              03890000
                            DSIDIN                             03930000
                            MODE-INVAR                         03910000
                            DATALOCA                           03920000
                            DATALENA                           03930000
                            MAXLEN.                            03940000
```

(continued)

Figure 14-1. (*Continued*)

```
          MOVE  RETURN-CODE  TO  ERROR-FLAG.                    03950000
                                                                03960000
          IF  ERROR-FLAG  >  8                                  03970000
                                                                03980000
                                                                03990000
              CALL  'ISPLINK'  USING  SETMSG                    04000000
                                      LMGET-FAILED-MSG.         04010000
                                                                04020000
                                                                04030000
 *                                                              04040000
 *   RETURN CODE OF 8 SIGNIFIES END-OF-FILE ON INPUT FILE:      04050000
 *                                                              04060000
                                                                04070000
          IF  ERROR-FLAG  =  8                                  04080000
                                                                04090000
              MOVE  'YES'  TO  LEAVE-FLAG                       04100000
                                                                04110000
              MOVE  0  TO  ERROR-FLAG.                          04120000
                                                                04130000
                                                                04140000
 *                                                              04150000
 *   IF A RECORD WAS READ, WRITE IT TO OUTPUT FILE:             04160000
 *                                                              04170000
                                                                04180000
          IF  ERROR-FLAG  =  0  AND  LEAVE-FLAG  =  'NO '       04190000
                                                                04200000
              CALL  'ISPLINK'  USING  LMPUT                     04210000
                                      DSIDOUT                   04220000
                                      MODE-INVAR                04230000
                                      DATALOCA                  04240000
                                      MAXLEN                    04250000
                                                                04260000
              MOVE  RETURN-CODE  TO  ERROR-FLAG                 04270000
                                                                04280000
              IF  ERROR-FLAG  >  0                              04290000
                                                                04300000
                  CALL  'ISPLINK'  USING  SETMSG               04310000
                                          LMPUT-FAILED-MSG      04320000
              ELSE                                              04330000
                                                                04340000
                  MOVE  'YES'  TO  PUT-FLAG.                    04350000
                                                                04360000
                                                                04370000
                                                                04380000
 COPY-PARAGRAPH-EXIT.                                           04390000
     EXIT.                                                      04400000
                                                                04410000
                                                                04420000
                                                                04430000
                                                                04440000
 DEFINE-VARIABLES.                                              04450000
                                                                04460000
                                                                04470000
                                                                04480000
 *                                                              04490000
 *   DEFINE NECESSARY VARIABLES TO ISPF DIALOG MANAGER:         04500000
 *                                                              04510000
          CALL  'ISPLINK'  USING  VDEFINE                       04520000
                                  DSIDIN-NAME                   04530000
                                  DSIDIN                        04540000
                                  CHAR                          04550000
                                  DSIDIN-LENGTH.                04560000
          CALL  'ISPLINK'  USING  VDEFINE                       04570000
                                  DSIDOUT-NAME                  04580000
                                  DSIDOUT                       04590000
                                  CHAR                          04600000
                                  DSIDOUT-LENGTH.               04610000
          CALL  'ISPLINK'  USING  VDEFINE                       04620000
                                  DATALOC-NAME                  04630000
                                  DATALOC                       04640000
                                  CHAR                          04650000
                                  DATALOC-LENGTH.               04660000
          CALL  'ISPLINK'  USING  VDEFINE                       04670000
                                  DATALEN-NAME                  04680000
                                  DATALEN                       04690000
                                  CHAR                          04700000
                                  DATALEN-LENGTH.               04710000
                                                                04720000
                                                                04730000
 DEFINE-VARIABLES-EXIT.                                         04740000
     EXIT.                                                      04750000
                                                                04760000
                                                                04770000
                                                                04780000
                                                                04790000
 DELETE-VARIABLES.                                              04800000
                                                                04810000
                                                                04820000
```

```
*                                                                04830000
*     DELETE ALL DIALOG MANAGER VARIABLES RE ISPF DIALOG MANAGER:  04840000
*                                                                04850000
                                                                 04860000
      CALL 'ISPLINK'   USING   VDELETE                           04870000
                               DSIDIN-NAME.                      04880000
      CALL 'ISPLINK'   USING   VDELETE                           04890000
                               DSIDOUT-NAME.                     04900000
      CALL 'ISPLINK'   USING   VDELETE                           04910000
                               DATALOC-NAME.                     04920000
      CALL 'ISPLINK'   USING   VDELETE                           04930000
                               DATALEN-NAME.                     04940000
                                                                 04950000
                                                                 04960000
  DELETE-VARIABLES-EXIT.                                         04970000
      EXIT.                                                      04980000
```

Figure 14-2. PDSCOPY CLIST function.

```
00010000   PROC 0
00020000   CONTROL LIST
00030000   /********************************************************************/
00040000   /* NAME: PDSCOPY                          BY: H. FOSDICK        */
00050000   /*                                                             */
00060000   /* PURPOSE: THIS CLIST COPIES A MEMBER FROM ONE ISPF           */
00070000   /* LIBRARY TO ANOTHER.  IT IS ASSUMED THAT THE MEMBER TO       */
00080000   /* COPY EXISTS AND THAT IT CONTAINS AT LEAST ONE RECORD.       */
00090000   /*                                                             */
00100000   /********************************************************************/
00110000
00120000   /*                                                             */
00130000   /*    INITIALIZE LIBRARY AND MEMBER NAMES FOR INPUT & OUTPUT:  */
00140000   /*                                                             */
00150000
00160000   SET   INPROJ    =  ZHMF01
00170000   SET   INGRP     =  PROGRAMS
00180000   SET   INTYPE    =  DATA
00190000   SET   INMEMBR   =  OLDMEMBR
00200000
00210000   SET   OUTPROJ   =  ZHMF01
00220000   SET   OUTGRP    =  PROGRAMS
00230000   SET   OUTTYPE   =  COBOL
00240000   SET   OUTMEMB   =  NEWMEMBR
00250000
00260000
00270000   /*                                                             */
00280000   /*    INITIALIZE FLAGS:                                        */
00290000   /*                                                             */
00300000
00310000   SET   ERROR   =  0       /* 0 MEANS AN ERROR HAS NOT OCCURRED. */
00320000   SET   ININIT  =  NO      /* THESE FOUR FLAGS INDICATE THE      */
00330000   SET   INOPEN  =  NO      /* STATUS OF THE INPUT AND OUTPUT     */
00340000   SET   OUTINIT =  NO      /* LIBRARIES & WHETHER THEY HAVE BEEN */
00350000   SET   OUTOPEN =  NO      /* INITIALIZED AND/OR OPENED.         */
00360000
00370000
00380000   /*                                                             */
00390000   /*    INITIALIZE THE INPUT FILE FOR THE COPY:                  */
00400000   /*                                                             */
00410000
00420000   ISPEXEC  LMINIT  DATAID(DSIDIN) +
00430000        DATASET('&INPROJ..&INGRP..&INTYPE')  ENQ(SHR)
00440000
00450000   SET   ERROR  =  &LASTCC
00460000
00470000   IF  &ERROR  >  0   THEN  +
00480000        ISPEXEC  SETMSG  MSG(WDAR001A)
00490000   ELSE  +
00500000        SET   ININIT  =  YES
00510000
00520000
00530000   /*                                                             */
00540000   /*  OPEN THE INPUT FILE FOR THE COPY:                          */
00550000   /*                                                             */
00560000
00570000   IF  &ERROR  =  0   THEN  DO
00580000
00590000        ISPEXEC  LMOPEN  DATAID(&DSIDIN)  OPTION(INPUT)
00600000
00610000        SET   ERROR  =  &LASTCC
00620000
00630000        IF  &ERROR  >  0   THEN  +
00640000            ISPEXEC  SETMSG  MSG(WDAR001B)
00650000        ELSE  +
00660000            SET   INOPEN  =  YES
00670000
00680000        END
00690000
00700000
00710000   /*                                                             */
00720000   /*  CALL 'LMMFIND' TO FIND THE MEMBER TO COPY:                 */
00730000   /*                                                             */
00740000
00750000   IF  &ERROR  =  0   THEN  DO
00760000
00770000        ISPEXEC  LMMFIND  DATAID(&DSIDIN)  MEMBER(&INMEMBR)
00780000
00790000        SET   ERROR  =  &LASTCC
00800000
00810000        IF  &ERROR  >  0   THEN  +
00820000            ISPEXEC  SETMSG  MSG(WDAR002A)
00830000
00840000        END
00850000
00860000
00870000   /*                                                             */
00880000   /*  INITIALIZE THE OUTPUT FILE FOR THE COPY:                   */
```

```
00890000   /*                                                             */
00900000
00910000   IF  &ERROR  =  0  THEN  DO
00920000
00930000       ISPEXEC  LMINIT  DATAID(DSIDOUT)    +
00940000           DATASET('&OUTPROJ..&OUTGRP..&OUTTYPE')  ENQ(EXCLU)
00950000
00960000       SET  ERROR  =  &LASTCC
00970000
00980000       IF  &ERROR  >  0  THEN  +
00990000           ISPEXEC  SETMSG  MSG(WDAR001C)
01000000       ELSE  +
01010000           SET  OUTINIT  =  YES
01020000
01030000       END
01040000
01050000
01060000   /*                                                             */
01070000   /*  OPEN THE OUTPUT FILE FOR THE COPY:                         */
01080000   /*                                                             */
01090000
01100000   IF  &ERROR  =  0  THEN  DO
01110000
01120000       ISPEXEC  LMOPEN  DATAID(&DSIDOUT)  OPTION(OUTPUT)
01130000
01140000       SET  ERROR  =  &LASTCC
01150000
01160000       IF  &ERROR  >  0  THEN  +
01170000           ISPEXEC  SETMSG  MSG(WDAR001D)
01180000       ELSE  +
01190000           SET  OUTOPEN  =  YES
01200000
01210000       END
01220000
01230000
01240000   /*                                                             */
01250000   /*  THE CODE IN THIS 'DO WHILE' LOOP COPIES THE RECORDS        */
01260000   /*  FROM THE LIBRARY MEMBER INPUT FILE TO THE OUTPUT MEMBER    */
01270000   /*  IN THE OTHER LIBRARY.  THE VARIABLE 'LEAVE' INDICATES      */
01280000   /*  END-OF-FILE ON THE INPUT FILE AND SIGNIFIES EXIT FROM      */
01290000   /*  THE 'DO WHILE' LOOP.  THE VARIABLE 'PUT' INDICATES         */
01300000   /*  WHETHER A SUCCESSFUL 'LMPUT' CALL OCCURRED:                */
01310000   /*                                                             */
01320000
01330000   SET  LEAVE  =  NO
01340000   SET  PUT    =  NO
01350000
01360000
01370000   DO  WHILE  &ERROR  =  0  AND  &LEAVE  =  NO
01380000
01390000
01400000       /*                                                         */
01410000       /*  RETRIEVE A RECORD FROM THE INPUT FILE:                 */
01420000       /*                                                         */
01430000
01440000       ISPEXEC  LMGET  DATAID(&DSIDIN)  MODE(INVAR)  +
01450000           DATALOC(RECORD)  DATALEN(RECLEN)  MAXLEN(80)
01460000
01470000       SET  ERROR  =  &LASTCC
01480000
01490000       IF  &ERROR  >  8  THEN  +
01500000           ISPEXEC  SETMSG  MSG(WDAR001E)
01510000
01520000       /*                                                         */
01530000       /*  RETURN CODE OF 8 SIGNIFIES END-OF-FILE ON INPUT FILE:  */
01540000       /*                                                         */
01550000
01560000       IF  &ERROR  =  8  THEN  DO
01570000           SET  LEAVE  =  YES
01580000           SET  ERROR  =  0
01590000           END
01600000
01610000
01620000       /*                                                         */
01630000       /*  IF A RECORD WAS READ, WRITE IT TO OUTPUT FILE:         */
01640000       /*                                                         */
01650000
01660000       IF  &ERROR  =  0   AND  &LEAVE  =  NO  THEN  DO
01670000
01680000           ISPEXEC  LMPUT  DATAID(&DSIDOUT)  MODE(INVAR)   +
01690000               DATALOC(RECORD)  DATALEN(&RECLEN)
01700000
01710000           SET  ERROR  =  &LASTCC
01720000
01730000           IF  &ERROR  >  0  THEN  +
01740000               ISPEXEC  SETMSG   MSG(WDAR001F)
```

(continued)

Figure 14-2. (*Continued*)

```
01750000                  ELSE  +
01760000                      SET  PUT  =  YES
01770000
01780000                  END
01790000
01800000    END
01810000
01820000
01830000
01840000    /*                                                                 */
01850000    /*  IF 'LMPUT' WAS PROPERLY EXECUTED FOR OUTPUT, CALL              */
01860000    /*  'LMMREP' TO REPLACE OUTPUT MEMBER.  RETURN CODE OF 8 IS        */
01870000    /*  OK - IT MEANS THE MEMBER IS ADDED, BECAUSE IT DID NOT          */
01880000    /*  PREVIOUSLY EXIST:                                              */
01890000    /*                                                                 */
01900000
01910001    IF  &ERROR = 0  AND  &PUT = YES  THEN  DO
01920000
01930002        ISPEXEC LMMREP DATAID(&DSIDOUT)  MEMBER(&OUTMEMB)
01940000
01950002        IF  &LASTCC  >  8  THEN  DO
01960000            SET  ERROR  =  &LASTCC
01970002            ISPEXEC  SETMSG  MSG(WDAR002B)
01980000            END
01990000
02000000        END
02010000
02020000
02030000
02040000    /*                                                                 */
02050000    /*  IF THE INPUT FILE WAS OPENED, CLOSE IT:                        */
02060000    /*                                                                 */
02070000
02080000    IF  &INOPEN  =  YES  THEN  DO
02090000
02100000        ISPEXEC  LMCLOSE  DATAID(&DSIDIN)
02110000
02120000        IF  &LASTCC  >  0  THEN  DO
02130000            SET  ERROR  =  &LASTCC
02140000            ISPEXEC  SETMSG  MSG(WDAR001G)
02150000            END
02160000
02170000        END
02180000
02190000
02200000    /*                                                                 */
02210000    /*  IF THE INPUT FILE WAS INITIALIZED, FREE IT:                    */
02220000    /*                                                                 */
02230000
02240000    IF  &ININIT  =  YES  THEN  DO
02250000
02260000        ISPEXEC  LMFREE  DATAID(&DSIDIN)
02270000
02280000        IF  &LASTCC  >  0  THEN  DO
02290000            SET  ERROR  =  &LASTCC
02300000            ISPEXEC  SETMSG  MSG(WDAR001H)
02310000            END
02320000
02330000        END
02340000
02350000
02360000    /*                                                                 */
02370000    /*  IF THE OUTPUT FILE WAS OPENED, CLOSE IT:                       */
02380000    /*                                                                 */
02390000
02400000    IF  &OUTOPEN  =  YES  THEN  DO
02410000
02420000        ISPEXEC  LMCLOSE  DATAID(&DSIDOUT)
02430000
02440000        IF  &LASTCC  >  0  THEN  DO
02450000            SET  ERROR  =  &LASTCC
02460000            ISPEXEC  SETMSG  MSG(WDAR001I)
02470000            END
02480000
02490000        END
02500000
02510000
02520000    /*                                                                 */
02530000    /*  IF THE OUTPUT FILE WAS INITIALIZED, FREE IT:                   */
02540000    /*                                                                 */
02550000
02560000    IF  &OUTINIT  =  YES  THEN  DO
02570000
02580000        ISPEXEC  LMFREE  DATAID(&DSIDOUT)
02590000
02600000        IF  &LASTCC  >  0  THEN  DO
02610000            SET  ERROR  =  &LASTCC
```

```
02620000          ISPEXEC  SETMSG  MSG(WDAR001J)
02630000          END
02640000
02650000     END
02660000
02670000
02680000 /*                                                */
02690000 /*  IF ALL WENT WELL, WRITE A MESSAGE.  THEN EXIT CLIST:    */
02700000 /*                                                */
02710000
02720000 IF  &ERROR = 0  THEN +
02730002     ISPEXEC  SETMSG  MSG(WDAR002C)
02740000
02750000
02760000 EXIT  CODE(&ERROR)
```

Figure 14-3. PDSLISTC COBOL function.

```
        IDENTIFICATION DIVISION.                                  00010000
        PROGRAM-ID. PDSLISTC.                                     00020000
        ***********************************************************00030000
        *  NAME: PDSLISTC                           BY: H. FOSDICK *00040000
        *                                                         *00050000
        *  PURPOSE: THIS PROGRAM CREATES AN MVS SEQUENTIAL FILE   *00060000
        *  CONTAINING A SORTED LIST OF ALL THE MEMBERS FROM AN MVS *00070000
        *  PARTITIONED DATA SET.  PDS STATISTICS ARE ASSOCIATED WITH*00080000
        *  EACH MEMBER LISTED.  ISPF BROWSE IS USED TO VIEW THE    *00090000
        *  NEWLY-CREATED FILE OF MEMBER NAMES AND STATISTICS.      *00100000
        *                                                         *00110000
        ***********************************************************00120000
        ENVIRONMENT DIVISION.                                     00130000
        DATA DIVISION.                                            00140000
                                                                  00150000
                                                                  00160000
        WORKING-STORAGE SECTION.                                  00170000
                                                                  00180000
                                                                  00190000
                                                                  00200000
        *  SERVICE CALL TYPES:                                    00210000
                                                                  00220000
        01  VDEFINE          PIC X(8)      VALUE 'VDEFINE '.       00230006
        01  VDELETE          PIC X(8)      VALUE 'VDELETE '.       00240006
                                                                  00250000
                                                                  00260000
        *  FLAG INDICATES ERROR HAS OCCURRED IF NOT 0:            00270000
                                                                  00280000
        01  ERROR-FLAG       PIC S9(8)     VALUE +0  COMP.         00290000
                                                                  00300000
                                                                  00310000
        *  THESE FOUR FLAGS INDICATE THE STATUS OF THE INPUT AND OUTPUT00320023
        *  FILES AND WHETHER THEY HAVE BEEN INITIALIZED AND/OR OPENED:00330000
                                                                  00340000
        01  ININIT           PIC X(3)      VALUE 'NO '.            00350000
        01  INOPEN           PIC X(3)      VALUE 'NO '.            00360000
        01  OUTINIT          PIC X(3)      VALUE 'NO '.            00370000
        01  OUTOPEN          PIC X(3)      VALUE 'NO '.            00380000
                                                                  00390000
                                                                  00400000
        *  THE BUFFER AND BUFFER LENGTH FOR THE 'ISPEXEC'-FORMAT CALLS:00410020
                                                                  00420000
        01  BUFFER           PIC X(120)    VALUE SPACES.           00430000
        01  BUFFER-LENGTH    PIC 9(8)      VALUE 120  COMP.        00440000
                                                                  00450000
                                                                  00460000
        *  FOR DATA SET ID'S RETURNED VIA 'LMINIT' INITIALIZATION SERVICE:00470000
                                                                  00480000
        01  DSIDIN           PIC X(8)      VALUE SPACES.           00490000
        01  DSIDOUT          PIC X(8)      VALUE SPACES.           00500000
                                                                  00510000
                                                                  00520000
        *  FLAG INDICATES END-OF-FILE CONDITION ON INPUT PDS LIST DURING00530020
        *  THE RETRIEVAL OF MEMBER NAMES:                         00540020
                                                                  00550000
        01  LEAVE-FLAG       PIC X(3)      VALUE 'NO '.            00560000
                                                                  00570000
                                                                  00580000
        *  FLAG INDICATES WHETHER ANY RECORD(S) HAVE BEEN WRITTEN TO00590000
        *  THE OUTPUT MEMBER:                                     00600000
                                                                  00610000
        01  PUT-FLAG         PIC X(3)      VALUE 'NO '.            00620000
                                                                  00630001
                                                                  00640001
        *  FLAG INDICATES WHETHER THE FIRST 'LMMLIST' CALL SUCCEEDED.00650001
        *  IF SO, ANOTHER 'LMMLIST' WITH THE 'FREE' OPTION SHOULD OCCUR:00660001
                                                                  00670001
        01  LISTED-FLAG      PIC X(3)      VALUE 'NO '.            00680001
                                                                  00760003
                                                                  00770003
        *  EACH MEMBER NAME RETRIEVED VIA 'LMMLIST' IS MOVED HERE: 00780003
                                                                  00790003
        01  MEMVAR           PIC X(8)      VALUE SPACES.           00800022
                                                                  00810004
                                                                  00820004
        *  SYSTEM VARIABLES RETRIEVED BY 'STATS' OPTION:          00830004
                                                                  00840004
        01  ZLUSER           PIC X(8)      VALUE SPACES.           00850004
        01  ZLMDATE          PIC X(8)      VALUE SPACES.           00860004
        01  ZLCNORC          PIC X(8)      VALUE SPACES.           00870004
                                                                  00880004
                                                                  00890004
        *  OUTPUT RECORD FOR COLUMN HEADER FOR NAME/STATISTICS FILE:00900010
                                                                  00910004
        01  HEADER           PIC X(80)                            00920010
            VALUE 'MEMBER:  USERID:  LAST MOD:  # RECS:'.          00930026
                                                                  00940004
                                                                  00950004
```

```
*    OUTPUT RECORD WITH MEMBER NAME AND STATISTICS:                00960004
                                                                   00970004
     01  OUTREC.                                                   00980023
         05   MEM-OUT         PIC  X(9)    VALUE   SPACES.          00990004
         05   USER-OUT        PIC  X(9)    VALUE   SPACES.          01000004
         05   DATE-OUT        PIC  X(9)    VALUE   SPACES.          01010004
         05   LCNORC-OUT      PIC  X(9)    VALUE   SPACES.          01020004
         05   FILLER          PIC  X(44)   VALUE   SPACES.          01030014
                                                                   01040000
                                                                   01050000
*    PARAMETERS USED IN 'VDEFINE' OF VARIABLES TO ISPF:            01060000
                                                                   01070000
     01  DSIDIN-LENGTH        PIC  9(6)    VALUE   8  COMP.         01080004
     01  DSIDOUT-LENGTH       PIC  9(6)    VALUE   8  COMP.         01090004
     01  HEADER-LENGTH        PIC  9(6)    VALUE   80 COMP.         01120011
     01  MEMVAR-LENGTH        PIC  9(6)    VALUE   8  COMP.         01130022
     01  OUTREC-LENGTH        PIC  9(6)    VALUE   80 COMP.         01140023
     01  ZLUSER-LENGTH        PIC  9(6)    VALUE   8  COMP.         01150015
     01  ZLMDATE-LENGTH       PIC  9(6)    VALUE   8  COMP.         01160018
     01  ZLCNORC-LENGTH       PIC  9(6)    VALUE   8  COMP.         01170018
                                                                   01180000
     01  DSIDIN-NAME          PIC  X(8)    VALUE   '(DSIDIN)'.      01190004
     01  DSIDOUT-NAME         PIC  X(9)    VALUE   '(DSIDOUT)'.     01200004
     01  HEADER-NAME          PIC  X(8)    VALUE   '(HEADER)'.      01230011
     01  MEMVAR-NAME          PIC  X(8)    VALUE   '(MEMVAR)'.      01240022
     01  OUTREC-NAME          PIC  X(8)    VALUE   '(OUTREC)'.      01250023
     01  ZLUSER-NAME          PIC  X(8)    VALUE   '(ZLUSER)'.      01260015
     01  ZLMDATE-NAME         PIC  X(9)    VALUE   '(ZLMDATE)'.     01270018
     01  ZLCNORC-NAME         PIC  X(9)    VALUE   '(ZLCNORC)'.     01280018
                                                                   01290000
     01  CHAR                 PIC  X(8)    VALUE   'CHAR    '.      01300004
                                                                   01310000
                                                                   01320000
                                                                   01330000
                                                                   01340000
     PROCEDURE DIVISION.                                           01350000
                                                                   01360000
                                                                   01370000
                                                                   01380000
*                                                                  01390000
*    DEFINE NECESSARY VARIABLES TO ISPF:                           01400000
*                                                                  01410000
                                                                   01420000
         PERFORM DEFINE-VARIABLES THROUGH DEFINE-VARIABLES-EXIT.   01430000
                                                                   01440000
                                                                   01450000
*                                                                  01460000
*    INITIALIZE THE INPUT PDS FOR THE MEMBER LIST:                 01470001
*                                                                  01480000
                                                                   01490000
         MOVE  'LMINIT  DATAID(DSIDIN)  DDNAME(INFILE)  ENQ(SHR)'  01510020
               TO  BUFFER.                                         01520000
                                                                   01530000
         CALL  'ISPEXEC'  USING  BUFFER-LENGTH  BUFFER.            01540000
                                                                   01550000
         MOVE  RETURN-CODE  TO  ERROR-FLAG.                        01560000
                                                                   01570000
         IF  ERROR-FLAG  >  0                                      01580000
                                                                   01590002
             MOVE  'SETMSG MSG(WDAR001A)'  TO  BUFFER              01600002
                                                                   01610002
             CALL  'ISPEXEC'  USING  BUFFER-LENGTH  BUFFER         01620002
                                                                   01630002
         ELSE                                                      01640000
                                                                   01650000
             MOVE  'YES'  TO  ININIT.                              01660000
                                                                   01670000
                                                                   01680000
*                                                                  01690000
*    OPEN THE INPUT PDS FOR THE MEMBER LIST:                       01700001
*                                                                  01710000
                                                                   01720000
         IF  ERROR-FLAG  =  0                                      01730000
                                                                   01740000
             MOVE  'LMOPEN  DATAID(&DSIDIN)  OPTION(INPUT)'        01750020
                   TO  BUFFER                                      01760001
                                                                   01770001
             CALL  'ISPEXEC'  USING  BUFFER-LENGTH  BUFFER         01780001
                                                                   01790000
             MOVE  RETURN-CODE  TO  ERROR-FLAG                     01800000
                                                                   01810000
             IF  ERROR-FLAG  >  0                                  01820000
                                                                   01830000
                 MOVE  'SETMSG MSG(WDAR001B)'  TO  BUFFER          01840002
                                                                   01850002
                 CALL  'ISPEXEC'  USING  BUFFER-LENGTH  BUFFER     01860002
```

(continued)

Figure 14-3. (Continued)

```
            ELSE                                                    01870000
                                                                    01880000
                MOVE 'YES' TO INOPEN.                               01890000
                                                                    01900000
                                                                    01910000
                                                                    01920000
*                                                                   01930000
* INITIALIZE THE OUTPUT FILE FOR THE MEMBER LIST.                   01940001
*                                                                   01950000
                                                                    01960000
        IF  ERROR-FLAG = 0                                          01970000
                                                                    01980000
            MOVE                                                    01990000
            'LMINIT DATAID(DSIDOUT) DDNAME(NEWFILE) ENQ(EXCLU)'     02000022
                 TO  BUFFER                                         02010000
                                                                    02020000
            CALL 'ISPEXEC' USING BUFFER-LENGTH BUFFER              02030000
                                                                    02040000
            MOVE RETURN-CODE TO ERROR-FLAG                          02050000
                                                                    02060000
            IF  ERROR-FLAG > 0                                      02070000
                                                                    02080000
                MOVE 'SETMSG MSG(WDAR001C)' TO BUFFER               02090000
                                                                    02100002
                CALL 'ISPEXEC' USING BUFFER-LENGTH BUFFER          02110002
                                                                    02120002
            ELSE                                                    02130000
                                                                    02140000
                MOVE 'YES' TO OUTINIT.                              02150000
                                                                    02160000
                                                                    02170000
*                                                                   02180001
* OPEN THE OUTPUT FILE FOR THE OUTPUT MEMBER LIST.  WRITE A         02190001
* COLUMN HEADER TO THAT FILE IF OPEN SUCCEEDS:                      02200001
*                                                                   02210001
                                                                    02220000
        IF  ERROR-FLAG = 0                                          02230000
                                                                    02240000
            MOVE 'LMOPEN DATAID(&DSIDOUT) OPTION(OUTPUT)'           02250008
                 TO  BUFFER                                         02260001
                                                                    02270001
            CALL 'ISPEXEC' USING BUFFER-LENGTH BUFFER              02280001
                                                                    02290000
            MOVE RETURN-CODE TO ERROR-FLAG                          02300000
                                                                    02310000
            IF  ERROR-FLAG > 0                                      02320000
                                                                    02330000
                MOVE 'SETMSG MSG(WDAR001D)' TO BUFFER               02340002
                                                                    02350002
                CALL 'ISPEXEC' USING BUFFER-LENGTH BUFFER          02360002
                                                                    02370000
            ELSE                                                    02380000
                                                                    02390000
                MOVE 'YES' TO OUTOPEN                               02400001
                                                                    02410001
                MOVE 'LMPUT DATAID(&DSIDOUT) MODE(INVAR)           02420008
                'DATALOC(HEADER) DATALEN(80)' TO BUFFER            02430013
                                                                    02440001
                CALL 'ISPEXEC' USING BUFFER-LENGTH BUFFER          02450001
                                                                    02460001
                MOVE RETURN-CODE TO ERROR-FLAG                      02470001
                                                                    02480001
                IF  ERROR-FLAG > 0                                  02490001
                                                                    02500001
                    MOVE 'SETMSG MSG(WDAR001F)' TO BUFFER           02510002
                                                                    02520002
                    CALL 'ISPEXEC' USING BUFFER-LENGTH BUFFER.     02530002
                                                                    02540000
                                                                    02550000
*                                                                   02560000
* GET THE PDS MEMBER NAMES ALONG WITH THEIR STATISTICS, PLACE       02570001
* THEM IN THE NEWLY-CREATED MVS SEQUENTIAL FILE IN SORTED ORDER:    02580001
*                                                                   02590000
                                                                    02600000
        PERFORM LIST-PARAGRAPH THRU LIST-PARAGRAPH-EXIT            02610001
            UNTIL ERROR-FLAG NOT = 0                                02620000
            OR    LEAVE-FLAG NOT = 'NO '.                           02630000
                                                                    02640000
                                                                    02650000
*                                                                   02660000
* IF A 'LMMLIST' CALL SUCCEEDED, ISSUE THE 'LMMLIST' SERVICE        02670001
* AGAIN, THIS TIME SPECIFYING THE 'FREE' OPTION:                    02680001
*                                                                   02690000
                                                                    02700000
        IF  LISTED-FLAG = 'YES'                                     02710001
                                                                    02720000
            MOVE 'LMMLIST DATAID(&DSIDIN) OPTION(FREE)'             02730008
                 TO  BUFFER                                         02740001
```

```
              CALL  'ISPEXEC'  USING  BUFFER-LENGTH  BUFFER          02750001
                                                                     02760001
          IF  RETURN-CODE  >  0                                      02770000
                                                                     02780001
                  MOVE  RETURN-CODE  TO  ERROR-FLAG                  02790000
                                                                     02800000
                                                                     02810000
                  MOVE  'SETMSG  MSG(WDAR003B)'  TO  BUFFER          02820002
                                                                     02830002
                  CALL  'ISPEXEC'  USING  BUFFER-LENGTH  BUFFER.     02840002
                                                                     02850000
                                                                     02860000
*                                                                    02870000
**  IF THE INPUT FILE WAS OPENED, CLOSE IT:                          02880000
*                                                                    02890000
                                                                     02900000
      IF  INOPEN  =  'YES'                                           02910000
                                                                     02920000
          MOVE  'LMCLOSE  DATAID(&DSIDIN)'  TO  BUFFER               02930008
                                                                     02940001
          CALL  'ISPEXEC'  USING  BUFFER-LENGTH  BUFFER              02950001
                                                                     02960000
          IF  RETURN-CODE  >  0                                      02970000
                                                                     02980000
                  MOVE  RETURN-CODE  TO  ERROR-FLAG                  02990000
                                                                     03000000
                  MOVE  'SETMSG  MSG(WDAR001G)'  TO  BUFFER          03010002
                                                                     03020002
                  CALL  'ISPEXEC'  USING  BUFFER-LENGTH BUFFER.      03030002
                                                                     03040000
                                                                     03050000
*                                                                    03060000
**  IF THE INPUT FILE WAS INITIALIZED, FREE IT:                      03070000
*                                                                    03080000
                                                                     03090000
      IF  ININIT  =  'YES'                                           03100000
                                                                     03110000
          MOVE  'LMFREE  DATAID(&DSIDIN)'  TO  BUFFER                03120008
                                                                     03130001
          CALL  'ISPEXEC'  USING  BUFFER-LENGTH  BUFFER              03140001
                                                                     03150000
          IF  RETURN-CODE  >  0                                      03160000
                                                                     03170000
                  MOVE  RETURN-CODE  TO  ERROR-FLAG                  03180000
                                                                     03190000
                  MOVE  'SETMSG  MSG(WDAR001H)'  TO  BUFFER          03200002
                                                                     03210002
                  CALL  'ISPEXEC'  USING  BUFFER-LENGTH BUFFER.      03220002
                                                                     03230000
                                                                     03240000
                                                                     03250000
*                                                                    03260000
**  IF THE OUTPUT FILE WAS OPENED, CLOSE IT:                         03270000
*                                                                    03280000
                                                                     03290000
      IF  OUTOPEN  =  'YES'                                          03300000
                                                                     03310000
          MOVE  'LMCLOSE  DATAID(&DSIDOUT)'  TO  BUFFER              03320008
                                                                     03330001
          CALL  'ISPEXEC'  USING  BUFFER-LENGTH  BUFFER              03340001
                                                                     03350000
          IF  RETURN-CODE  >  0                                      03360000
                                                                     03370000
                  MOVE  RETURN-CODE  TO  ERROR-FLAG                  03380000
                                                                     03390000
                  MOVE  'SETMSG  MSG(WDAR001I)'  TO  BUFFER          03400002
                                                                     03410002
                  CALL  'ISPEXEC'  USING  BUFFER-LENGTH BUFFER.      03420002
                                                                     03430000
                                                                     03440001
                                                                     03450001
*                                                                    03460001
**  IF NO ERROR HAS OCCURRED, ALLOW USER TO BROWSE THE              03470001
**  NEWLY-CREATED DATA SET OF MEMBER NAMES AND THEIR STATISTICS:     03480001
*                                                                    03490001
      IF  ERROR-FLAG  =  0  AND  PUT-FLAG  =  'YES'                  03500001
                                                                     03510001
          MOVE  'BROWSE  DATAID(&DSIDOUT)'  TO  BUFFER               03520008
                                                                     03530001
          CALL  'ISPEXEC'  USING  BUFFER-LENGTH  BUFFER              03540001
                                                                     03550001
          MOVE  RETURN-CODE  TO  ERROR-FLAG                          03560001
                                                                     03570001
          IF  ERROR-FLAG  >  0                                       03580001
                                                                     03590001
                  MOVE  'SETMSG  MSG(WDAR003C)'  TO  BUFFER          03600002
                                                                     03610002
                  CALL  'ISPEXEC'  USING  BUFFER-LENGTH BUFFER.      03620002
```

(continued)

Figure 14-3. (*Continued*)

```
                                                                          03630001
                                                                          03640000
 *                                                                        03650000
 *    IF THE OUTPUT FILE WAS INITIALIZED, FREE IT:                        03660000
 *                                                                        03670000
                                                                          03680000
       IF  OUTINIT  =  'YES'                                              03690000
                                                                          03700000
            MOVE  'LMFREE  DATAID(&DSIDOUT)'  TO  BUFFER                  03710008
                                                                          03720001
            CALL  'ISPEXEC'  USING  BUFFER-LENGTH  BUFFER                 03730001
                                                                          03740000
            IF  RETURN-CODE  >  0                                         03750000
                                                                          03760000
                 MOVE  RETURN-CODE  TO  ERROR-FLAG                        03770000
                                                                          03780000
                 MOVE  'SETMSG  MSG(WDAR001J)'  TO  BUFFER                03790002
                                                                          03800002
                 CALL  'ISPEXEC'  USING  BUFFER-LENGTH BUFFER.            03810002
                                                                          03820000
                                                                          03830000
 *                                                                        03840000
 *    IF ALL WENT WELL, WRITE A MESSAGE.  'VDELETE' ALL VARIABLES         03850000
 *    KNOWN TO ISPF AND EXIT:                                             03860000
 *                                                                        03870000
                                                                          03880000
       IF  ERROR-FLAG  =  0                                               03890000
                                                                          03900000
            MOVE  'SETMSG  MSG(WDAR003D)'  TO  BUFFER                     03910002
                                                                          03920002
            CALL  'ISPEXEC'  USING  BUFFER-LENGTH BUFFER.                 03930002
                                                                          03940000
                                                                          03950000
                                                                          03960000
       PERFORM DELETE-VARIABLES THROUGH DELETE-VARIABLES-EXIT.           03970000
                                                                          03980000
                                                                          03990000
       MOVE  ERROR-FLAG  TO  RETURN-CODE.                                04000000
       GOBACK.                                                           04010000
                                                                          04020000
 MAIN-LINE-EXIT.                                                          04030000
                                                                          04040000
                                                                          04050000
                                                                          04060000
                                                                          04070000
 LIST-PARAGRAPH.                                                          04080001
                                                                          04090000
                                                                          04100000
 *                                                                        04110000
 *    GET A MEMBER AND ITS ASSOCIATED STATISTICS:                         04120001
 *                                                                        04130000
                                                                          04140000
       MOVE  'LMMLIST  DATAID(&DSIDIN)  OPTION(LIST)                      04150008
            'MEMBER(MEMVAR)  STATS(YES)'   TO BUFFER                      04160022
                                                                          04170001
       CALL  'ISPEXEC'  USING  BUFFER-LENGTH  BUFFER                     04180001
                                                                          04190000
       MOVE  RETURN-CODE  TO  ERROR-FLAG.                                04200000
                                                                          04210000
       IF  ERROR-FLAG  >  8                                              04220020
                                                                          04230000
            MOVE  'SETMSG  MSG(WDAR003A)'  TO  BUFFER                     04240000
                                                                          04250004
            CALL  'ISPEXEC'  USING  BUFFER-LENGTH BUFFER.                04260002
                                                                          04270002
       IF  ERROR-FLAG  =  0                                              04280017
                                                                          04290017
            MOVE  'YES'  TO  LISTED-FLAG.                                04300017
                                                                          04310017
                                                                          04320017
                                                                          04330000
 *                                                                        04340000
 *    RETURN CODE OF 8 SIGNIFIES END-OF-FILE ON INPUT FILE:               04350000
 *                                                                        04360000
                                                                          04370000
       IF  ERROR-FLAG  =  8                                              04380000
                                                                          04390000
            MOVE  'YES'  TO  LEAVE-FLAG                                   04400000
                                                                          04410000
            MOVE  0  TO  ERROR-FLAG.                                     04420000
                                                                          04430000
                                                                          04440000
 *                                                                        04450000
 *    IF A RECORD WAS READ, WRITE IT TO OUTPUT FILE:                      04460000
 *                                                                        04470000
                                                                          04480000
       IF  ERROR-FLAG  =  0  AND  LEAVE-FLAG  =  'NO '                   04490000
                                                                          04500000
```

```
            MOVE   MEMVAR   TO   MEM-OUT     OF  OUTREC          04510004
            MOVE   ZLUSER   TO   USER-OUT    OF  OUTREC          04520023
            MOVE   ZLMDATE  TO   DATE-OUT    OF  OUTREC          04530023
            MOVE   ZLCNORC  TO   LCNORC-OUT  OF  OUTREC          04540023
                                                                04550023
                                                                04560014
            MOVE 'LMPUT  DATAID(&DSIDOUT)   MODE(INVAR)          04570014
            'DATALOC(OUTREC)  DATALEN(80)'  TO  BUFFER           04580008
                                                                04590023
            CALL  'ISPEXEC' USING  BUFFER-LENGTH  BUFFER         04600004
                                                                04610004
            MOVE  RETURN-CODE  TO  ERROR-FLAG                    04620000
                                                                04630000
            IF  ERROR-FLAG  >  0                                 04640000
                                                                04650000
                MOVE  'SETMSG MSG(WDAR001F)'  TO  BUFFER         04660000
                                                                04670005
                CALL  'ISPEXEC'  USING  BUFFER-LENGTH BUFFER     04680004
                                                                04690006
            ELSE                                                 04700004
                                                                04710004
                MOVE  'YES'  TO  PUT-FLAG.                       04720000
                                                                04730000
                                                                04740000
                                                                04750000
                                                                04760000
    LIST-PARAGRAPH-EXIT.                                         04770001
        EXIT.                                                    04780000
                                                                04790000
                                                                04800000
                                                                04810000
                                                                04820000
    DEFINE-VARIABLES.                                            04830000
                                                                04840000
                                                                04850000
                                                                04860000
*                                                               04870000
**  DEFINE NECESSARY VARIABLES TO ISPF DIALOG MANAGER:           04880000
*                                                               04890000
        CALL 'ISPLINK'  USING   VDEFINE                          04900000
                                DSIDIN-NAME                      04910000
                                DSIDIN                           04920000
                                CHAR                             04930000
                                DSIDIN-LENGTH.                   04940000
        CALL 'ISPLINK'  USING   VDEFINE                          04950000
                                DSIDOUT-NAME                     04960000
                                DSIDOUT                          04970000
                                CHAR                             04980000
                                DSIDOUT-LENGTH.                  04990000
        CALL 'ISPLINK'  USING   VDEFINE                          05100011
                                HEADER-NAME                      05110011
                                HEADER                           05120011
                                CHAR                             05130011
                                HEADER-LENGTH.                   05140011
        CALL 'ISPLINK'  USING   VDEFINE                          05150011
                                MEMVAR-NAME                      05160022
                                MEMVAR                           05170022
                                CHAR                             05180011
                                MEMVAR-LENGTH.                   05190022
        CALL 'ISPLINK'  USING   VDEFINE                          05200014
                                OUTREC-NAME                      05210023
                                OUTREC                           05220023
                                CHAR                             05230014
                                OUTREC-LENGTH.                   05240023
        CALL 'ISPLINK'  USING   VDEFINE                          05250015
                                ZLUSER-NAME                      05260015
                                ZLUSER                           05270015
                                CHAR                             05280015
                                ZLUSER-LENGTH.                   05290015
        CALL 'ISPLINK'  USING   VDEFINE                          05300018
                                ZLMDATE-NAME                     05310018
                                ZLMDATE                          05320018
                                CHAR                             05330018
                                ZLMDATE-LENGTH.                  05340018
        CALL 'ISPLINK'  USING   VDEFINE                          05350018
                                ZLCNORC-NAME                     05360018
                                ZLCNORC                          05370018
                                CHAR                             05380018
                                ZLCNORC-LENGTH.                  05390018
                                                                05400000
                                                                05410000
    DEFINE-VARIABLES-EXIT.                                       05420000
        EXIT.                                                    05430000
                                                                05440000
                                                                05450000
                                                                05460000
                                                                05470000
```

(continued)

Figure 14-3. (*Continued*)

```
   DELETE-VARIABLES.                                             05480000
                                                                 05490000
                                                                 05500000
 *                                                               05510000
 *   DELETE ALL DIALOG MANAGER VARIABLES RE ISPF DIALOG MANAGER: 05520000
 *                                                               05530000
                                                                 05540000
       CALL 'ISPLINK'  USING  VDELETE                            05550000
                              DSIDIN-NAME.                       05560000
       CALL 'ISPLINK'  USING  VDELETE                            05570000
                              DSIDOUT-NAME.                      05530000
       CALL 'ISPLINK'  USING  VDELETE                            05630014
                              HEADER-NAME.                       05640014
       CALL 'ISPLINK'  USING  VDELETE                            05650014
                              MEMVAR-NAME.                       05660022
       CALL 'ISPLINK'  USING  VDELETE                            05670014
                              OUTREC-NAME.                       05680023
       CALL 'ISPLINK'  USING  VDELETE                            05690015
                              ZLUSER-NAME.                       05700015
       CALL 'ISPLINK'  USING  VDELETE                            05710018
                              ZLMDATE-NAME.                      05720018
       CALL 'ISPLINK'  USING  VDELETE                            05730018
                              ZLCNORC-NAME.                      05740018
                                                                 05750000
                                                                 05760000
   DELETE-VARIABLES-EXIT.                                        05770000
       EXIT.                                                     05780000
```

Figure 14-4. **PDSLIST** CLIST function.

```
00010000   PROC 0
00020000   CONTROL LIST
00030000   /**************************************************************/
00040000   /* NAME: PDSLIST                          BY: H. FOSDICK     */
00050000   /*                                                          */
00060000   /* PURPOSE: THIS CLIST CREATES AN MVS SEQUENTIAL FILE       */
00070000   /* CONTAINING A SORTED LIST OF ALL THE MEMBERS FROM AN MVS  */
00080000   /* PARTITIONED DATA SET.  PDS STATISTICS ARE ASSOCIATED     */
00090000   /* WITH EACH MEMBER LISTED.  ISPF BROWSE IS USED TO VIEW    */
00100000   /* THE NEWLY-CREATED FILE OF MEMBER NAMES AND STATISTICS.   */
00110000   /*                                                          */
00120000   /**************************************************************/
00130000
00140000   /*                                                          */
00150000   /*   FREE PREVIOUS FILE ALLOCATION AND ALLOCATE THE OUTPUT  */
00160000   /*   DATA SET FOR THE COPY:                                 */
00170000   /*                                                          */
00180000
00190000   DELETE  'ZHMF01.STATS.DATA'
00200000   FREE   FILE(NEWFILE)
00210000   FREE   ATTRLIST(ATTR1)
00220000
00230000   ATTR ATTR1  BLKSIZE(6080)  LRECL(80)  RECFM(F B)  DSORG(PS)
00240001   ALLOCATE  FILE(NEWFILE)  DA('ZHMF01.STATS.DATA')  +
00250001       NEW  SPACE(3)  TRACKS  USING(ATTR1)
00260000
00270000
00280000   /*                                                          */
00290000   /*   INITIALIZE FLAGS:                                      */
00300000   /*                                                          */
00310000
00320000   SET   ERROR   = 0       /* 0 MEANS AN ERROR HAS NOT OCCURRED. */
00330000   SET   ININIT  = NO      /* THESE FOUR FLAGS INDICATE THE      */
00340000   SET   INOPEN  = NO      /* STATUS OF THE INPUT AND OUTPUT     */
00350001   SET   OUTINIT = NO      /* FILES AND WHETHER THEY HAVE BEEN   */
00360000   SET   OUTOPEN = NO      /* INITIALIZED AND/OR OPENED.         */
00370000
00380000
00390000   /*                                                          */
00400002   /*   INITIALIZE VARIABLES FOR THE INPUT MVS PDS:            */
00410000   /*                                                          */
00420000
00430002   SET   PROJECT = ZHMF01     /* THE MVS PARTITIONTED DATA SET  */
00440012   SET   GROUP   = PROGRAMS   /* FROM WHICH TO GET THE          */
00450012   SET   TYPE    = COBOL      /* MEMBER LIST.                   */
00460002
00470002
00480002   /*                                                          */
00490002   /*   INITIALIZE THE INPUT PDS FOR THE MEMBER LIST:          */
00500002   /*                                                          */
00510002
00520002
00530002   ISPEXEC  LMINIT  DATAID(DSIDIN)  +
00540002       DATASET('&PROJECT..&GROUP..&TYPE')  ENQ(SHR)
00550002
00560000   SET   ERROR  = &LASTCC
00570000
00580000   IF  &ERROR  >  0  THEN  +
00590000       ISPEXEC  SETMSG  MSG(WDAR001A)
00600000   ELSE  +
00610000       SET  ININIT  = YES
00620000
00630000
00640000   /*                                                          */
00650002   /*   OPEN THE INPUT PDS FOR THE MEMBER LIST:                */
00660000   /*                                                          */
00670000
00680000   IF  &ERROR  =  0  THEN  DO
00690000
00700000       ISPEXEC  LMOPEN  DATAID(&DSIDIN)  OPTION(INPUT)
00710000
00720000       SET  ERROR  = &LASTCC
00730000
00740000       IF  &ERROR  >  0  THEN  +
00750000           ISPEXEC  SETMSG  MSG(WDAR001B)
00760000       ELSE  +
00770000           SET  INOPEN  = YES
00780000
00790000       END
00800000
00810000
00820000   /*                                                          */
00830002   /*   INITIALIZE THE OUTPUT FILE FOR THE OUTPUT MEMBER LIST: */
00840000   /*                                                          */
00850000
00860000   IF  &ERROR  =  0  THEN  DO
00870000
00880004       ISPEXEC  LMINIT  DATAID(DSIDOUT)  DDNAME(NEWFILE)  ENQ(EXCLU)
```

(continued)

Figure 14-4. *(Continued)*

```
00890000
00900000          SET   ERROR  = &LASTCC
00910000
00920000          IF  &ERROR  >  0  THEN  +
00930000              ISPEXEC  SETMSG  MSG(WDAR001C)
00940000          ELSE  +
00950000              SET  OUTINIT  =  YES
00960000
00970000          END
00980000
00990000
01000000   /*                                                            */
01010002   /*  OPEN THE OUTPUT FILE FOR THE OUTPUT MEMBER LIST.  WRITE */
01020002   /*  A COLUMN HEADER TO THAT FILE IF THE OPEN SUCCEEDS:        */
01030000   /*                                                            */
01040000
01050000   IF  &ERROR  =  0  THEN  DO
01060000
01070000       ISPEXEC  LMOPEN  DATAID(&DSIDOUT)  OPTION(OUTPUT)
01080000
01090000       SET  ERROR  =  &LASTCC
01100000
01110000       IF  &ERROR  >  0  THEN  +
01120000           ISPEXEC  SETMSG  MSG(WDAR001D)
01130002
01140002       ELSE  DO
01150002
01160002           SET  OUTOPEN  =  YES
01170000
01180002           SET  HEADER  = &STR(MEMBER:  USERID:  LAST MOD:   # RECS:)
01190002
01200002           ISPEXEC  LMPUT  DATAID(&DSIDOUT)  MODE(INVAR)  +
01210002               DATALOC(HEADER)  DATALEN(80)
01220002
01230002           SET  ERROR  =  &LASTCC
01240002
01250002           IF  &ERROR  >  0  THEN  +
01260002               ISPEXEC  SETMSG  MSG(WDAR001F)
01270002
01280002
01290000       END
01300002       END
01310000
01320000
01330000
01340000   /*                                                            */
01350002   /*  THE CODE IN THIS 'DO WHILE' LOOP GETS THE PDS MEMBER     */
01360002   /*  NAMES VIA REPEATED USE OF THE 'LMMLIST' SERVICE.  THIS   */
01370002   /*  SERVICE ALSO RETURNS MEMBER STATISTICS.  THE LIST IS     */
01380002   /*  SORTED BY MEMBER NAME.  THE CODE HERE ALSO PERFORMS AN   */
01390002   /*  'LMPUT' FOR EACH MEMBER NAME RETRIEVED, WRITING THIS     */
01400002   /*  DATA TO THE NEWLY-CREATED MVS SEQUENTIAL FILE:           */
01410000   /*                                                            */
01420000
01430002   SET  LEAVE  =  NO
01440000   SET  PUT    =  NO
01450002   SET  LISTED =  NO
01460000
01470000   DO  WHILE &ERROR  =  0  AND  &LEAVE  =  NO
01480000
01490000
01500000           /*                                                    */
01510002           /*  GET A MEMBER NAME AND ITS ASSOCIATED STATISTICS:  */
01520002           /*                                                    */
01530000
01540002           ISPEXEC  LMMLIST  DATAID(&DSIDIN)  OPTION(LIST)  +
01550000               MEMBER(MEMVAR)  STATS(YES)
01560000
01570000           SET  ERROR  =  &LASTCC
01580000
01590000           IF  &ERROR  >  8  THEN  +
01600000               ISPEXEC  SETMSG  MSG(WDAR003A)
01610002
01620002           IF  &ERROR  =  0  THEN  +
01630002               SET  LISTED  =  YES
01640000
01650000           /*                                                    */
01660000           /*  RETURN CODE OF 8 SIGNIFIES END-OF-FILE ON INPUT FILE:  */
01670000           /*                                                    */
01680000
01690000           IF  &ERROR  =  8  THEN  DO
01700000               SET  LEAVE  =  YES
01710000               SET  ERROR  =  0
01720000               END
01730000
01740000
01750000           /*                                                    */
01760000           /*  IF A RECORD WAS READ, WRITE IT TO OUTPUT FILE:    */
```

```
01770000           /*                                                        */
01780000
01790002           IF  &ERROR = 0    AND  &LEAVE = NO  THEN  DO
01800002
01810002              SET  OUTPUT = &STR(&MEMVAR &ZLUSER &ZLMDATE &ZLCNORC)
01820002
01830000              ISPEXEC  LMPUT  DATAID(&DSIDOUT)  MODE(INVAR)   +
01840002                  DATALOC(OUTPUT)  DATALEN(80)
01850000
01860000              SET  ERROR  =  &LASTCC
01870000
01880000              IF  &ERROR  >  0  THEN  +
01890000                  ISPEXEC  SETMSG   MSG(WDAR001F)
01900000              ELSE  +
01910000                  SET  PUT  =  YES
01920000
01930000              END
01940000
01950000    END
01960000
01970000
01980000
01990000    /*                                                        */
02000004    /*  IF A 'LMMLIST' COMMAND SUCCEEDED, ISSUE THE 'LMMLIST'   */
02010004    /*  SERVICE AGAIN, THIS TIME SPECIFYING THE 'FREE' OPTION:  */
02020000    /*                                                        */
02030000
02040002    IF  &LISTED  =  YES  THEN  DO
02050000
02060002        ISPEXEC  LMMLIST  DATAID(&DSIDIN)  OPTION(FREE)
02070000
02080002        IF  &LASTCC  >  0  THEN  DO
02090002            SET  ERROR  =  &LASTCC
02100002            ISPEXEC  SETMSG  MSG(WDAR003B)
02110000            END
02120000
02130000        END
02140000
02150000
02160000
02170000    /*                                                        */
02180000    /*  IF THE INPUT FILE WAS OPENED, CLOSE IT:                 */
02190000    /*                                                        */
02200000
02210000    IF  &INOPEN  =  YES  THEN  DO
02220000
02230000        ISPEXEC  LMCLOSE  DATAID(&DSIDIN)
02240000
02250000        IF  &LASTCC  >  0  THEN  DO
02260000            SET  ERROR  =  &LASTCC
02270000            ISPEXEC  SETMSG  MSG(WDAR001G)
02280000            END
02290000
02300000        END
02310000
02320000
02330000    /*                                                        */
02340000    /*  IF THE INPUT FILE WAS INITIALIZED, FREE IT:             */
02350000    /*                                                        */
02360000
02370000    IF  &ININIT  =  YES  THEN  DO
02380000
02390000        ISPEXEC  LMFREE  DATAID(&DSIDIN)
02400000
02410000        IF  &LASTCC  >  0  THEN  DO
02420000            SET  ERROR  =  &LASTCC
02430000            ISPEXEC  SETMSG  MSG(WDAR001H)
02440000            END
02450000
02460000        END
02470000
02480000
02490000    /*                                                        */
02500000    /*  IF THE OUTPUT FILE WAS OPENED, CLOSE IT:                */
02510000    /*                                                        */
02520000
02530000    IF  &OUTOPEN  =  YES  THEN  DO
02540000
02550000        ISPEXEC  LMCLOSE  DATAID(&DSIDOUT)
02560000
02570000        IF  &LASTCC  >  0  THEN  DO
02580000            SET  ERROR  =  &LASTCC
02590000            ISPEXEC  SETMSG  MSG(WDAR001I)
02600000            END
02610000
02620000        END
02630002
```

(continued)

Figure 14-4. (*Continued*)

```
02640002
02650002   /*                                                           */
02660002   /*  IF NO ERROR HAS OCCURRED, ALLOW USER TO BROWSE THE         */
02670002   /*  CREATED DATA SET OF MEMBER NAMES AND THEIR STATISTICS:     */
02680002   /*                                                           */
02690002
02700002   IF  &ERROR = 0  AND  &PUT = YES  THEN  DO
02710002
02720002      ISPEXEC  BROWSE  DATAID(&DSIDOUT)
02730002
02740002      SET  &ERROR = &LASTCC
02750002
02760002      IF  &ERROR > 0  THEN +
02770002          ISPEXEC  SETMSG  MSG(WDAR003C)
02780002
02790002      END
02800000
02810000
02820000   /*                                                           */
02830000   /*  IF THE OUTPUT FILE WAS INITIALIZED, FREE IT:               */
02840000   /*                                                           */
02850000
02860000   IF  &OUTINIT = YES  THEN  DO
02870000
02880000      ISPEXEC  LMFREE  DATAID(&DSIDOUT)
02890000
02900000      IF  &LASTCC > 0  THEN  DO
02910000          SET  ERROR = &LASTCC
02920000          ISPEXEC  SETMSG  MSG(WDAR001J)
02930000          END
02940000
02950000      END
02960000
02970000
02980000   /*                                                           */
02990000   /*  IF ALL WENT WELL, WRITE A MESSAGE.  THEN EXIT CLIST:        */
03000000   /*                                                           */
03010000
03020000   IF  &ERROR = 0  THEN +
03030002      ISPEXEC  SETMSG  MSG(WDAR003D)
03040000
03050000
03060000   EXIT  CODE(&ERROR)
```

Figure 14-5. Browsing **PDSLISTC** (and **PDSLIST**) function output.

```
 BROWSE  - ZHMF01.STATS.DATA -------------------------LINE 000000 COL   001 080
  COMMAND ===>                                            SCROLL ===> PAGE
 ******************************** TOP OF DATA  ********************************
 MEMBER:   USERID:   LAST MOD:  # RECS:
 AV1844V2 ZPOLK1    85/08/22     5
 NNJ443V1 ZHMF01    85/07/12     8
 SPUFI1   ZHMF01    85/08/21     5
 SU0500   ZJJJ01    85/12/12     1
 SU0600   ZAJAB3    85/09/22     2
 TESTMEM  ZHMF01    85/08/20     7
 ********************************BOTTOM OF DATA ********************************
```

15

Using the Dialog Manager with IBM's Relational Database Management Systems

Version 2 of the ISPF Dialog Manager supports IBM's relational database management systems, DB2 and SQL/DS. Recall that DB2 and SQL/DS are parallel relational offerings. DB2 runs under MVS, and SQL/DS is offered for the VM and VSE environments.

This chapter presents a simple dialog function that accesses both ISPF Dialog Manager services and IBM's DB2 database management system. The example is provided only in a compiled programming language (COBOL). It is not shown in a command procedure language like CLIST because command procedures cannot interface with DB2.

The sample program is a stand-alone application. It is not part of the West Department Accounts Receivable System used as the dialog example previously in this book. Instead the example COBOL ISPF/DB2 program supports an online company employee directory, the *Company Employee Directory System*.

USER VIEW OF THE COMPANY EMPLOYEE DIRECTORY SYSTEM

In order to access the Company Employee Directory System, the terminal user executes an initializing CLIST. At this point, he or she sees the panel depicted in figure 15-1 on the terminal screen. The user enters an employee's name into the requested data entry field. This name indicates the employee record that the COBOL program will retrieve from the DB2 table supporting the application.

If the employee name matches an entry in the DB2 employee table, the system displays the screen of figure 15-2. This panel contains the appropriate employee's information, as shown. If an exact match is not found for the name entered by the terminal user, the screen of figure 15-2 is displayed with an "Employee Not Found" message. Whether the employee is found in the database or not, the system then returns the terminal user to the data query screen of figure 15-1. Now the user may elect to enter another employee query or exit the dialog by pressing the **END** program function key.

DISCUSSION OF THE EXAMPLE COBOL ISPF/DB2 PROGRAM

The Company Employee Directory System is entered by the terminal user through execution of an initialization CLIST. This CLIST allocates the necessary libraries for the ISPF Dialog Manager environment, exactly as seen in the **XDM2** and **XDMC** CLISTs of figures 2-2 and A-1. Recall that these CLISTs established the appropriate ISPF environment for the West Department Accounts Receivables System, as described in chapter 2 and appendix A. The only difference between the CLIST that initiates the Company Employee Directory System and the earlier example dialog is this last line in the CLIST:

> **ISPSTART CMD(CSTART)**

The initiating CLIST for this system thus selects a CLIST called **CSTART** for execution upon entry to the ISPF Dialog Manager. Figure 15-3 contains the code of CLIST **CSTART**. This CLIST establishes the DB2 system environment by issuing a DB2 **DSN** command. It then runs the ISPF Dialog Manager/DB2 sample COBOL program via the DB2 subcommand **RUN**:

> **DSN SYSTEM(DB2P)**
> **RUN PROGRAM(CDIRECT) PLAN(CDIRECT) LIB(RUNLIB.LOAD)**

The sample COBOL program is therefore called **CDIRECT**. Its application plan is also named **CDIRECT**. **RUNLIB.LOAD** is the relevant program library.

The **CSTART** CLIST demonstrates one way in which to run a program that uses both ISPF Dialog Manager and DB2 subsystem services.*

Figure 15-4 contains the sample COBOL program **CDIRECT**. Because the only purpose of the program is to illustrate use of the Dialog Manager and DB2 together, its code is quite simple. The Dialog Manager coding portions of the WORKING-STORAGE SECTION of this program should look familiar; nothing is different from the examples

---

*Assuming ISPF Version 2 and DB2 Release 1, programs that use both ISPF and DB2 services are executed in this manner. First, invoke the DB2 DSN command processor from within ISPF through ISPF's select services. Then attach the application program under the DSN command processor through the **DSN** subcommand **RUN**.

ISPF Version 1 imposes a subtasking restriction on full use of ISPF and DB2 services. ISPF Version 1 programs can only use DB2 services under certain conditions.

Refer to the vendor's manual *IBM Database 2: TSO Usage Guide* for discussion and examples of how to execute programs so that they use both ISPF and DB2 services under ISPF Versions 1 and 2.

provided in the West Department Accounts Receivables System. The data definitions include those necessary for service calls, panel names, messages, and storage space for dialog variables used by this application.

The DB2 declarations in the WORKING-STORAGE SECTION are new to this program, however. As required by DB2, the storage area includes definition of the SQL Communications Area (SQLCA) and the SQL Table Declaration. The SQL Table Declaration shows how the one table used by this program to support the Company Employee Directory System was defined. This definition was accomplished by using the SQL language under DB2 prior to encoding the COBOL program.

The PROCEDURE DIVISION of the program again looks similar in terms of its use of the ISPF Dialog Manager; nothing is changed from those examples provided previously. Once again, however, new code is added to support DB2.

In the PROCEDURE DIVISION logic, the program first defines necessary variables to the Dialog Manager. Next, the program sets up SQL exception processing via the embedded SQL **WHENEVER** sentences.

Now program initialization is completed. The program displays the "employee name" data entry panel to the terminal user via an ISPF Dialog Manager **DISPLAY** service CALL. If the user enters an employee name, the program executes paragraph **QUERY-DISPLAY**. The function of this paragraph is to attempt direct retrieval on the employee name key of the single DB2 table supporting this application, done in the SQL **SELECT** statement at the beginning of the paragraph. If retrieval is successful, the **CDIRECT** program displays the data output panel to the terminal user with the appropriate employee information displayed. If retrieval is not successful, **CDIRECT** displays the same output display panel but with an "Employee Not Found" message. Output display fields are blank in this instance.

Then the program redisplays the original data query panel to the terminal user so that he or she can enter another employee's name for searching.

EXAMPLE COBOL ISPF/DB2 PROGRAM SUMMARY

The ISPF Dialog Manager CALLs in the **CDIRECT** program make plain the fact that the CALLs to the Dialog Manager are encoded exactly the same in this ISPF Dialog Manager/DB2 program as in any other Dialog Manager function. This particular program example made use of only the Dialog Manager's display, variable, and message services, but all other services of the Dialog Manager were available to it as well.

Storage definitions in ISPF Dialog Manager/DB2 programs are also encoded as previously described in this book. The only difference between this program and those seen earlier is in the added presence of DB2 statements.

Thus, in order to design ISPF Dialog Manager/DB2 programs, all you must do is add any required DB2 code to standard ISPF dialog functions.

Of course, this example assumes use of Time Sharing Option (TSO) as the MVS teleprocessing monitor under which the application runs. With DB2, installations also have the option to use the Customer Information Control System (CICS) or Information Management System/Data Communications (IMS-DC) monitors. Use of the ISPF Dialog Manager requires installation and selection of TSO as the teleprocessing monitor supporting the application.

ISPF DIALOG MANAGER SERVICES
VERSUS DB2 AND SQL/DS

Given that ISPF Dialog functions can utilize DB2 (or SQL/DS) for their database needs, you might wonder when you would use ISPF's own services for data storage and management. Recall that the Dialog Manager's services pertaining to this area include Table Services, Variable Services, and the File Tailoring Services. When would you use ISPF services, and when would you use database management system facilities?

In approaching this issue, remember that you can freely intermix use of ISPF services and database management system CALLSs within programs. There are no artificial restrictions forcing use of one system or the other. You can use ISPF and relational database management systems capabilities from your programs in the manner you consider most appropriate.

Second, certain ISPF services may initially appear to offer capabilities that duplicate those supported by DB2, but they in fact do not. For example, File Tailoring Services automatically processes input file skeletons and prompts the Dialog Manager to perform dynamic variable substitution. Recall that the Dialog Manager's file tailoring processing can be directed by *control records* within the input skeleton.

Obviously programmers could duplicate ISPF's File Tailoring Services from within DB2 programs using only DB2 capabilities, but use of the ISPF Dialog Manager is much more convenient for this purpose.

The Dialog Manager's Variable Services may also at first glance appear to duplicate DB2's features. But again the two products are differentiated. Remember that the Variable Services groups variables into three separate pools: the *function pool* (variables associated with a particular dialog function), the *shared pool* (variables shared by all functions in a dialog), and the *application profile pool* (the set of variables associated with a particular application and saved across sessions). Implementation of equivalent functionality through use of DB2 or SQL/DS (without ISPF) is possible. Once again, however, it is more convenient to use Dialog Manager services provided specifically for these purposes. A good example is the Dialog Manager's application profile pool. As shown in chapter 5, it is probably easier to save information for each terminal user via the ISPF application profile pool services than to use DB2 or SQL/DS tables for this purpose.

The Dialog Manager's Table Services constitute the only direct example of duplication between ISPF and DB2 services. For applications involving small tables or simple data storage needs, it is often convenient to use the Dialog Manager's Table Services. For programs manipulating large tables or having complex data storage requirements, however, DB2 and SQL/DS offer much stronger capability. As two of IBM's premier database management systems, DB2 and SQL/DS provide full relational database management systems features; the ISPF Dialog Manager's Table Services do not. Furthermore, DB2 and SQL/DS are specifically designed and optimized to work with voluminous data storage requirements. Use them whenever your application requires full DBMS functionality.

CONCLUSION

The ISPF Dialog Manager offers many services that have no equivalents under DB2 and SQL/DS. These include the Dialog Manager's Display and Message services.

Several ISPF services pertaining to data storage might appear, at first to duplicate DB2 or SQL/DS functions, but in fact they do not. Examples include File Tailoring Services and Dialog Variable Services.

The Dialog Manager's Table Services do provide some of the same functionality provided by IBM's relational database management systems, DB2 and SQL/DS. However, you should use DB2 and SQL/DS in conjunction with the Dialog Manager whenever dialog functions require full DBMS functionality.

The addition of DB2 and SQL/DS database management system capability to ISPF dialogs greatly increases the utility of dialogs. The ISPF Dialog Manager can provide Display, Message, File Tailoring, Variable, Table, and Miscellaneous Services to user-written dialogs, while the relational DBMS's provide full relational database management capability. Together the two products offer state-of-the-art facilities for software design.

The accessibility of complete and powerful relational database management systems to functions written for the Dialog Manager underlines the central role of ISPF in IBM's plans. It also ensures ever-increasing usage of the ISPF Dialog Manager.

Figure 15-1. Company employee directory system data query screen.

```
---------------- COMPANY EMPLOYEE DIRECTORY SYSTEM --------------------------



ENTER EMPLOYEE NAME ON WHICH TO SEARCH:



        EMPLOYEE NAME ===>_





PRESS END KEY TO EXIT
```

Figure 15-2. Company employee directory system employee data display screen.

```
--------------- COMPANY EMPLOYEE DIRECTORY SYSTEM ---------------------------



   FOR EMPLOYEE NAME: BECKLEY


           OFFICE     : DENVER
           BUILDING   : 1400
           DEPARTMENT: ACTG
           TITLE      : ACCOUNTANT



PRESS END KEY TO EXIT
```

Figure 15-3. CSTART CLIST function.

```
00010000   PROC 0
00020000   CONTROL MSG NOFLUSH
00030000   /******************************************************************/
00040001   /* NAME: CSTART                            BY: H. FOSDICK      */
00050000   /*                                                            */
00060002   /* PURPOSE: THIS CLIST SETS UP THE DB2 ENVIRONMENT, AND       */
00070002   /* RUNS THE COBOL/DB2 PROGRAM 'CDIRECT'.  THIS PROGRAM        */
00080002   /* USES THE ISPF DIALOG MANAGER AND SUPPORTS THE 'COMPANY     */
00090002   /* EMPLOYEE DIRECTORY' APPLICATION.                           */
00100000   /*                                                            */
00110000   /******************************************************************/
00120002
00130002   DSN SYSTEM(DB2P)
00140002   RUN PROGRAM(CDIRECT) PLAN(CDIRECT) LIB(RUNLIB.LOAD)
00150004   END
00160002
00170002   EXIT CODE(0)
```

Figure 15-4. CDIRECT COBOL function.

```
 IDENTIFICATION DIVISION.                                        00010000
 PROGRAM-ID. CDIRECT.                                            00020001
***************************************************************00030000
*  NAME: CDIRECT                               BY: H. FOSDICK *00040001
*                                                             *00050000
*  PURPOSE: THIS PROGRAM ILLUSTRATES USE OF THE ISPF DIALOG   *00060017
*  MANAGER SERVICES FOR SCREEN HANDLING FROM A DB2 PROGRAM.   *00070000
*                                                             *00080000
*  THIS COBOL/DB2 PROGRAM SUPPORTS A SIMPLE ONLINE COMPANY    *00090017
*  EMPLOYEE DIRECTORY.  THE PROGRAM DISPLAYS AN INITIAL SCREEN*00100017
*  THROUGH WHICH THE TERMINAL USER SPECIFIES A COMPANY EMPLOYEE*00110017
*  CONCERNING WHOM HE DESIRES INFORMATION.  IN RESPONSE, THIS *00120017
*  PROGRAM EITHER DISPLAYS THAT EMPLOYEE'S INFORMATION FROM THE*00130017
*  DB2 TABLE; OR, IT DISPLAYS AN 'EMPLOYEE NOT FOUND' MESSAGE.*00140017
*  THE PROGRAM THEN RE-DISPLAYS THE ORIGINAL EMPLOYEE QUERY   *00150017
*  PANEL.                                                     *00160017
*                                                             *00170000
*  NOTE: IT IS KNOWN THAT THE EMPLOYEE NAME (KEY) IS UNIQUE.  *00180005
*                                                             *00190005
***************************************************************00200000
 ENVIRONMENT DIVISION.                                           00210000
 DATA DIVISION.                                                  00220000
                                                                 00230000
                                                                 00240000
 WORKING-STORAGE SECTION.                                        00250000
                                                                 00260000
                                                                 00270000
*  SERVICE CALL TYPES:                                           00280000
                                                                 00290000
 01  DISPLAY-PANEL        PIC X(8)      VALUE 'DISPLAY '.         00300000
 01  VDEFINE              PIC X(8)      VALUE 'VDEFINE '.         00310000
 01  VDELETE              PIC X(8)      VALUE 'VDELETE '.         00320000
                                                                 00330000
                                                                 00340000
*  THE NAME OF THE DATA QUERY PANEL:                             00350002
                                                                 00360000
 01  INPUT-PANEL          PIC X(8)      VALUE 'CDIRECT1'.         00370002
                                                                 00380000
                                                                 00390000
*  THE NAME OF THE DATA OUTPUT PANEL:                            00400002
                                                                 00410000
 01  OUTPUT-PANEL         PIC X(8)      VALUE 'CDIRECT2'.         00420002
                                                                 00430000
                                                                 00440000
*  VARIABLE TYPE FOR VARIABLE DEFINITION TO ISPF DIALOG MANAGER: 00450000
                                                                 00460000
 01  CHAR                 PIC X(8)      VALUE 'CHAR    '.         00470000
                                                                 00480000
                                                                 00490000
*  MESSAGES:                                                     00500000
                                                                 00510000
                                                                 00520000
 01  NAME-NOT-FOUND-MSG      PIC X(8)      VALUE 'CDAR001A'.      00530003
                                                                 00540000
                                                                 00550000
*  DEFINE STORAGE SPACE FOR DIALOG VARIABLES:                    00560000
                                                                 00570000
                                                                 00580000
 01  FNAME                PIC X(20)     VALUE  SPACES.            00590003
 01  OFFICE               PIC X(8)      VALUE  SPACES.            00600003
 01  BLDG                 PIC X(4)      VALUE  SPACES.            00610003
 01  DEPT                 PIC X(4)      VALUE  SPACES.            00620003
 01  TITLE                PIC X(12)     VALUE  SPACES.            00630003
                                                                 00640000
                                                                 00650000
*  DEFINE THE LENGTH OF EACH DIALOG VARIABLE:                    00660000
                                                                 00670000
                                                                 00680000
 01  FNAME-LENGTH         PIC 9(6)      VALUE  20   COMP.         00690003
 01  OFFICE-LENGTH        PIC 9(6)      VALUE  8    COMP.         00700003
 01  BLDG-LENGTH          PIC 9(6)      VALUE  4    COMP.         00710003
 01  DEPT-LENGTH          PIC 9(6)      VALUE  4    COMP.         00720003
 01  TITLE-LENGTH         PIC 9(6)      VALUE  12   COMP.         00730003
                                                                 00740000
                                                                 00750000
*  DEFINE DIALOG VARIABLE NAMES FOR ISPF DIALOG MANAGER:         00760000
                                                                 00770000
                                                                 00780000
 01  FNAME-NAME           PIC X(7)      VALUE  '(FNAME)'.         00790003
 01  OFFICE-NAME          PIC X(8)      VALUE  '(OFFICE)'.        00800003
 01  BLDG-NAME            PIC X(6)      VALUE  '(BLDG)'.          00810003
 01  DEPT-NAME            PIC X(6)      VALUE  '(DEPT)'.          00820003
 01  TITLE-NAME           PIC X(7)      VALUE  '(TITLE)'.         00830003
                                                                 00840005
                                                                 00850005
*  SQL COMMUNICATIONS AREA (SQLCA):                              00860005
                                                                 00870005
```

(continued)

Figure 15-4. *(Continued)*

```
        EXEC SQL                                                        00880005
                                                                        00890010
            INCLUDE  SQLCA                                              00900010
                                                                        00910010
        END-EXEC.                                                       00920010
                                                                        00930012
                                                                        00940013
    *  SQL TABLE DECLARATION:                                           00950013
                                                                        00960013
                                                                        00970013
        EXEC SQL                                                        00980013
                                                                        00990014
            DECLARE  ZHMF01.EMPTAB  TABLE                               01000014
                (FNAME          CHAR(20)          NOT NULL,             01010014
                 OFFICE         CHAR(8)           NOT NULL,             01020014
                 BLDG           CHAR(4)           NOT NULL,             01030014
                 DEPT           CHAR(4)           NOT NULL,             01040014
                 TITLE          CHAR(12)          NOT NULL)             01050014
                                                                        01060014
        END-EXEC.                                                       01070014
                                                                        01080014
                                                                        01090000
                                                                        01100005
                                                                        01110000
     PROCEDURE DIVISION.                                                01120000
                                                                        01130000
                                                                        01140000
                                                                        01150018
    *                                                                   01160018
    *  DEFINE ALL DIALOG FUNCTION VARIABLES TO ISPF DIALOG MANAGER:     01170018
    *                                                                   01180018
                                                                        01190018
        PERFORM DEFINE-VARIABLES THRU DEFINE-VARIABLES-EXIT.            01200018
                                                                        01210022
                                                                        01220018
    *                                                                   01230018
    *  SET UP SQL EXCEPTION CONDITIONS:                                 01240018
    *                                                                   01250018
                                                                        01260018
                                                                        01270018
        EXEC SQL  WHENEVER  NOT FOUND   CONTINUE  END-EXEC.             01280018
                                                                        01290018
        EXEC SQL  WHENEVER  SQLERROR    CONTINUE  END-EXEC.             01300018
                                                                        01310018
        EXEC SQL  WHENEVER  SQLWARNING  CONTINUE  END-EXEC.             01320018
                                                                        01330018
                                                                        01340000
    *                                                                   01350000
    *  DISPLAY DATA QUERY PANEL, AND RETRIEVE EMPLOYEE INFORMATION      01360000
    *  CONTINUALLY UNTIL USER PRESSES 'END' KEY:                        01370020
    *                                                                   01380004
                                                                        01390004
        CALL  'ISPLINK'  USING  DISPLAY-PANEL                           01400000
                                INPUT-PANEL.                            01410004
                                                                        01420004
        IF  RETURN-CODE  =  0                                           01430004
                                                                        01440004
                                                                        01450004
            PERFORM  QUERY-DISPLAY  THROUGH  QUERY-DISPLAY-EXIT         01460004
                UNTIL  RETURN-CODE  NOT = 0.                            01470005
                                                                        01480004
                                                                        01490004
    *                                                                   01500000
    *  DELETE ALL DIALOG FUNCTION VARIABLES RE ISPF DIALOG MANAGER      01510000
    *  AND EXIT:                                                        01520004
    *                                                                   01530004
                                                                        01540000
        PERFORM DELETE-VARIABLES THRU DELETE-VARIABLES-EXIT.            01550000
                                                                        01560000
        MOVE 0 TO RETURN-CODE.                                          01570004
                                                                        01580004
        GOBACK.                                                         01590000
                                                                        01600000
                                                                        01610000
     MAIN-LINE-EXIT.                                                    01620004
                                                                        01630000
                                                                        01640000
                                                                        01650021
                                                                        01660021
                                                                        01670000
     QUERY-DISPLAY.                                                     01680004
                                                                        01690004
    *                                                                   01700004
    *  SQL DIRECT RETRIEVAL OF USER-SPECIFIED EMPLOYEE NAME:            01710004
    *                                                                   01720004
                                                                        01730004
        EXEC SQL                                                        01740021
                                                                        01750005
```

```
              SELECT  FNAME,  OFFICE,  BLDG,  DEPT,  TITLE          01760005
              INTO    :FNAME, :OFFICE, :BLDG, :DEPT, :TITLE         01770008
              FROM    ZHMF01.EMPTAB                                 01780008
              WHERE   FNAME  =  :FNAME                              01790009
                                                                   01800005
         END-EXEC.                                                 01810005
                                                                   01820021
                                                                   01830005
                                                                   01840005
    *                                                              01850004
    *  IF RETRIEVAL SUCCEEDS, DISPLAY EMPLOYEE INFORMATION.        01860005
    *  OTHERWISE, DISPLAY ERROR MESSAGE:                           01870004
    *                                                              01880004
                                                                   01890021
         IF  SQLCODE  =  0                                         01900005
                                                                   01910004
              CALL 'ISPLINK'  USING  DISPLAY-PANEL                 01920004
                                     OUTPUT-PANEL                  01930011
                                                                   01940004
         ELSE                                                      01950004
                                                                   01960021
              MOVE  SPACES  TO  OFFICE, BLDG, DEPT, TITLE          01970016
                                                                   01980005
              CALL 'ISPLINK'  USING  DISPLAY-PANEL                 01990004
                                     OUTPUT-PANEL                  02000004
                                     NAME-NOT-FOUND-MSG.           02010005
                                                                   02020004
                                                                   02030004
    *                                                              02040004
    *  DISPLAY THE QUERY DATA ENTRY PANEL FOR NEXT RETRIEVAL ATTEMPT:  02050005
    *                                                              02060004
         CALL  'ISPLINK'  USING  DISPLAY-PANEL                     02070004
                                 INPUT-PANEL.                      02080004
                                                                   02090004
                                                                   02100004
                                                                   02110004
     QUERY-DISPLAY-EXIT.                                           02120004
         EXIT.                                                     02130004
                                                                   02140004
                                                                   02150004
                                                                   02160004
                                                                   02170000
                                                                   02180000
     DEFINE-VARIABLES.                                             02190000
                                                                   02200000
    *                                                              02210000
    *  THIS PARAGRAPH DEFINES DIALOG VARIABLES TO THE DIALOG MANAGER:  02220000
    *                                                              02230000
                                                                   02240000
         CALL 'ISPLINK'  USING  VDEFINE                            02250000
                                FNAME-NAME                         02260003
                                FNAME                              02270003
                                CHAR                               02280000
                                FNAME-LENGTH.                      02290003
         CALL 'ISPLINK'  USING  VDEFINE                            02300000
                                OFFICE-NAME                        02310003
                                OFFICE                             02320003
                                CHAR                               02330000
                                OFFICE-LENGTH.                     02340003
         CALL 'ISPLINK'  USING  VDEFINE                            02350000
                                BLDG-NAME                          02360003
                                BLDG                               02370003
                                CHAR                               02380000
                                BLDG-LENGTH.                       02390003
         CALL 'ISPLINK'  USING  VDEFINE                            02400000
                                DEPT-NAME                          02410003
                                DEPT                               02420003
                                CHAR                               02430000
                                DEPT-LENGTH.                       02440003
         CALL 'ISPLINK'  USING  VDEFINE                            02450000
                                TITLE-NAME                         02460003
                                TITLE                              02470003
                                CHAR                               02480000
                                TITLE-LENGTH.                      02490003
                                                                   02500000
     DEFINE-VARIABLES-EXIT.                                        02510000
         EXIT.                                                     02520000
                                                                   02530000
                                                                   02540000
                                                                   02550000
     DELETE-VARIABLES.                                             02560000
                                                                   02570000
    *                                                              02580000
    *  THIS PARAGRAPH DELETES DIALOG VARIABLES RE THE DIALOG MANAGER:  02590000
    *                                                              02600000
                                                                   02610000
```

(continued)

Figure 15-4. *(Continued)*

```
        CALL 'ISPLINK'   USING   VDELETE                              02620000
                                 FNAME-NAME.                          02630003
        CALL 'ISPLINK'   USING   VDELETE                              02640000
                                 OFFICE-NAME.                         02650003
        CALL 'ISPLINK'   USING   VDELETE                              02660000
                                 BLDG-NAME.                           02670003
        CALL 'ISPLINK'   USING   VDELETE                              02680000
                                 DEPT-NAME.                           02690003
        CALL 'ISPLINK'   USING   VDELETE                              02700000
                                 TITLE-NAME.                          02710003
                                                                      02720000
    DELETE-VARIABLES-EXIT.                                            02730000
        EXIT.                                                         02740000
```

16

Conclusion: The Future of ISPF

This chapter offers some perspective on the role and future of ISPF and its Dialog Manager. How does ISPF fit with other IBM program product offerings? What are its strengths and weaknesses? How is the vendor improving this product? What facilities will likely be added? In short, what will be the role of the ISPF Dialog Manager in the future, and how will the product evolve to fulfill this role?

HISTORY OF ISPF

In order to project the future role of the Dialog Manager, it is helpful to look at the product's past. ISPF has evolved over a decade in which its use has continually widened across the spectrum of IBM software and hardware offerings. Moreover, the functionality inherent in the product has expanded in parallel to this widening accessibility.

The predecessor product to ISPF, the Structured Programming Facility (SPF), was announced for the MVS operating system in 1974. It ran only on large IBM mainframe computers. SPF was made available under the VM/CMS operating system by 1979.

The original SPF was comprised of only that dialog that today is referred to as the ISPF/PDF. In other words, old SPF was a single dialog consisting of an editor and associated utilities designed to aid programmers in the building and maintenance of their applications. It did not offer programmers the ability to create dialogs via the CALL-able Dialog Manager service routines, nor did it provide the integrated Dialog Test facility that would evolve to support dialog development.

Sophisticated installations soon found that old SPF could in fact be extended into a more broadly based tool; the dialog could be extended to do much more than the code distributed by the vendor. However, these dialog extensions were installation dependent. Any site developing such extensions also had to accept the maintenance burden for that code.

By 1980, pressure from user organizations resulted in IBM's replacement of the original SPF by a new SPF. Although the product acronym remained unchanged, the full name of the new product became System Productivity Facility. The major feature of this new product was that the SPF's internal service routines were documented and made publicly available. Thus, for the first time, SPF provided a well-defined external interface to applications programmers. The Dialog Manager service routines described in this book were now CALLable from programming languages. The languages supported were COBOL and PL/I for compiled languages and CLIST and EXEC2 for command procedures (under MVS and VM, respectively). Using these languages, programmers could create *dialogs* whose user interface appeared similar to that of IBM's SPF dialog itself.

In 1982, SPF was renamed again, this time as the Interactive System Productivity Facility (ISPF). ISPF's Dialog Manager capabilities were augmented and extended to new programming languages.

For the first time, the IBM-provided dialog for the editor and associated utilities was broken out into a separately purchased product, ISPF/PDF. This means that only ISPF (the Dialog Manager) may be required for machines that run dialogs. Dialog development machines require both ISPF and ISFP/PDF. At the same time, ISPF/PDF was improved to provide facilities for dialog design and testing. These features included the ISPF/PDF Editor **MODEL** command and a complete, integrated Dialog Test facility.

Also in 1982, the ISPF Dialog Manager and ISPF/PDF for the VSE operating system were announced. This VSE/ICCF product became available in 1983.

Since 1982, several important ISPF announcements have followed in rapid succession. IBM introduced ISPF Version 2, which added some two dozen new Dialog Manager services while enhancing 14 existing functions. Terminal support was improved to include the Graphical Data Display Manager (GDDM), table services were significantly improved, library access services were introduced, and programs using the Dialog Manager could now use DB2 and SQL/DS database management services. This last feature is especially important because it means that programs running under the ISPF Dialog Manager now have access to a functionally complete and robust database management system. (This assumes, of course, that an installation has installed one of these separately purchased database management products.) Additionally, ISPF Dialog Manager support was extended to the programming languages APL2, VS FORTRAN, and REXX. Finally, the ISPF products were made available under the SSX/VSE operating system.

IBM's expansion of its ISPF offerings were not limited to the mainframes. In 1984, the company introduced the EZ-VU Development Facility, a version of the ISPF Dialog Manager for the IBM personal computer family. (Appendix E describes this product in some detail.) EZ-VU was rapidly followed by an ISPF/PDF Editor product for personal computers in 1985.

This dizzying procession of IPSF product announcements is sum-

Table 16-1. Evolution of the ISPF Dialog Manager

1974	Structured Programming Facility introduced for MVS
1979	Structured Programming Facility introduced for VM
1980	System Productivity Facility introduced.
	Dialog Manager services introduced and made available to programs written in COBOL, PL/I, CLIST, EXEC2
1982	Interactive System Productivity Facility (ISPF) introduced
	ISPF/PDF now a separately purchased product
	ISPF/PDF enhanced to include support for dialog development
	Dialog Manager services extended to new programming languages
1983	ISPF Dialog Manager and ISPF/PDF available under VSE
1984	EZ-VU Development Facility introduced under PC-DOS for IBM personal computers
1984/ 1985	ISPF Version 2 introduced; support for new terminal devices, expanded table services, new library access services, compatibility with DB2 and SQL/DS, etc.
	Language support extended for VS FORTRAN, Pascal, APL2, REXX
	Operating system support extended to SSX/VSE
1985	IBM introduces ISPF/PDF Editor under PC-DOS for IBM personal computer family
1986	EZ-VU-II Development Facility available for IBM personal computers

marized in table 16-1. Notice that the velocity of product introductions has increased over the past several years.

WHITHER ISPF?

The ISPF Dialog Manager works:

with all major terminal devices (3278, 3178, 3270PC, 3290, 3279, etc.),

with all major programming languages (COBOL, PL/I, VS FORTRAN, FORTRAN IV, Assembler, Pascal, RPG II, APL2, CLIST, EXEC2, REXX),

across all strategic operating systems (MVS/TSO, VM/CMS, DOS/ VSE, SSX/VSE, PC-DOS), VM/PC, VM/E), and

across most major machine families (309X, 308X, 303X, 43XX, 370, IBM PC/XT/AT family, IBM XT/AT/370).

The ISPF Dialog Manager's companion product, ISPF/PDF, provides menu-driven interface to most major IBM products. For example, dialog interfaces for new products such as the Application Development Facility (IADF) and Database 2 (DB2I) have recently been added. As noted in this book's Introduction, over 70 IBM (and 60 non-IBM) program products interface to ISPF. It is IBM's stated direction to expand ISPF as the common dialog manager for all new and existing products wherever feasible.

Thus, it is clear the ISPF Dialog Manager and ISPF/PDF represent *strategic products* for IBM. The central positioning of these two products in IBM's plans, present and future, is quite apparent.

Key to ISPF's central role is its cross-system compatibility. IBM offers very few other program products across such a wide spectrum of operating systems. In fact, it would be difficult to point to examples of other products that so widely touch upon the otherwise-disparate offerings in the vendor's product line.

ADVANTAGES OF THE ISPF DIALOG MANAGER

It is worthwhile to enumerate briefly the Dialog Manager's advantages to program developers:

High Programmer Productivity.   One can develop procedural code quite quickly using the ISPF Dialog Manager services.

Less Programmer Expertise Required.   The ISPF Dialog Manager requires less time to learn and less expertise to use than do many other program development products (such as IMS and CICS).

Transportability of Programmer Skills.   The fact that the Dialog Manager runs under so many major operating systems renders Dialog Manager skills applicable across operating environments. In an era when programmer and education costs are paramount, this is a key ISPF advantage. The availability of Dialog Manager interfaces to nearly all major programming languages reinforces skill transferability, as does the common dialog testing environment of ISPF/PDF.

Code Transportability.   The ISPF Dialog Manager offers a high degree of code portability across operating systems. The product is designed to increase portability to the extent possible. As one example, the library access services associate data set names with a *dataid*, thereby limiting the coding impact of operating system dependent file naming conventions on code transportability.

Front-Ends for Existing Batch Applications.   The Dialog Manager is ideal for creating dialog front-ends for existing batch applications. One can often create such front-ends without affecting existing code. The "batch online" approach outlined in chapter 6 thus gives such systems some of the advantages of online systems without altering existing programs.

Consistent User Interface.   The ISPF Dialog Manager leads to a consistent user interface for applications on both a single computer and across operating systems. The product offers programmers the tools needed to ensure interface consistency and simplicity regardless of the nature of their applications or their target operating systems.

Easy-to-Use Applications.   The Dialog Manager's user interface is based on such principles of user-friendly systems as menu-driven selection, a full "help" system, tutorial panels, and consistent program function key settings.

Integrated Support Facilities.   The Dialog Manager's related ISPF/ PDF component provides a powerful editor, uniform access to operating system utilities, and integrated Dialog Test facilities. ISPF/PDF provides an exceptional programmer's workbench for dialog development.

Relational Database Management System Compatibility.   Programs written with the Dialog Manager can also use the relational database management system capabilities of DB2 and SQL/DS. No special changes need be made to the Dialog Manager portion of the programs in order to use these database managers. These database management systems provide strong support to ISPF programs, including database backup, auditing, and restoration functions; relational database operators; database integrity and security; and powerful data modeling capability. DB2 and SQL/DS are separately purchased program products.

PRODUCT POSITIONING OF THE ISPF DIALOG MANAGER

Given the Dialog Manager's strengths, how does this product fit into IBM's product line? Of special interest is where ISPF fits with IBM's strategic products, Information Management System (IMS) and Customer Information Control System (CICS). Like the ISPF Dialog Manager, these products support the development of interactive applications.

Comparison of the ISPF Dialog Manager with IMS and CICS can best be approached by enumerating the relative strengths of the products. This is done in table 16-2. This table provides rough comparison only because the comparisons heavily depend on how the products are configured.

Compared to IMS or CICS, the Dialog Manager offers these advantages:

higher programmer productivity
greater ease of use
more rapid application development
better suitability for prototyping
greater transportability of code across operating systems
greater transferability of programmer skills across operating systems
minimally disruptive online front-ends to existing batch applications
consistent user interface across operating systems
wider variety of services other than those for screen control and data
    storage (for example, message services with complete "help" and
    tutorial system support, file tailoring services, embedded ISPF/
    PDF Editor support, and split-screen)

IMS and CICS, however, offer applications generators that are not currently available for the ISPF Dialog Manager. Use of applications generators like the Application Development Facility (ADF) for IMS

Table 16-2. When to Use ISPF Dialog Manager versus IMS and CICS

ISPF Dialog Manager	IMS and CICS
Faster application development (for procedural code)	
Higher programmer productivity (for procedural code)	
Command procedure support	
Good for prototyping	Good for prototyping only
Easier to learn and use	through application generators
Nondisruptive front-end for existing applications	like ADF-II
Higher degree of code portability across operating systems	(Can offer applications portability through CSP only)
Higher degree of skills transferability across systems	(Can offer skills transferability through CSP only)
	Provide application generators (ADF and CSP)
	Volume online, transaction-oriented systems, especially involving updates
	More concurrent users of an application
Access to DB2 and SQL/DS databases	Access to DB2 and SQL/DS databases
	Access to IMS (or DL/1) databases
Easy access to built-in Editor (ISPF/PDF **EDIT** and **BROWSE**)	
Access to many other kinds of ISPF services (Message, Variable, File Tailoring, Misc.)	
Easy access to complete tutorial/ "help" system	

or Cross-System Product (CSP) for CICS tends to even the comparison in the areas of high programmer productivity, rapid applications development, and suitability of these systems for prototyping. CSP also offers cross-systems advantages similar to those of the Dialog Manager in terms of transportability of code and transferability of programmer skills across operating systems.

With or without applications generators, IMS and CICS are superior to the Dialog Manager for applications involving large numbers of concurrent users. They better support high-transaction-volume online systems. IMS and CICS remain IBM's primary offerings for transaction-oriented processing.

IBM's new relational database management systems products, DB2 and SQL/DS, significantly strengthen the Dialog Manager's suitability for production systems. ISPF programmers now have access to full-fledged database management capabilities, including the data backup, recovery, and security features provided by these products. Now that the Dialog Manager can be used in database programs, the positioning of this product should become more pronounced.

The relative advantages and disadvantages of the ISPF Dialog Manager versus IMS and CICS depend on the nature of the applications. Although such precise comparisons are not possible here, this brief discussion and table 16-2 should indicate when use of the Dialog Manager can prove most beneficial.

ROLE AND FUTURE OF ISPF

How can the ISPF Dialog Manager and ISPF/PDF provide such diverse advantages as skill transferability, code transportability, and consistent user interface? Part of the reason lies in the fact that the products together constitute a *shell*. The concept of a shell, derived from the UNIX operating system, has been applied to various operating systems such as PC-DOS. A shell is a layer of software that surrounds the operating system. It provides a different interface to its programmers and users than does the operating system itself. Users interact with the operating system through this shell; it is through the shell that they request system functions and utilities.

In this sense of the definition, ISPF is IBM's shell. The shell provides portability of skills and code to each operating system under which it runs. The ISPF/PDF portion of the shell comprises a consistent user interface through which its users (programmers) access the operating system and its functions. The Dialog Manager services component provides programmers with an extendable applications shell. These services render the shell programmable. Through use of the consistent shell interface represented by Dialog Manager services, an installation can build applications whose user interface resembles that of the shell itself.

The ISPF Dialog Manager and ISPF/PDF together represent IBM's shell of choice. IBM conceives a strategic role for this shell, tying together otherwise diverse operating systems, programming languages, and computer hardware. Together the ISPF Dialog Manager and ISPF/ PDF constitute the foundation for IBM's software offerings for years to come.

Defining Libraries to the Dialog Manager

The following steps describe the general procedure for installing and working with the ISPF Dialog Manager:

1. Establish the libraries for the dialog components. These libraries hold the source code for dialog panels, messages, file skeletons, and so forth.
2. Create a procedure containing the necessary statements to define the libraries to ISPF.
3. Create such dialog components as panels, messages, and file skeletons by directly entering source code definitions for these elements into library members.
4. Create the dialog functions in languages appropriate to the operating environment and place them into suitable libraries.
5. Test dialog components through the features of the Dialog Test facility described in chapter 8.
6. Set up the dialog such that it can be invoked for regular use. This can be done in several ways, as described in chapter 1.

Although these steps describe a general approach to working with the Dialog Manager, definition of the required libraries is operating-system dependent. The sections that follow provide an overview of library requirements for each of the three major operating systems: MVS, VM, and VSE. *Be aware that the specifics of installation are highly site-dependent*. This appendix only supplies an example. You should consult the vendor's reference manuals and your system administrator for more detailed information.

MVS LIBRARY REQUIREMENTS

Under MVS, a *library* is defined as a *partitioned data set*. Such files as panel and skeleton definitions constitute individual members within their respective libraries. The Dialog Manager requires use of the following libraries in the MVS environment:

ISPPLIB (Panel Library),
ISPMLIB (Message Library),
ISPSLIB (Skeleton Library),
ISPTLIB (Table Input Library), and
ISPPROF (User Profile Library).

The data set names (DSNAMEs) for these libraries at an installation depend on the version and release of ISPF in use at that site, as well as the naming choices of the systems programmers. You should contact your system administrator or project leader for these data set names.

In addition to ISPF-provided libraries, you will want to create application libraries that hold your own panels, messages, file skeletons, and tables. These must have block sizes at least as big as the distribution libraries and should be concatenated ahead of their respective ISPF product libraries. Many installations have their own standards concerning library concatenation order.

Refer to the section entitled "Library Requirements" in the vendor's manual, *Interactive System Productivity Facility: Dialog Management Services* for specific details relating to your own release of the Dialog Manager.

In addition to the required libraries, the following data sets may be needed where an application uses table or file tailoring services:

ISPTABL (Table Output Library) and
ISPFILE (File Tailoring Output).

The Table Output Library is a partitioned data set that may be either the same data set or a different one as the Table Input Library (**ISPTLIB**). If a dialog updates a table and intends to process that updated version later, these data set names must be the same. Another alternative is for a dialog to allocate **ISPTABL** dynamically and free it after use.

The File Tailoring Output data set may be a sequential or a partitioned data set. Like **ISPTABL**, **ISPFILE** may be dynamically allocated by a dialog and freed after use. A File Tailoring Output data set need not be allocated for a dialog that writes file tailoring output to the temporary sequential data set provided by the Dialog Manager. ISPF takes care of the necessary allocation in this case.

Finally, CLIST and program functions have their own special library requirements. CLISTs are defined as members of the partitioned data set procedure library allocated to the DDNAME **SYSPROC**. This allocation must occur prior to invocation of the Dialog Manager. Many programmers define this CLIST library during their TSO LOGON procedures.

Program functions must be compiled and link edited prior to use in dialogs. The link edit step includes a reference to the **ISPLINK** interface routine seen in the sample programs.* (Recall that this routine is named **ISPLNK** for FORTRAN programs.) Ask your system programmer or look in the vendor's manual for the proper data set name under which to access this ISPF routine. Program function load modules are often placed in a partitioned data set allocated to the DDNAME **IS-PLLIB**.

An example of the details of library allocation should make them more clear. Figure A-1 provides such an example. This is the CLIST used in allocating the files and in issuing the **ISPSTART** command for the COBOL version of the sample dialog discussed in this book.

In its first statement, the CLIST first frees any previous allocations for the DDNAMEs to which it subsequently refers. Then it proceeds to allocate the panel, message, file tailoring skeleton, and table input libraries. In each of these cases, the user's application library in which these dialog components reside is called **PROGRAMS.TEST**. The system libraries at the installation in the example all start with the high-level qualifier **SYS1**. This may not be the same at your installation. Notice that each of these allocations specifies the sharable and reusable attributes (**SHR REUSE**). These parameters are recommended in the product reference manual.

The last of the five required libraries allocated is the User Profile Library. Assigned the DDNAME **ISPPROF**, this allocation refers to a locally defined data set name. Since the User Profile Library is allocated on a per user basis, the user's high-level TSO qualifier serves to render the data set name unique. The vendor reference manual recommends that this data set be given the attributes of **OLD REUSE**.

Since the sample dialog uses the Dialog Manager's table services for creating and maintaining a permanent table, the next allocation defines the table output library **PROGRAMS.TEST**. The table output library references the same data set name as the table input library because the dialog updates the table and processes this updated version later.

This CLIST uses only the single library **PROGRAMS.TEST** because this is a sample application. In a production environment, different libraries would most likely be specified for each dialog component type. That is, all the panel definitions would reside in one library, all the message definitions in another, the file skeleton definitions in another, and so on.

Next the program function library is allocated to the DDNAME **ISPLLIB**. This is where the COBOL program functions reside under the member names referred to in the selection panel definitions of the sample dialog. Remember that these program functions must have been linked with the ISPF interface service routine.† This module is called **ISPLINK** for all programming languages except FORTRAN, which references it as **ISPLNK**.

For a dialog using CLISTs, a command procedure library must be

---

*Programs can also dynamically call ISPF.

†Program functions can also link to **ISPLINK** dynamically.

allocated to the DDNAME **SYSPROC** prior to invoking the Dialog Manager. This is not shown in the figure because it was accomplished through these statements in the developer's TSO LOGON procedure:

```
FREE FILE(SYSPROC)
ALLOCATE FILE(SYSPROC) +
          DA(MY.CLIST.LIBRARY 'OTHER.CLIST.LIBRARIS') SHR
```

The last statement in the CLIST example contains the **ISPSTART** command. This command initiates the Dialog Manager and tells it to display the selection panel **WMENUC**. **WMENUC** is the member name of the application master menu panel definition stored in the panel library **PROGRAMS.TEST**.

The single difference between the versions of this CLIST for the COBOL and CLIST implementations of the sample dialog exists in the panel reference of last line. In the COBOL version, this statement refers to panel **WMENUC**; the CLIST implementation first displays panel **WMENU**. The two panel definitions are different because selection panels must indicate whether they **SELECT** functions written as command procedures or compiled programs (explained in chapter 3).

In this CLIST, the Table Input Library and Table Output Library are assigned to the same partitioned data set because the dialog updates a Dialog Manager–maintained table and later reprocesses it. The File Tailoring Output Library (DDNAME of **ISPFILE**) is not allocated in this CLIST because the sample dialog writes its file tailoring output to a temporary sequential data set. The allocation for this temporary data set is automatically provided by the Dialog Manager.

VM LIBRARY REQUIREMENTS

Use of the Dialog Manager under VM requires definition of the five same libraries mandatory under MVS (see table A-1). These libraries are CMS MACLIBs.

It is assumed that the user's virtual device 191 is accessible as the A-disk. If you are interested in the Dialog Manager's support of shared minidisks, consult the section "VM/SP: Use of Shared Minidisks" in the vendor reference manual *Interactive System Productivity Facility: Dialog Management Services*.

The User Profile Library is allocated on a per user basis and is maintained by ISPF.

As in the MVS environment, user libraries for panels, messages, skeletons, and so forth should be concatenated ahead of the ISPF distribution libraries. This can be accomplished either through the CMS **PROFILE EXEC** or through a command procedure written to start a specific dialog. For example, where a user-developed dialog uses the **ABCPANLS**, **ABCMSGS**, and **ABCSKELS** MACLIBs for its panel, message, and skeleton libraries, **FILEDEF**s such as the following could be employed:

Table A-1. Required ISPF Libraries for VM

DDNAME	Description	FILE NAME
ISPPLIB	Panel Library	ISPPLIB MACLIB
ISPMLIB	Message Library	ISPMLIB MACLIB
ISPSLIB	Skeleton Library	ISPSLIB MACLIB
ISPTLIB	Table Input Library	ISPTLIB MACLIB
ISPPROF	User Profile Library	User selected

```
FILEDEF ISPPLIB  DISK ABCPANLS  MACLIB * (PERM CONCAT
FILEDEF ISPPLIB  DISK ISPPLIB    MACLIB * (PERM CONCAT
FILEDEF ISPMLIB  DISK ABCMSGS    MACLIB * (PERM CONCAT
FILEDEF ISPMLIB  DISK ISPMLIB    MACLIB * (PERM CONCAT
FILEDEF ISPSLIB  DISK ABCSKELS   MACLIB * (PERM CONCAT
FILEDEF ISPSLIB  DISK ISPSLIB    MACLIB * (PERM CONCAT
```

The Table Output Library and File Tailoring Output Library are both optionally defined by the dialog developer. These are allocated via **FILEDEF** statements in a manner similar to that shown above.

The Table Output Library must be a MACLIB allocated to the DDNAME of **ISPTABL**. If a dialog updates and then processes a Dialog Manager table, the Table Output Library filename must be the same as the Table Input Library filename assigned to the DDNAME of **ISPTLIB**.

The File Tailoring Output allocation may refer to either a MACLIB or a sequential file, or this file may be dynamically allocated by the dialog itself. Another alternative is for the dialog to write its file tailoring output to the temporary sequential file provided by ISPF. In this case, any necessary file allocation is automatically performed by the Dialog Manager.

Dialog functions written in the EXEC2 or REXX command languages must reside on minidisks that have been linked and accessed prior to their use with the Dialog Manager.

Dialog functions written in compiled programming languages can either be invoked in object (text) module format or in load module format. The DDNAMEs normally used are as follows:

ISPXLIB (Text Module Library, **TXTLIB**) and
ISPLLIB (Load Module Library, **LOADLIB**).

FILEDEF statements are used to allocate these libraries as needed. Details concerning these libraries are available in the vendor's reference manual.

VSE LIBRARY REQUIREMENTS

The VSE environment requires use of source statement libraries to contain dialog element definitions, as shown in table A-2.

Table A-2. Sublibraries for Dialog Components

Type	Sublibrary
MESSAGES	M
PANELS	N
SKELETONS	S
TABLES	T

The sublibrary for file tailoring skeletons includes file tailoring output also. These sublibraries are defined through **ISPDEF** control statements contained in the ICCF procedure used to start the Dialog Manager. Details on encoding **ISPDEF** control statements can be found in the vendor's reference manual *Interactive System Productivity Facility: Dialog Management Services*.

Use of the Dialog Manager in the VSE environment requires definition of the same five libraries mandatory under MVS and VM. All five libraries are distributed with the ISPF product, except the User Profile Library, which is dynamically generated and updated during execution of ISPF. The dialog developers' application libraries are concatenated ahead of the Dialog Manager distribution libraries.

The Table Output Library and the File Tailoring Output definitions are optional. The Table Output Library must specify the same library as the Table Input Library if dialogs intend to update tables and later reprocess them.

The File Tailoring Output definition can be accomplished through the **ISPDEF** statement for **ISPFILE**. If file tailoring output is written to a temporary file, it is output to a temporary sequential data set defined under the filename **ISPCTLx**.

Figure A-1. XDMC CLIST.

```
00010000  PROC 0
00020000  CONTROL MSG NOFLUSH
00030000  /*****************************************************************/
00040000  /* NAME: XDMC                          BY: H. FOSDICK       */
00050000  /*                                                         */
00060000  /* PURPOSE: THIS CLIST SETS UP THE ENVIRONMENT NECESSARY   */
00070000  /* TO ENTERING THE 'WEST DEPARTMENT ACCOUNTS RECEIVABLE'   */
00080000  /* SYSTEM.  IT ALLOCATES ALL LIBRARIES REQUIRED BY THE USER */
00090000  /* WHEN ENTERING A DIALOG MANAGER APPLICATION, THEN ISSUES */
00100000  /* THE 'ISPSTART' COMMAND TO SELECT THE APPLICATION MASTER */
00110000  /* MENU.   THE MASTER APPLICATION MENU THEN CALLS COBOL    */
00120000  /* PROGRAMS APPROPRIATE TO PROCESS THE USER'S SELECTED     */
00130000  /* OPTION.                                                 */
00140000  /*                                                         */
00150000  /*****************************************************************/
00160000
00170000  /*                                                         */
00180000  /*   FREE ANY PREVIOUS ISPF/DIALOG MANAGER ALLOCATIONS:    */
00190000  /*                                                         */
00200000
00210000  FREE FILE(ISPPLIB ISPMLIB ISPSLIB ISPTLIB ISPPROF ISPTABL ISPLLIB)
00220000
00230000
00240000  /*                                                         */
00250000  /*   ALLOCATE THE PANEL LIBRARIES:                         */
00260000  /*                                                         */
00270000
00280003  ALLOCATE FILE(ISPPLIB) DA(PROGRAMS.TEST    'SYS1.PANELS')  SHR REUSE
00290000
00300000
00310000  /*                                                         */
00320000  /*   ALLOCATE THE MESSAGE LIBRARIES:                       */
00330000  /*                                                         */
00340000
00350003  ALLOCATE FILE(ISPMLIB) DA(PROGRAMS.TEST    'SYS1.MSGS')  SHR REUSE
00360000
00370000
00380000  /*                                                         */
00390000  /*   ALLOCATE THE SKELETON JCL LIBRARIES:                  */
00400000  /*                                                         */
00410000
00420003  ALLOCATE FILE(ISPSLIB) DA(PROGRAMS.TEST    'SYS1.SKELS')  SHR REUSE
00430000
00440000
00450000  /*                                                         */
00460000  /*   ALLOCATE THE TABLE INPUT LIBRARIES:                   */
00470000  /*                                                         */
00480000
00490003  ALLOCATE FILE(ISPTLIB) DA(PROGRAMS.TEST    'SYS1.TABLES')  SHR REUSE
00500000
00510000
00520000  /*                                                         */
00530000  /*   ALLOCATE THE USER PROFILE LIBRARY:                    */
00540000  /*                                                         */
00550000
00560000  ALLOCATE FILE(ISPPROF) DA('&SYSUID..ISPF.PROFILE') OLD REUSE
00570000
00580000
00590000  /*                                                         */
00600000  /*   ALLOCATE THE TABLE OUTPUT LIBRARY:                    */
00610000  /*                                                         */
00620000
00630001  ALLOCATE FILE(ISPTABL) DA(PROGRAMS.TEST)  SHR REUSE
00640000
00650000
00660000  /*                                                         */
00670000  /*   ALLOCATE THE PROGRAM FUNCTION LOAD LIBRARY:           */
00680000  /*                                                         */
00690000
00700000  ALLOCATE FILE(ISPLLIB) DA(C.LOAD)  SHR REUSE
00710000
00720000
00730000  /*                                                         */
00740000  /*   ISSUE THE 'ISPSTART' COMMAND TO DISPLAY THE MASTER    */
00750000  /*   APPLICATION MENU TO THE USER:                         */
00760000  /*                                                         */
00770000
00780000  ISPSTART PANEL(WMENUC)
```

Appendix B
Reference Manuals

Appendix B summarizes IBM's ISPF reference manuals and provides sources for further information on the topics discussed in this book.

The most introductory of the ISPF manuals are the *ISPF and ISPF/PDF General Information* manual and the *ISPF and ISPF/PDF Primer*. The *General Information* manual provides an overview of the purpose and functions of the product, and the *Primer* presents a tutorial. The *Primer* was first published in ISPF Version 2.

The reference manuals most pertinent to the material in this book are the *ISPF Dialog Management Services*—a complete reference to programming with ISPF, and the *ISPF Dialog Management Services Examples*—containing program examples in a wide variety of programming languages.

The ISPF library access services described in chapters 13 and 14 of this book are referenced in *ISPF/PDF Dialog Services*. These services are new in Version 2 of ISPF. The new features of ISPF Version 2 summarized in chapter 12 are presented in *ISPF and ISPF/PDF: What's New in ISPF?* This manual analyzes differences between ISPF Versions 1 and 2.

Tables B-1, B-2, and B-3 list the major manuals for the various mainframe and microcomputer ISPF products. IBM is presently improving the ISPF documentation and revising the manual numbers. This information represents the best available at the time of publication.

Table B-1. Major ISPF and ISPF/PDF Reference Manuals

Publication	Operating System			
	MVS	VM	VSE	PC/370
ISPF and ISPF/PDF General Information	GC34-4041	GC34-4036	GC34-2078	GC34-2078
ISPF and ISPF/PDF Primer		SC34-4017		
ISPF Dialog Management Services	SC34-4021	SC34-4010	SC34-2088	SC34-2088
ISPF Dialog Management Services Examples	SC34-4022	SC34-4010	SC34-2085	SC34-2085
ISPF Dialog Management Reference Card	SC34-2109	SC34-4101	SC34-2109	SC34-2109
ISPF Dialog Management Guide		SC34-4009		
ISPF/PDF Dialog Services	SC34-4023	SC34-4012		
ISPF and ISPF/PDF Installation and Customization	SC34-4019	SC34-4015	SC34-2080	SC34-2083
ISPF Version 2 for MVS Installation and Use	GG24-1706			
ISPF/PDF Program References	SC34-4024	SC34-4011	SC34-2079	SC34-2090
ISPF/PDF Library Management	SC34-4025	SC34-4013		
ISPF Licensed Program Specifications	GC34-4039	GC34-4034		
ISPF/PDF Licensed Program Specifications	GC34-4040	GC34-4035		

Table B-2. Supporting ISPF Reference Material

ISPF Articles from *IBM Systems Journal:*

Joslin, P. H., 1981, System Productivity Facility, in *IBM Systems Journal,* vol. 20, no. 4, IBM reprint form number G321-5155, pp. 388–406.

Maurer, M. E., 1983, Full-Screen Testing of Interactive Applications, in *IBM Systems Journal,* vol. 22, no. 3, IBM reprint form number G321–5194, pp. 246–261.

Course Material:

ISPF Dialog Management Services Self Study (Course Code 32302)
Introduction to ISPF Dialog Manager (Videotape SV24-0260 Beta, SV24-0261 VHS)

Presentation Guides:

ISPF and ISPF/PDF Presentation Guide (G320-6506)
ISPF/PDF Library Management Presentation Guide (G320-0740)

Miscellaneous:

Version 2: What's New in ISPF? (GC34-2172)
ISPF Product Reference Card (GC34-2169)

Table B-3. EZ-VU Product Reference Material*

EZ-VU Development Facility for the IBM Personal Computer (6410980)
ISPF/PDF (EZ-VU) Editor (6466974)
ISPF/PC (EZ-VU): Hints and Tips (GC34-4103)
EZ-VU Information Brochure (GC34-4001)
EZ-VU Presentation Guide (GC34-2167)
EZ-VU II Information Brochure (G520-6006)
EZ-VU II Presentation Guide (G520–6007)

*This chart represents the information available at the time of publication.

Table B-4. Other Reference Manuals

COBOL References:

VS COBOL for OS/VS (GC26-3857)
OS/VS COBOL Compiler and Library Programmer's Guide (SC28-6483)

CLIST References:

TSO Terminal User's Guide (GC28-0645)
TSO Command Language Reference (GC28-0646)

JCL Reference:

MVS/XA JCL (GC28-1148)

DB2 and SQL/DS References:

IBM Database 2: Introduction to SQL (GC26-4082)
IBM Database 2: General Information (GC26-4073)
IBM Database 2: Application Programming Guide for TSO Users (SH26-4081)
SQL/Data System: General Information for VSE (GH24-5012)
SQL/Data System: Application Programming for VSE (SH24-5018)

Dialog Diagrams for the West Department Accounts Receivable System

COBOL version.

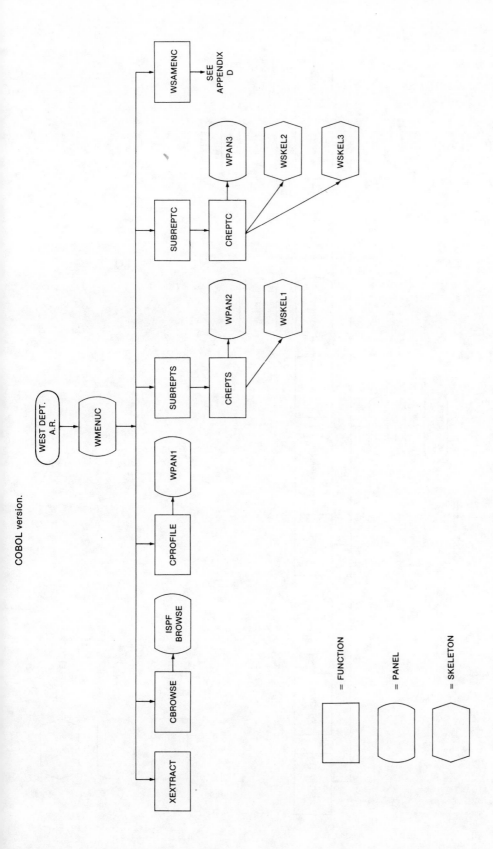

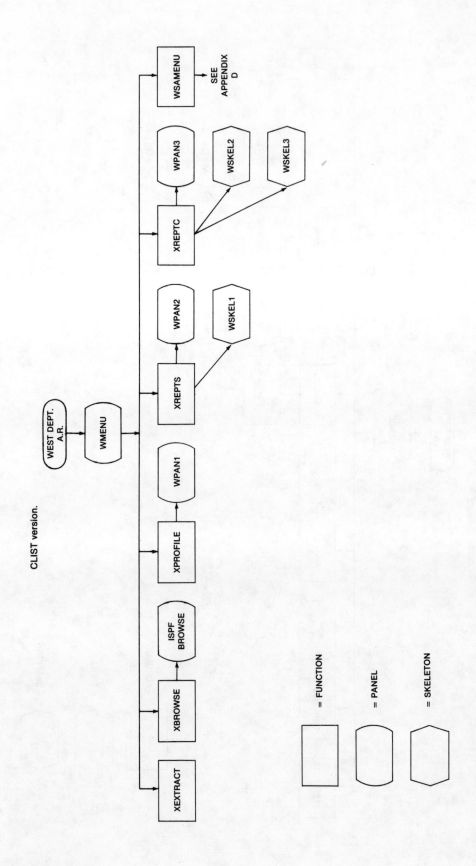

CLIST version.

= FUNCTION

= PANEL

= SKELETON

Dialog Diagrams for the Accounting Control Administration Subsystem of the West Department Accounts Receivable System

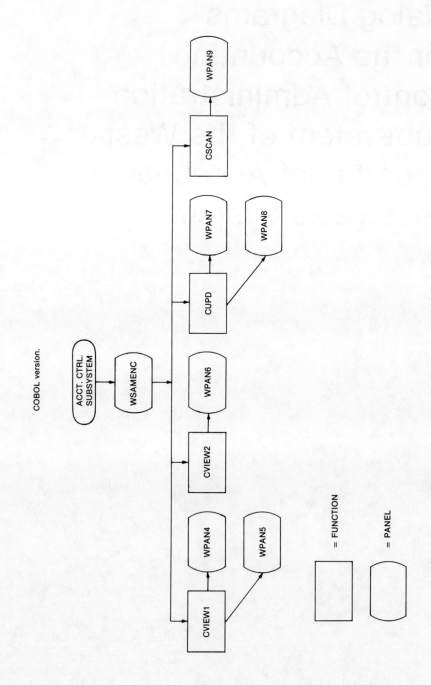

COBOL version.

= FUNCTION

= PANEL

CLIST version.

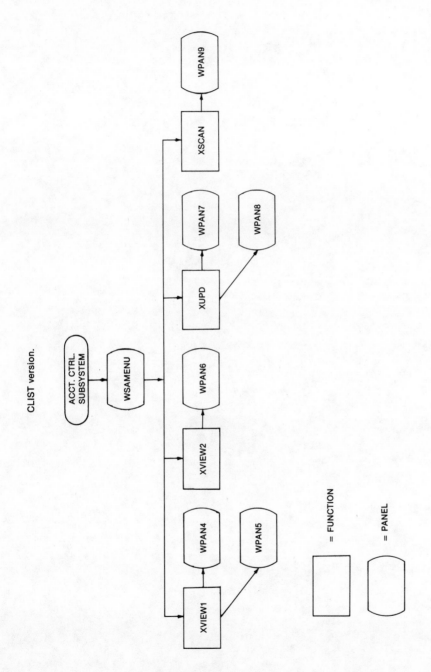

ACCT. CTRL.
SUBSYSTEM

WSAMENU

XVIEW1

WPAN4

WPAN5

XVIEW2

WPAN6

XUPD

WPAN7

WPAN8

XSCAN

WPAN9

☐ = FUNCTION

⬓ = PANEL

255

Appendix E

EZ-VU Development Facility

This appendix provides a brief overview of the EZ-VU Development Facility. This product runs on members of the IBM personal computer family, including the PC, XT, and AT.

The EZ-VU product is modeled on the ISPF Dialog Manager; however, it is not code compatible with it. Use of the ISPF Dialog Manager is extremely similar on computers running versions of the MVS, VM, and VSE operating systems, leading to a high degree of code compatibility among dialogs for these systems. This is not the case with the EZ-VU product, which is best considered a functional subset of the mainframe Dialog Manager adapted to the unique operating environment of the personal computer.

The EZ-VU Development Facility consists of two components.

The *EZ-VU Runtime Facility Program Product* provides the interface between the dialog program(s) and the terminal user. It is also called the *Dialog Manager* or (DM).

The *EZ-VU Development Facility Program Product* aids developers in design and generation of their panels. This facility is also referred to as the *Screen Design Facility* (SDF).

Finally, several example programs are distributed with the EZ-VU product. These provide complete dialog samples written in the BASIC and Pascal programming languages. Printing and studying these examples is the best way to learn to use the product.

DIALOG MANAGER OVERVIEW

Similar to ISPF Dialog Manager functions, applications written with EZ-VU invoke DM services through calls to an interface routine. Programs may be developed in BASIC, Pascal, COBOL, FORTRAN, and Macro Assembler.

DM services divide into four basic groups: *select services*, *display services*, *variable services*, and *system services*. The select services allow the microcomputer user to invoke the dialog and display an initial panel or execute a first program function. The display services aid programs in the control and display of panels to the screen. The variable services allow dialogs to define and use variables in terms of the same three variable pools recognized by the ISPF Dialog Manager. Finally, the system services offer an interface to PC-DOS services.

Of these four groups of services, three mimic the facilities provided by the ISPF Dialog Manager. They provide services similar to those of the mainframe-developed product except that they offer their features on a much-reduced scale.

The fourth group, system services, differentiates EZ-VU from its mainframe product counterpart because it extends control of the personal computer environment to the user's dialog application. For example, system services permit dialog control of the various personal computer displays and floppy diskette mounting.

The initial release of the DM supports these service calls:

CONTROL
DISPLAY
MOUNT
RUN
SETMSG
VDEFARR
VDEFINE
VDELETE
VGET
VPUT

The functions of several of these services are similar to their mainframe ISPF counterparts. These include **DISPLAY, SETMSG, VDEFINE, VDELETE, VGET,** and **VPUT**. Other services are unique to the personal computers. For example, **CONTROL** defines the dialog processing options for screen display. It permits control of both color and monochrome displays, as well as dynamic specification of attribute characters. **MOUNT** provides for file access and automatic prompting for insertion of a required diskette. **RUN** allows a dialog function to issue a PC-DOS command or execute a batch file.

As in the ISPF Dialog Manager, each DM service is invoked through a CALL to the DM interface routine in the user's application program. The EZ-VU manual lists and illustrates these service invocations for each DM service. The syntax of each service invocation is appropriate to the programming language used. The DM communicates success or failure of all invocations through a return code defined in the user program.

SCREEN DESIGN FACILITY OVERVIEW

EZ-VU's Screen Design Facility offers a *screen painting* approach to definition of screen panels. Screen painting means that developers draw their panels on the screen under control of SDF in order to define them. This panel design process may be called *function key driven* since extensive use of function keys supplies many of the important features required in panel definition.

When interacting with SDF to create panels, the purposes of the function keys are labeled on the bottom of the screen. The function keys provide for the definition and placement of data fields and literals, input editing criteria, display attributes, and color selection. (SDF supports both color and monochrome displays.) Special screens within SDF also allow for translation and validation of source strings upon entry by the user. These capabilities are analogous to those provided through the **TRANS, TRUNC,** and **VER** functions of the ISPF Dialog Manager panel definition language.

Screen Design Facility generates three kinds of panel definitions: selection (or menu) panels, data entry panels, and help panels. These types of panels have roles similar to their counterparts in the mainframe ISPF Dialog Manager.

The panel definition process may be referred to as a "what you see is what you get" approach. Since the panel definition notation of the ISPF Dialog Manager is not used in EZ-VU, the product includes the *Screen Development Utility* program to allow designers to print their screens. The listing includes attribute and other information defined through use of the function keys during the screen definition process.

The Screen Development Utility also outputs comment statements describing fields within the panel in any of the programming languages that may be used with EZ-VU. These descriptive comments on fields can be output to user-named files. Since they are written in programming-language syntax, they may be directly incorporated into the source code of programs that manipulate the panels with which they are associated.

SCREEN DESIGN FACILITY SUMMARY

The Screen Design Facility epitomizes the personal computer approach to product development in its visual orientation. It is easy to use and largely self-explanatory. Its use is not extensively illustrated in this appendix because users can easily generate screens after only a few minutes of practice with the product.

EZ-VU's screen-painting methodology contrasts with the code-oriented panel definitions required by the mainframe-based ISPF Dialog Manager. The ISPF Dialog Manager requires familiarity with a coding syntax defined explicitly for panel definition. In this respect it is less visually oriented than its microcomputer product counterpart.

EZ-VU II

In 1986, IBM introduced EZ-VU II, an enhanced version of the EZ-VU product. New features in EZ-VU II include:

selection fields,
panel libraries,
picture edit,
floating point support,
C language support,
multiple active panels, and
a new PC-host panel conversion utility.

Primary sources for information on this new version of EZ-VU include the *EZ-VU II Presentation Guide* and the *EZ-VU II Information Brochure*. See Appendix B for further sources of information on EZ-VU II and EZ-VU.

ASSOCIATED PRODUCTS

IBM also vends a microcomputer version of the ISPF/Program Development Facility (ISPF/PDF) Editor, often referred to as the EZ-VU Editor. As in the mainframe world, the personal computer version of ISPF/PDF provides a complementary product to the EZ-VU Dialog Manager product. It supplies the program editor useful to developing programs and dialogs with EZ-VU. The EZ-VU Runtime Facility Program Product is required on the personal computer in order to use this microcomputer version of the ISPF/PDF Editor.

Several competing vendors offer similar microcomputer-based products closely modeled on the ISPF/PDF Editor. Among them are Micro/SPF, vended by Digital Research Inc., Pacific Grove, California and SPF/PC, from Command Technology Corp., Oakland, California. These products offer varying degrees of similarity to the IBM product with which they compete.

SUMMARY

With IBM's introduction of the EZ-VU Editor, the company offers a complete set of ISPF-related products for both mainframes and microcomputers. Table E-1 diagrams the situation. IBM vends ISPF, also called the ISPF Dialog Manager, the subject of this book. The microcomputer (PC-DOS operating system) equivalent of the mainframe-based ISPF Dialog Manager consists of two separately purchased products; the EZ-VU Development Facility and the EZ-VU Runtime Facility.

The ISPF/PDF program product complements the use of the ISPF Dialog Manager on mainframe computers. ISPF/PDF is an editor and utilities that help programmers design and debug ISPF dialogs and other mainframe programs.

Similarly, the EZ-VU Editor product provides a microcomputer equivalent of the mainframe ISPF/PDF Editor. This PC-DOS version of ISPF/PDF aids in the development of dialog applications designed with the EZ-VU Development and Runtime Facilities.

Table E-1. IBM's ISPF-Related Program Products

Mainframe Products*	Microcomputer Products
ISPF (also known as ISPF Dialog Manager or Dialog Manager)	EZ-VU Development Facility EZ-VU Runtime Facility (Together often referred to as EZ-VU; they include the Screen Design Facility and the Screen Development Utility)
ISPF/PDF (also known as Program Development Facility)	EZ-VU Editor (also known as ISPF/PDF Editor for PC-DOS)

*These mainframe products run on microcomputers that support versions of the VM/CMS operating system, such as the XT/370 and AT/370.

In summary, IBM currently vends two complete sets of ISPF-based program products. One set, the group upon which this book is based, is available for mainframe computers. These products run under such mainframe operating systems as MVS, VM, VSE, and SSX/VSE. (This group of products also runs on microcomputers supporting versions of the VM/CMS operating system, such as the XT/370 and AT/370.) The other set, described in this appendix, is designed for PC-DOS-based microcomputers. IBM is aggressively broadening the functionality of its mainframe- and microcomputer-based ISPF products and continues integration of these products with others in its software product line.

Glossary

Application Master Menu   The first menu panel displayed to a user upon invoking a Dialog Manager application.

Application Profile Pool   The group of dialog variables associated with an application and saved across sessions.

Attribute Byte   A special character that indicates how a field is to be displayed on a terminal. Also referred to as an *attribute character*.

Attribute Section   That part of a panel definition that defines special characters to denote attribute characteristics.

Background Job   A noninteractive batch job.

Body Section   The part of a panel definition that defines the panel layout as it will display on the screen.

Breakpoint   A point within a dialog where processing is suspended so that the user may inspect the values of variables, tables, and so forth during use of the Dialog Test facility.

CLIST   A command language supported in the MVS environment by the Dialog Manager for user development of functions. Also written as Clist.

Command   A character string entered by a terminal user in order to request a specific processing function. System commands are provided for by the Dialog Manager; application and function commands are supported by user-developed functions.

Command Language   An interpretive language featuring the ability to issue commands to the operating system. The Dialog Manager supports the use of the CLIST and EXEC2 command languages under MVS and VM, respectively. ISPF Version 2 for VM also supports REXX.

Command Procedure   A user-developed Dialog Manager function written in a command language such as the CLIST language under MVS or the EXEC2 language under VM.

Continuation Panel A panel definition designated as a connecting panel to another panel definition.

Cross-systems Compatible Program products that offer a large degree of code compatibility and a similar user interface across several different operating systems.

Current Row Pointer (CRP) An indicator of the current row in a table selected for processing.

Data Entry Panel A panel definition through which the user enters information.

DB2 A relational database management system (DBMS) vended by IBM for the MVS environment. Programs written in compiled programming languages (such as COBOL and PL/I) that use Dialog Manager services may also use DB2 for database management. This assumes that TSO is used as a teleprocessing monitor in conjunction with DB2.

Defined Variable A dialog variable created explicitly by a program function through use of the **VDEFINE** service.

Dialog An interactive, full-screen application that runs under control of the Dialog Manager.

Dialog Test That part of the ISPF/Program Development Facility that supports the design and testing of user-developed dialogs.

Dialog Variable A character string referred to by a symbolic name and used in the panels, file tailoring skeletons, messages, and functions that make up a dialog.

Display Services The ability to display information and receive responses from the terminal user provided as part of the Dialog Manager. The major display services are provided through **SELECT** (to select and display a panel), **DISPLAY** (to display a panel), **TBDISPL** (to display a table), and **SETMSG** (to display a message on the next panel viewed).

DOS *See* VSE.

DOS/VSE *See* VSE.

EXEC2 A command language supported in the VM environment by the Dialog Manager for user development of functions. Also written as **Exec 2**, **Exec2**, and **EXEC 2**.

Explicit Chain Mode Setting up an explicit hierarchical chaining of panels through the use of the **ZPARENT** system variable for indicating the parent panel.

Extension Variables Variables stored in a table row that were not specified when the table was created.

EZ-VU Development Facility A microcomputer dialog development product similar to and modeled on the ISPF Dialog Manager product for mainframe computers. This product does not support code compatibility with dialogs developed for the ISPF Dialog Manager.

Field Name Placeholder Use of the **Z** system variable allows definition of short field names within panel definitions for fields for which the length of the variable name would otherwise exceed the length of the field.

File   Under MVS, a sequential data set; under VM, a sequential CMS file; under VSE, a sequential file or library.

File Tailoring Services   The ability to process genericized file skeletons provided by the Dialog Manager for user-developed dialogs. These services include the capability to dynamically substitute variables into file skeletons and the ability to conditionally include records in the output file. File Tailoring Services do not directly update the input file skeletons; all processing effects are reflected in file tailoring output files.

File Tailoring Skeleton   A file processed via Dialog Manager's file tailoring services. Skeletons often consist of Job Control Language statements tailored to create individual batch jobs.

Function   A user-developed command procedure or program that runs under control of the Dialog Manager.

Function Pool   The group of dialog variables associated with a particular function.

"Help" Panel   A type of panel definition designed to provide the terminal user with context-sensitive explanatory ("help") information.

Index Panel   A tutorial panel definition designated by use of the **ZHINDEX** system variable and providing the terminal user with index selection of tutorial topics.

Initialization Section   The part of a panel definition that describes processing to occur prior to display of the panel.

Interactive System Productivity Facility (ISPF)   A program product consisting of the Dialog Manager and the services it supports.

ISPF Services   Commands accessible through user-developed functions via the ISPF interface.

Jump Function   Use of the **RETURN** command via a program function key and a menu option number preceded by an equal sign.

Library   Under MVS, a partitioned data set (PDS); under VM, a MACLIB; under VSE, a system or private library.

Literal   A character string that appears exactly as written in a panel display.

Log Services   The feature of ISPF services that allows user-developed functions to write messages to the ISPF log file.

Message   Information displayed on the user's terminal screen.

Message Definition   An informational or error message structured according to the requirements of the Dialog Manager's services for message display.

Message Services   The ability to display context-sensitive messages through the Dialog Manager.

Menu   A screen panel definition providing for user selection of one of a number of actions.

Model Section   The part of a panel definition used in conjunction with table display services to display all or part of a table on the screen.

MVS   A major operating system on large mainframe computers. One of the operating systems under which the ISPF Dialog Manager may be installed. Also loosely referred to as OS, OS/VS2, MVS/XA, MVS/SP, or MVS/TSO.

Panel Definition   A file containing a definition of a screen panel for display under control of the Dialog Manager.

PC-DOS   A major personal computer operating system under which the EZ-VU Development Facility product may be run.

Permanent Table   A table that will be saved across terminal sessions on disk.

Pool   A grouping of dialog variable values.

Primary Option Menu   *See* Application Master Menu.

Processing Section   The part of a panel definition that describes processing to occur after the panel has been displayed, upon receipt of some information from the terminal user.

Program   A user-developed Dialog Manager function written in one of the supported compiled programming languages.

Program Development Facility (PDF)   A program product based on the ISPF Dialog Manager. PDF is a dialog designed to aid programmers in designing, editing, and debugging programs and in performing related tasks.

Return Code   A value set by the Dialog Manager and accessible to user-developed functions in order to determine the success or failure of a Dialog Manager invocation. User-developed functions may also issue return codes as a mode of communication to other functions.

Screen Design Facility   The part of the EZ-VU Development Facility that supports design and development of panels for full-screen terminal input-output by application programs.

Screen Development Utility   The part of the Screen Design Facility that prints design criteria for panels.

Selection Panel   *See* Menu.

Shared Pool   The group of dialog variables associated with a particular dialog application.

Shell   A software product that surrounds an operating system. Shells consist of two logical components: the *command interpreter*, which translates user-input commands into the appropriate operating system commands, and a *programmable extension*, a command language that allows programming the command interpreter. In IBM's ISPF products, ISPF/PDF represents the command interpreter portion of the shell, and the ISPF Dialog Manager is the programming interface.

Skeleton   *See* **File Tailoring Skeleton**.

Split Screen   The ability to partition the display screen into two logical sessions as a result of keying in the **SPLIT** command or pressing an associated program function key. Split-screen capability is provided to application dialogs by the Dialog Manager in a manner transparent to user-developed functions.

SQL/DS A relational database management system (DBMS) vended by IBM for the VM and VSE environments. Programs written in compiled programming languages (such as COBOL and PL/I) that use Dialog Manager services may also use database management provided by SQL/DS.

SSX/VSE A version of the DOS/VSE operating system for entry-level mainframes.

Stacking Defining a single dialog variable more than once through the **VDEFINE** service in a program function. Each definition thereby associates a different program variable with the dialog variable name.

System Productivity Facility (SPF) Formerly known as Structured Programming Facility, a predecessor product to ISPF. Code developed under the System Productivity Facility is largely compatible with the ISPF Dialog Manager.

System Variable A variable provided and maintained by the Dialog Manager. These variables begin with the letter **Z** and provide certain kinds of information to user-developed functions.

Table A two-dimensional collection of data that may be saved temporarily or permanently across sessions. Tables are created and maintained through invocation of the Dialog Manager's table services.

Table Services The ability to maintain tabular data provided by the Dialog Manager for user-developed dialogs.

Temporary Table A table that is not written to disk; it exists on a temporary basis in memory only.

Trace The saving of information upon occurrence of a specified event within a dialog.

TSO The teleprocessing monitor with which the ISPF Dialog Manager runs under the MVS operating system.

Tutorial Panel A display panel containing "help" or tutorial information displayed under control of the Dialog Manager as part of its tutorial services.

Variable *See* Dialog Variable.

VM/PC A microcomputer variant of the VM operating system under which the ISPF Dialog Manager may be run.

VM A major operating system on mainframe computers. One of the operating systems under which the ISPF Dialog Manager may be installed. Also referred to as VM/SP, VM/CMS, and VM/370.

VSE A major operating system on mid-range to smaller mainframe computers. One of the operating systems under which the ISPF Dialog Manager may be installed. Also loosely referred to as DOS/VSE, DOS/ICCF, or just DOS.

Index